VIRGINIA

OFF THE BEATEN PATH®

OFF THE BEATEN PATH® SERIES

TWELFTH EDITION

VIRGINIA

OFF THE BEATEN PATH®

DISCOVER YOUR FUN

JUDY COLBERT

Globe
Pequot

Guilford, Connecticut

All the information in this guidebook is subject to change. We recommend that you call ahead to obtain current information before traveling.

Globe Pequot

An imprint of The Rowman & Littlefield Publishing Group, Inc.
4501 Forbes Blvd., Ste. 200
Lanham, MD 20706
www.rowman.com

Distributed by NATIONAL BOOK NETWORK

Copyright © 2019 by Judy Colbert

Maps by Equator Graphics for The Rowman & Littlefield Publishing Group, Inc.

ISSN 1539-8110
ISBN 978-1-4930-4265-4 (paperback)
ISBN 978-1-4930-4266-1 (e-book)

∞™ The paper used in this publication meets the minimum requirements of American National Standard for Information Sciences—Permanence of Paper for Printed Library Materials, ANSI/NISO Z39.48-1992

Contents

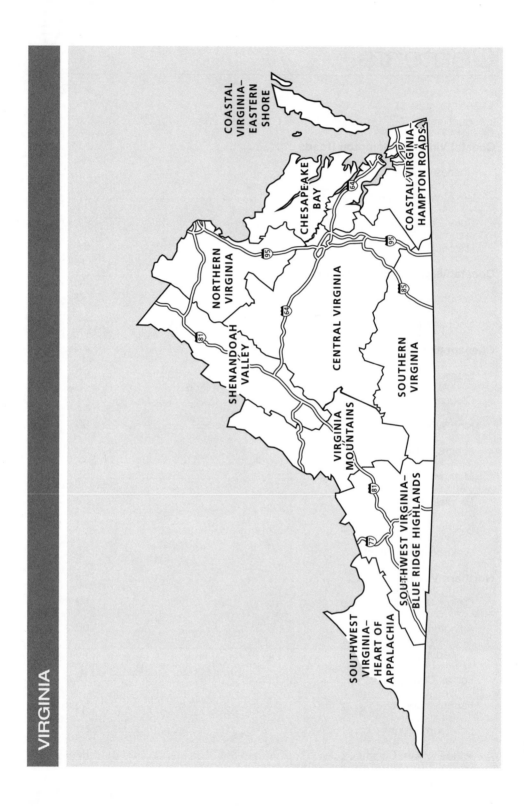

VIRGINIA

COASTAL VIRGINIA–EASTERN SHORE

CHESAPEAKE BAY

COASTAL VIRGINIA–HAMPTON ROADS

NORTHERN VIRGINIA

CENTRAL VIRGINIA

SHENANDOAH VALLEY

SOUTHERN VIRGINIA

VIRGINIA MOUNTAINS

SOUTHWEST VIRGINIA–BLUE RIDGE HIGHLANDS

SOUTHWEST VIRGINIA–HEART OF APPALACHIA

About the Author

Judy Colbert is a native Washingtonian (DC, not the state) whose mother grew up in a large family in Virginia's Tidewater or Hampton Roads area. Family visits were frequent, and much of the history and attractions (natural and man-made) of the state seeped in as if by osmosis. "One activity my mother loved was 'getting lost,' and I relished those days when we drove around and explored and were misplaced almost beyond belief. This was long before GPS programs. We always knew someone would be around the corner to tell us how to make it back home," says Judy.

A natural-born storyteller who has honed her craft for many years, Judy is thrilled when someone says, "I didn't know that" about a place that's right down the street or across the county line. Judy likes to wander into restaurants, libraries, and even beauty parlors to listen to the locals as they tell her, "Go talk to Uncle Fred. He invented the wooden leg." "I don't know if that's true or they're pulling mine. It doesn't matter," she says. "There's bound to be a story there."

Judy is an award-winning writer and photographer who has been writing about the mid-Atlantic and other areas for decades and is the author of *Maryland & Delaware Off the Beaten Path, 100 Things to Do in Baltimore Before You Die, Insiders' Guide to Baltimore, Chesapeake Bay Crabs Cookbook, Country Towns of Maryland and Delaware, Fun Places to Go with Children in Washington, D.C., Peaceful Places Washington, D.C., It Happened in Maryland,* and *It Happened in Delaware*. She has written hundreds—if not thousands—of articles that have appeared in international, national, regional, and local publications and websites, including ThePointsGuy.com, medium.com, BinduTrips .com, NextAvenue.com, Geniionline.com, *Northern Virginia* magazine, *GO AAA Carolinas,* and *Southern Maryland This Is Living.*

After thoroughly exploring the mid-Atlantic, Judy would like to spend a year or two on a cruise ship exploring other parts of the world.

She is a member of the American Society of Authors and Journalists, Society of Professional Journalists, Maryland Writers Association, Sisters in Crime, and a retired member of Screen Actors Guild and American Federation of Television Arts and Sciences.

Acknowledgments

I would like to thank the Virginia Division of Tourism and all the wonderful Virginians who took the time to assist in researching and updating *Off the Beaten Path Virginia*. This book could not be attempted, much less completed, without the assistance of many people. Therefore, thanks (and I hope I don't miss anyone) go to Emily Allen, Kerry Allison, Tim Ayers, Pam Barefoot, Becky Barnhardt, Renee Bayliss, Corinne Becker, Mindy Bianca, Andy Bittner, Krista Boothby, Sierra Brown, Tom Budesheim, Amy Burkert, Becky Crouch, Robert Culp, Rebecca M. Cutchins, John DeDakis, Jasmine De Jesus, Ryan Downey, Lexi Dwyer, Kris Ferraro, Fran Folsom, Catherine Fox, Erin Framel, Meghan Gearino, Morgan Gilbert, Rich Gilbert, Liz Griffin, Candy Harrington, Felicia Hart, Sarah Hodges, Stephanie Holguin, Shiloh Holley, Lisa Hull, Philip Irwin, Robin Jay, Daniel Jones, Suzanne Joyella, Len Kaufman, Justin Kerns, Mary Kester, James King, Lee Langston-Harrison, Sara Martin, Ashley Mason-Greene, Cyndi Masterstaff, Peg McGuire, Claire Mouledoux, Dianne Murphy, Mary-Lynne Neil, Sunny Nelson, Bruce L. Newton, Tiffany Niide, Gail Mesa Norman, Marie O'Day, Tom O'Day, Cara O'Donnell, Sherry Olstein, Myron Olstein, Liza Peltola, Tracy Perkins, Charles Price, Michael Quonce, Nancy Rader, Marie Rajtik, Karen Riddle, Louise Ripley, Kevin P. Sary, Ilene Schneider, David S. Schulte, Jim Sears, Elizabeth Severs, Lisa Shannon, Jennifer Sigal, Emmy Simpson, Taylor Spellman, Amy Steele, Mark Stevens, Beth Stinnett, Mike Stommel, Karen Sutter, Lynn Swann, Gordon Taplin, Laura Torpy, Janie Tross, Sergei Troubetzkoy, Sally Van Wieren, Nancy Vaughan, Sheryl Wagner, Judy Sluser Walter, Nicole Warner, Ed Wetschler, Mike Whiteside, Gina Wills, Dan Wilson, Judy Winslow, and Michele Wojciechowski.

Introduction

Whatever frame of mind you're in, there's a place for you in Virginia. From mountains to beaches, from cosmopolitan to country, from great dining and fine lodging to down-home cooking and rustic campsites, you can look to Virginia for a special time in your life.

If you rearrange "getaway" it becomes "gateway," and Virginia certainly is the gateway to so many fascinating and unusual attractions and events.

Virginia's famed tourism slogan, "Virginia Is for Lovers," will be celebrating its 50th anniversary in 2019! The slogan means that Virginia is for lovers of mountain climbing, catching some rays, seeing both innovative modern architecture or log cabins from a previous century, horseback riding, auto racing, outlet shopping, covered bridges, gristmills, wineries, and just about anything else you can imagine. Okay, so it's not great for extreme skiing, but you can downhill and cross-country ski.

Several years ago, the Virginia Tourism Corporation started erecting LOVE signs throughout the commonwealth (most permanent, some temporary), with 127 as of October 2018. A list of the LOVEworks can be found at virginia .org/LOVE. When you find one, take a picture, and then post it on the Facebook page, Facebook.com/VirginiaisforLovers (or Twitter or Pinterest with #LOVEVA).

Travel a little and you can find the most bodacious barbecue and a library designed by noted postmodernist architect Michael Graves. Varieties of tomatoes and cantaloupes are grown here that are grown nowhere else. Smithfield ham can only come from Smithfield, Virginia.

Remember, whatever you love in a vacation, you can find in Virginia.

Virginia is the fourth largest South Atlantic state and 35th in size among all the states. It extends 200 miles from north to south and about 430 miles from east to west. It's the 12th most populous state in the country, with nearly three-fourths of the population living in cities. Within its woodlands are 12 varieties of oak, 5 of pine, and 2 of walnut, as well as locust, gum, and poplar. Its indigenous mammals include the white-tailed Virginia deer, elk, black bear, bobcat, woodchuck, raccoon, opossum, and nutria.

Firsts of Virginia

Among the many "firsts" of Virginia was the establishment of a statewide birding and wildlife trail so visitors can view some of the 400 species of birds, 250 species of fish, 150 species of terrestrial and marine mammals, 150 species of amphibians and reptiles, and who knows how many aquatic and terrestrial invertebrates. Three guides are available: a 200-page Mountain Area (everything west of US 29), an 84-page Piedmont Area (central portion), and the 100-page Coastal Area (eastern Virginia and the Eastern Shore). It's a partnership between the Department of Game and Inland Fisheries and the Virginia Tourism Corporation (VTC). In promoting Mother Nature's fall foliage fashion show, the VTC joined with the Virginia Department of Forestry and Virginia State Parks.

Operation Wildflower is a combined program of the Virginia Department of Transportation and the Virginia Federation of Garden Clubs, Inc., that has grown from 25 plots of wildflowers planted in 1976 to hundreds of acres of assorted species planted along state highways today. From Apr through Oct, you'll see (seasonally) black-eyed Susans, New England asters, oxeye sunflower, New York ironweed, butterfly weed, lance-leaved coreopsis, purple coneflower, tickseed-sunflower (all native to Virginia), Indian blanket (central United States), plains coreopsis (southern United States), sulphur cosmos and mixed cosmos (Mexico), and corn poppy (Europe). If you don't know a sunflower from an aster, pick up a *Wildflowers Color Virginia* brochure at a welcome station, or call (804) 371-6825 or (800) 774-3382.

Home-grown Goodness

Fall is the time to pick that perfect pumpkin or wonderful apples for pies and more. Many farms offer a pick-your-own option, nature studies for your young ones without being in a classroom, and fun outdoor activities. As many of these farms now earn more from two months of corn or hay maze and related sales than they do from farming all year, the options have grown exponentially.

Wineries

Vineyards and wineries populate almost every corner of the state, from the Blue Ridge to the Eastern Shore. Most wineries are open for tours and tastings and some offer overnight accommodations.

Look for wine-related events almost throughout the year. Some programs include Valentine's Day–themed wine pairings, an *annual wine expo* (virginia wineexpo.com), a "Wines and Wags" event that includes showing off dogs and wines, a wine and bluegrass festival, a wine and garlic festival, hot-air balloon and wine festival, and the *annual state wine fest* (virginiawinefest.com). That is only a sip out of a barrelful of occasions. A statewide organization, the *Virginia Wine Marketing Office,* has valuable information about the wineries, recipes using local wines, tours, and festivals in their Richmond office, 600 E. Main St., Ste. 308, Richmond 23219; on their website, virginiawine.org; or by calling (804) 344-8200.

Rails-to-Trails

Virginia has been active in the Rails-to-Trails program that converts the old railroad right-of-way into a pedestrian-friendly trail. Because the trains had to be able to climb any incline, you can figure the trails will be fairly flat and any incline will be moderate. *The Rails-To-Trails Conservancy Guidebook* for the mid-Atlantic area includes 107 trails in Virginia for walkers, hikers, history buffs, and bicycle riders. They go through Civil War battlefields, wetlands, and small and large towns. A mid-Atlantic guide to 57 trails in Virginia, Maryland, Delaware, West Virginia, and Washington, DC, is available from the Conservancy website, railstotrails.org, either in print or as an ebook.

General Notes

As this book highlights unique places, there is less emphasis on the major tourism destinations and sites. Some are mentioned, with a focus on what's unique about those popular sites and destinations. To find those roads more traveled, call (800) VISIT-VA (847-4882) for a Virginia vacation guide, or write to the *Virginia Tourism Corporation* at 901 E. Cary St., Ste. 900, Richmond 23219. The tourism division (virginia.org) can also provide more specific information about a particular area. They have many special-interest brochures that will help you in your search for the perfect bed-and-breakfast, African-American and Hispanic sites and events, and other destinations.

Much of Virginia is old, and many buildings were constructed before wheelchair access and special needs were a public concern. While most, if not all, public buildings have been made accessible or comply with the Americans with Disabilities Act, this is not always the case. A building in Williamsburg may not have an elevator to the second floor. It probably will have a narrated video of the areas you can't access that you can watch instead. For specific information about public accessibility, check the *Virginia Travel Guide for Persons with Disabilities* at accessiblevirginia.org (the TDD number is 804-371-0327).

This is not always the case with accommodations. Even a bed-and-breakfast that's on one floor may have steps to a porch. As I have limited the number of chain hotels and motels listed in this book and made an emphasis on individually owned and operated accommodations, you may find properties that are not accessible. Restaurants, too, may be downstairs or upstairs or have tables set close to each other. Sometimes, they will offer to carry a person in a wheelchair (sitting in the chair) to a table.

Be sure to call any place you plan to visit to determine whether the facility is wheelchair accessible or if there are special provisions for those who have visual or hearing impairments.

birthplace of presidents

You may have heard that Virginia is the birthplace of presidents because eight men from this state held that office—George Washington, Thomas Jefferson, James Madison, James Monroe, William Henry Harrison, John Tyler, Zachary Taylor, and Woodrow Wilson. A ninth Virginian, Joseph Jenkins Roberts, became the first African-American governor (president) of the African colony of Liberia in 1841.

Virginia has 95 counties, 40 independent cities, and 189 incorporated towns. This can be a little confusing, particularly when trying to locate and visit an independent city that's located within a county. Avoid trying to figure out the difference between Fairfax County, Fairfax city, Alexandria, Arlington, etc. Just plug the location information into your GPS or find an online map. Persevere, please.

This book is divided into 10 sections, matching the geographical areas as designated by Virginia tourism. They are Hampton Roads, Eastern Shore, Chesapeake Bay, Northern Virginia, Central Virginia, Southern Virginia, Shenandoah Valley, Virginia Mountains, Blue Ridge Highlands, and Heart of Appalachia. Within each area, the counties and cities are listed alphabetically rather than geographically. It might seem a little confusing to find two adjacent counties not listed one after the other, but there is no one way to tour the state, so I went with the alpha listing.

By the way, Virginia is a commonwealth—a term first used in Jamestown in 1619—not a state. Kentucky, Massachusetts, and Pennsylvania also use the term *commonwealth*.

When I started researching and writing the first edition of *Virginia Off the Beaten Path,* we did not have websites and the state certainly didn't have seven telephone area codes. Now, almost every place listed has a presence on the internet, growing from being part of a regional organization to individual sites. Some places have entered the 21st century and can be found on Facebook, Twitter, Instagram, and other social networking sites. The URLs, addresses, phone numbers, prices, rates, and times of operation listed in this guidebook were confirmed at press time. Note that many places are closed for national holidays. We recommend that you call establishments before traveling to obtain current information.

Virginia Tourism Resources

VIRGINIA TOURISM

Virginia Tourism Corporation, 901 E. Cary St., Ste. 900, Richmond 23219; (804) 545-5572, (800) 732-5827, or (800) VISIT-VA (847-4882); fax (804) 371-0327; TTY/TTD (804) 371-0327; Virginia.org

VIRGINIA WELCOME CENTERS

East Coast Gateway Welcome Center, I-64E, mile marker 213, New Kent 23124; (804) 966-7450

Welcome Center at New Church, US 13, 3420 Lankford Hwy., New Church 23415; (757) 824-5000

Welcome Center at Fredericksburg, I-95S, mile marker 132, Fredericksburg 22404; (540) 786-8344

Welcome Center at Manassas, I-66W, mile marker 48, 9915 Vandor Ln., Manassas 20109; (703) 361-2134

Welcome Center at Main Street Station, 1500 E. Main St., Richmond 23219; (804) 545-5581

Welcome Center at Bracey, I-85N, mile marker 1, Bracey 23919; (434) 689-2295

Welcome Center at Skippers, I-95N, mile marker 0, Skippers 23879; (434) 634-4113

Welcome Center at Clear Brook, I-81S, mile marker 320, Clear Brook 22624; (540) 722-3448

Welcome Center at Covington, I-64E, 1 Welcome Center Dr., Covington 24426; (540) 559-3010

Welcome Center at Bristol, I-81N, mile marker 0, 66 Island Rd., Bristol 24201; (276) 466-2932

Welcome Center at Rocky Gap, I-77S, mile marker 61, Rocky Gap 24366; (276) 928-1873

Welcome Center at Lambsburg, I-77N, mile marker 0, Lambsburg 24351; (276) 755-3931

Heart of Appalachia Tourist Information Center, 3028 4th Ave. Market Sq., St. Paul 24283; (276) 762-0011; heartofappalachia.com

VISITOR CENTERS

Coastal Virginia—Hampton Roads

Chesapeake Visitor Center, 1224 Progressive Dr., Chesapeake 23320; (757) 382-6411; visitchesapeake.com

Colonial Williamsburg Regional Visitor Center, 101 Visitor Center Dr., Williamsburg 23185; (800) 447-8679 or (757) 220-7645; colonialwilliamsburg.com/plan/visitor-center

Franklin/Southampton County Area Chamber of Commerce, 108 W. 3rd Ave., Franklin 23851 (757) 562-4900; fsachamber.com

Hampton Visitor Center, 120 Old Hampton Ln., Hampton 23669; (757) 727-1102; visithampton.com

High Street Information Center (Portsmouth), High and Water Streets, Portsmouth 23704; (757) 393-5111; visitportsva.com

New Kent Tourism, 7324 Vineyards Pkwy., New Kent 23124; (804) 966-8787; yesnewkent.com

Newport News Tourism, 702 Town Center Dr., Newport News 23606; (757) 926-1400; newport-news.org

Newport News Visitor Center, Newport News Park, 13560 Jefferson Ave., Newport News 23603; (888) 493-7386 or (757) 886-7777; newport-news.org

Portsmouth Visitor Information Center, 6 Crawford Pkwy., Portsmouth 23704; (757) 393-5111; visitportsva.com

Smithfield and Isle of Wight Convention & Visitor Bureau, 319 Main St., Smithfield 23431; (800) 365-9339 or (757) 357-5182; visitsmithfieldva.com

Suffolk Visitor Center, 524 N. Main St., Suffolk 23434; (757) 514-4130; visit suffolkva.com

Surry County Tourism & Visitors Center, 267 Church St., Surry 23883; (757) 294-5095; surrycountytourism.com

Virginia Beach Convention & Visitors Bureau, 2100 Parks Ave., Virginia Beach 23451; (757) 385-7873; visitvirginiabeach.com

Visit Norfolk, 232 E. Main St., Norfolk 23510; (757) 664-6620; visitnorfolk.com

Visit Williamsburg, 421 N. Boundary St., Williamsburg 23185; (757) 229-6511; visitwilliamsburg.com

Visit Yorktown, 301 Main St., Yorktown 23690; (757) 890-3500; visityorktown .org

Coastal Virginia—Eastern Shore

Cape Charles Museum & Welcome Center, 814 Randolph Ave., Cape Charles 23310; (757) 331-1008; smallmuseum.org/capechas.html

Chincoteague Chamber of Commerce & Certified Visitor Center, 6733 Maddox Blvd., Chincoteague Island 23336; (757) 336-6161; chincoteaguecham ber.com

Eastern Shore of VA Chamber of Commerce, 19056 Pkwy., Melfa 23410; (757) 787-2460; esvachamber.org

Eastern Shore of VA Welcome Center, 32383 Lankford Hwy., Cape Charles 23310; (757) 331-1660; esvatourism.org

Northampton County Chamber of Commerce, 16404 Courthouse Rd., Eastville 23347; (757) 678-0010

Chesapeake Bay

Colonial Beach Tourism, At Town Pier, Colonial Beach 22443; (804) 224-0732; colonialbeach.org

Gloucester Visitor Center, 6504 Main St., Gloucester 23061; (804) 824-2476; gloucesterva.info

Mathews County Visitor & Information Center, 239 Main St., Mathews 23109; (804) 725-4229; visitmathews.com

Middlesex County Visitor Center, 795 Chesty Puller Hwy., Saluda 23149; (804) 758-3663; co.middlesex.va.us

Northern Neck Tourism Commission, 457 Main St., Warsaw 22572; (804) 333-1919; northerneck.org

Westmoreland County Museum and Visitor Center, 43 Court Sq., Montross 22520; (804) 493-8440; westmoreland-county.org

West Point/Tri-Rivers Chamber of Commerce, 621 Main St., West Point 23181; (804) 843-4620; westpointvachamber.com

Northern Virginia

Alexandria Visitors Center, 221 King St., Alexandria 22314; (703) 838-5005 or (800) 388-9119; visitalexandriava.com

Arlington Convention and Visitors Services, 1100 N. Glebe Rd., Ste. 1500, Arlington 22201; (800) 677-6267; stayarlington.com

Caroline County Visitor Center, 23724 Rogers Clark Blvd., Ruther Glen 22546; visitcaroline.com

Culpeper Visitor's Center, 111 S. Commerce St., The Depot, Culpeper 22701; (540) 727-0611; visitculpeperva.com

Fairfax County/Capital Region Visitor Center–Tysons Corner, 1961 Chain Bridge Rd., 2nd Level, McLean 22102; (703) 752-9500; fxva.com/plan-your-trip/visitor-center

Fauquier County Department of Economic Development, 35 Culpeper St., Warrenton 20186; (540) 422-8270; visitfauquier.com

Fredericksburg Visitor Center, 706 Caroline St., Fredericksburg 22401; (800) 678-4748 or (540) 373-1776; visitfred.com

Historic Downtown Manassas Visitors Center, Train Depot, 9431 West St., Manassas 20110; (703) 361-6599; visitmanassas.org

Loudoun County Visitors Center, 112-G South St. SE, Leesburg 20175; (703) 771-2170; visitloudoun.org

Prince William County Office of Tourism, 14420 Bristow Rd., Manassas 20112; (703) 792-8420; visitpwc.com

Rappahannock County Visitor Center, 3 Library Rd., Washington 22747; (540) 675-3153; visitrappahannockva.com

Spotsylvania County Visitors Center, 4704 Southpoint Pkwy., Fredericksburg 22407; (540) 507-7090 or (877) 515-6197; visitspotsy.com/spotyslvania-history/spotsylvania-county-visitors-center/

Stafford Visitors Center, 224 Washington St., Falmouth 22405; (540) 654-1015; staffordcountyva.gov/64/Visiting

Visit Fairfax, 3702 Pender Dr., Ste. 420, Fairfax 22030; (703) 790-0643; fxva.com

Warrenton–Fauquier County Visitors Center, 33 N. Calhoun St., Warrenton 20186; (540) 422-8270 or (800) 820-1021; visitfauquier.com

Central Virginia

Appomattox Visitor Information Center, 214 Main St., Appomattox 24522; (434) 352-8999; historicappomattox.com

Ashland/Hanover Visitor Information Center, 112 N. Railroad Ave., Ashland 23005; (804) 752-6766; ashlandva.gov

Charlottesville Albemarle CVB—Downtown Visitor Center, 610 E. Main St., Charlottesville 22902; (877) 386-1103 or (434) 293-6789; visitcharlottesville.org

Greene County Visitor Center, 8315 Seminole Trail, Ste. 2, Ruckersville 22968; (434) 985-6663; exploregreene.com

Henrico County Visitor Center at Dobbs House, 3812 Nine Mile Rd., Henrico, 23223; (804) 652-3406; henricorecandparks.com

Hopewell/Prince George Visitor Welcome Center, 4100 Oaklawn Blvd., Hopewell 23860; (804) 458-5536; hpgchamber.org

Lake Anna Visitor Center, 208 Lake Front Dr., Mineral 23117; (540) 872-0684; lakeannavisitorcenter.com

Lynchburg Visitor Center, 216 12th St. at Church, Lynchburg 24504; (800) 732-5821 or (434) 847-1811; discoverLynchburg.org

Madison County Chamber of Commerce, 110 N. Main St., #A, Madison 22727; (540) 948-4455; madison-va.com

Nelson County Tourism & Visitors Bureau, 8519 Thomas Nelson Hwy. (US 29), Lovingston 22949; (800) 282-8223 or (434) 263-7015; nelsoncounty.com

Orange County Visitors Center, 122 E. Main St., Orange 22960; (877) 222-8072 or (540) 672-1653; visitorangevirginia.com

Petersburg Visitor's Center, 19 Bollingbrook St., Petersburg 23803; (804) 733-2400; petersburg-va.org

Richmond Region Tourism, 401 N. 3rd St, Richmond 23219; (804) 782-2777 or (888) RICHMOND; VisitRichmondVa.com

Richmond Region Visitor Center, 405 N. 3rd St., Richmond 23219; (804) 782-2777; VisitRichmondVa.com

Virginia's Heartland Regional Visitor Center, 121 E. 3rd St., Farmville 23901; (434) 392-1482; visitfarmville.com

Southern Virginia

Danville Welcome Center, 645 River Park Dr., Danville 24540; (434) 793-4636; playdanvilleva.com

Martinsville-Henry County Visitor Center, 191 Fayette St., Martinsville 24114; (888) PACE-4YU (722-3498) or (276) 632-8006; visitmartinsville.com

South Boston–Halifax County Visitor Center, 1180 Bill Tuck Hwy., South Boston 24592; (434) 572-2543; discoverHalifaxva.com

South Hill Tourist Information Center, 201 S. Mecklenburg Ave., South Hill 23970; (434) 447-4547; southhillchamber.com

Shenandoah Valley

Bridgewater Visitor's Center, 109 S. Main St., Bridgewater 22812; (540) 828-9986; bridgewatervahistmuseum.org

Buena Vista Regional Visitor Center, 595 E. 29th St., Buena Vista 24416; (540) 261-8004; lexingtonvirginia.com

Elkton Welcome Center, 306 W. Spotswood Ave., Elkton 22827; (504) 405-7084; elktonva.gov/elktonwelcomecenter.html

Front Royal–Warren County Visitor Center, 414 E. Main St., Front Royal 22630; (800) 338-2576 or (540) 635-5788; discoverfrontroyal.com

Hardesty-Higgins House Visitor Center, 212 S. Main St., Harrisonburg 22801; (540) 432-8935; visitharrisonburgva.com

Harrisonburg Tourism and Visitor Services, 212 S. Main St., Harrisonburg 22801; (540) 432-8940; visitharrisonburgva.com

Lexington & the Rockbridge Area Visitor Center, 106 E. Washington St., Lexington 24450; (540) 463-3777; lexingtonvirginia.com

Luray–Page County Chamber of Commerce & Visitor Center, 18 Campbell St., Luray 22835; (540) 743-3915 or (888) 743-3915; visit.luraypage.com

Rockfish Gap Tourist Information Center, 130 Afton Circle, Afton 22920; (540) 943-5187 or (540) 942-6644; visitwaynesboro.net

Shenandoah County Tourism, 600 N. Main St., Ste. 101, Woodstock 22664; (540) 459-6227 or (888) 367-4965; visitshenandoahcounty.com

Staunton Convention and Visitors Bureau, 116 W. Beverley St., 3rd Floor, Staunton 24401; (540) 332-3865; visitstaunton.com

Staunton Visitors Center, 35 S. New St., Staunton 24401; (540) 332-3971 or (800) 342-7982; visitstaunton.com

Waynesboro Department of Tourism, 301 W. Main St., Waynesboro 22980; (540) 942-6512; visitwaynesboro.net

Winchester–Frederick County Visitors Center, 1400 S. Pleasant Valley Rd., Winchester 22601; (877) 871-1326 or (540) 542-1326; visitwinchesterva.com

Virginia Mountains

Alleghany Highlands Chamber of Commerce & Tourism, 110 Mall Rd., Covington 24426; (540) 962-2178; visitalleghanyhighlands.com

Bedford Area Welcome Center, 816 Burks Hill Rd., Bedford 24523; (540) 587-5682 or (877) HI-PEAKS (447-3257); visitbedford.com

County of Bath Office of Tourism, 65 Courthouse Rd., Warm Springs 24484; (540) 839-7202; discoverbath.com

Craig County Tourism Commission, 108 Court St., New Castle 24127; (540) 864-5010; visitcraigcountyva.com

Franklin County Division of Tourism & Film, 1255 Franklin St., Ste. 112, Rocky Mount 24151; (540) 483-3030; visitfranklincountyva.org

Highland County Visitor's Center, 61 Highland Center Dr., Monterey 24465; (540) 468-2550; highlandcounty.org

Salem Visitor's Center, Salem Civic Center, 1001 Roanoke Blvd., Salem 24153; (888) VA-SALEM (725-2536) or (540) 375-4044; visitsalemva.com

Smith Mountain Lake Regional Chamber of Commerce & Visitors Center, 16430 Booker T. Washington Hwy., Unit 2, Moneta 24121; (540) 721-1203; visitsmithmountainlake.com

Virginia's Blue Ridge Visitor Information Center, 101 Shenandoah Ave. NE, Roanoke 24016; (540) 342-6025; visitvbr.com

Blue Ridge Highlands

Abingdon Convention & Visitors Bureau, 335 Cummings St., Abingdon 24210; (800) 435-3440 or (276) 676-2282; visitabingdonvirginia.com

Blue Ridge Plateau Regional Visitor Center, 239 Farmers Market Rd., Hillsville 24343; (276) 730-3100; visittheblueridge.com

Blue Ridge Travel Association, 2680 Grayson Pkwy., Independence 24348; (276) 773-0450; virginiablueridge.org

Blue Ridge Visitor Center, 2609 Jeb Stuart Hwy., Meadows of Dan 24120; (276) 694-6012; patrickchamber.com

Bristol Convention and Visitors Bureau, 20 Volunteer Pkwy., Bristol 24203; (423) 989-4850; discoverbristol.org

Floyd Chamber of Commerce, 109 E. Main St., Floyd 24091; (540) 745-4407; floydchamber.org

Floyd County Visitor Center & Tourism Office, 109 E. Main St., Floyd 24091; (540) 745-4407; visitfloydva.com

Galax Visitors Center, 110 E. Grayson St., Galax 24333; (276) 238-8130 or (888) 217-8823; visitgalax.com

Grayson County Tourist Office, 129 Davis St., Box 217, Independence 24348; (276) 773-2000; graysoncountyva.com

Montgomery County, Blacksburg, Christiansburg Regional Tourism Office, 755 Roanoke St., Christiansburg 24073; (540) 394-4470; gotomontva .com

Patrick County Tourism Office, 106 Rucker St., Stuart 24171; (276) 694-6094; visitpatrickcounty.org

Pulaski County Visitor Center, 4440 Cleburne Blvd., Dublin 24084; (540) 674-4161; pulaskichamber.info

City of Radford Visitor's Center, 400 Unruh Dr., Radford 24141; (540) 267-3153; visitradford.com

Smyth County Regional Visitor Center, 408 Whitetop Rd., Chilhowie 24319; (877) 255-9928; visitvirginiamountains.com

Town of Hillsville Visitors Center, 410 N. Main St., Hillsville 24343; (276) 728-2128; townofhillsville.com

Virginia Creeper Trail Welcome Center, 300 Green Spring Rd., Abingdon 24210; (276) 525-4457 or (800) 435-3440; visitabingdonvirginia.com

Wytheville Convention & Visitors Bureau and Regional Visitors Center, 975 Tazewell St., Wytheville 24382; (877) 347-8307; visitwytheville.com

Heart of Appalachia

Carmine's Big Stone Gap Visitor Center, 300 Wood Ave., Big Stone Gap 24219; (276) 523-2060; bigstonegap.com

Dickenson County Visitor's Center & Chamber of Commerce, 194 Main St., Clintwood 24228; (276) 926-6074; dickensonchamber.net

Greater Bluefield Area Chamber of Commerce, 619 Bland St., Bluefield 24701; (304) 327-7184; bluefieldchamber.com

Lee County Tourism Office, 33640 Main St., Jonesville 24263; (276) 346-7714; Ilovelee.org

Pennington Gap Visitor Center, 610 Old Zion Rd., Pennington Gap 24277; (276) 298-511; townofpenningtonva.gov

Russell County Tourism, 137 Highland Dr., Lebanon 24266; (276) 619-1817; experiencerussell.com

Scott County Tourism, 190 Beech St., Ste. 201, Gate City 24251; (276) 386-6521; explorescottcountyva.com

Southern Gap Outdoor Adventure Visitor Center, 1124 Chipping Sparrow Rd., Grundy 24614; (276) 244-1111; sgadventures.com

Wise County & City of Norton Chamber of Commerce, 765 Park Ave., Norton 24273; (276) 679-0961; wisecountychamber.org

Wise County Tourism, 206 E. Main St, Wise 24293; (276) 328-2321; visitwise county.com

USEFUL WEBSITES

Metropolitan Washington Airports, metwashairports.com
National Park Service, nps.gov
Virginia Tourism Corporation, virginia.org

MAJOR NEWSPAPERS

Alexandria Gazette Packet, 1606 King St., Alexandria 22314; (703) 778-9431; alexandriagazette.com
Bristol Herald-Courier/Virginia-Tennessean, 320 Bob Morrison Blvd., Bristol, VA 24201; (276) 669-2181; heraldcourier.com
Danville Register & Bee, 700 Monument St., Danville 24541; (434) 797-7900; godanriver.com
Free Lance–Star, 1340 Central Park Blvd., Ste. 100, Fredericksburg 22401; (540) 374-5000; fredericksburg.com
News Leader, 11 N. Central Ave., Staunton 24402; (540) 885-7281; newsleader .com
News-Virginian, 201 C. Rosser Ave., Waynesboro 22980; (540) 949-8213; daily progress.com/newsvirginian/
Richmond Times Dispatch, 300 E. Franklin St., Richmond 23219; (804) 649-6990; richmond.com/
Roanoke Times, 201Campbell Ave. SW, Roanoke 240711; (800) 346-1234; roanoke.com
Washington Post, 1150 15th St. NW, Washington, DC 20071; (202) 334-6000; washingtonpost.com

PUBLIC TRANSPORTATION

Amtrak, (800) USA-RAIL (872-7245), (888) 268-7251 or (888) AMTRAK1; amtrak.com
Newport News–Williamsburg International Airport, 900 Bland Blvd., Newport News 23602; (757) 877-0221; flyphf.com
Norfolk International Airport, 2200 Norview Ave., Norfolk 23518; (757) 857-3351; norfolkairport.com
Richmond International Airport, 1 Robert E. Byrd Terminal Dr., Richmond 23250; (804) 226-3000; flyrichmond.com
Roanoke-Blacksburg Regional Airport, 5202 Aviation Dr. NW, Roanoke 24012; (540) 362-1999; roanokeairport.com
Ronald Reagan National Airport, Arlington 22210; (703) 417-8600; metwash airports.com/dca/reagan-national-airport

Virginia Railway Express (VRE), 1500 King St., Ste. 202, Alexandria 22314; (703) 684-1001; vre.org

Washington Dulles International Airport, Herndon 22204; (703) 572-2700; metwashairports.com/iad/dulles-international-airport

Fast Facts About the Old Dominion

Area (land): 42,774 square miles; rank: 35

Capital: Richmond

Largest city: Virginia Beach, population 452,745 (2015 est.)

Number of counties: 95

Highest elevation: 5,729 feet, Mount Rogers

Lowest elevation: sea level, at the Atlantic Ocean

Population: 8,470,020 (2017 est.)

Population distribution: 88.5 percent in urban areas, 11.5 percent rural

Institutions of higher education: 95 colleges and universities (2018)

Median family income: $44,656 (2013)

Statehood: June 25, 1788; the 10th state

Nicknames: Old Dominion, Mother of Presidents

State flower/tree: dogwood

State motto: Sic Semper Tyrannis ("Thus Always to Tyrants")

State bird: northern cardinal

State shell: oyster shell

State fossil: *Chesapecten jeffersonius*

State dog: American foxhound

State drink: milk, rye whiskey

State insect: tiger swallowtail butterfly

State folkdance: square dancing

State boat: Chesapeake Bay Deadrise

State fish: striped bass

Climate Overview

Virginia's weather depends on the region and the season. The Tidewater area is relatively mild in the winter but can be quite humid in the summer. Northern Virginia also has hot, humid summer days and receives an average 20 inches of snow each winter. The mountains can receive severe winter storms and then enjoy delightful summer days.

Famous Sons & Daughters of Virginia

Richard Arlen, actor
Arthur Ashe, tennis champion
Stephen F. Austin, Texas founder
Pearl Bailey, singer
Russell Baker, columnist
Phil Balsley, singer
Warren Beatty, actor
George Bingham, painter
Richard Evelyn Bird, naval officer/explorer
Jeff Burton, NASCAR driver
Maybelle Carter, singer
June Carter Cash, singer
Willa Cather, novelist
Spencer Christian, TV weatherman
Roy Clark, country music artist
William Clark, soldier/explorer
Henry Clay, orator and statesman
Patsy Cline, singer
Joseph Cotten, actor
Ella Fitzgerald, jazz singer
Jimmy Fortune, singer
William Henry Harrison, US president
Patrick Henry, statesman
Sam Houston, political leader
Thomas Jefferson, US president
Henry "Light-Horse Harry" Lee, public official
Robert E. Lee, Confederate general
Meriwether Lewis, explorer
Shirley MacLaine, actress
James Madison, US president
John Marshall, US chief justice
Dave Matthews, singer

Cyrus Hall McCormick, inventor

James Monroe, US president

Wayne Newton, entertainer

Opechancanough, Powhatan leader

John Payne, actor

Pocahontas, Indian princess

Walter Reed, army surgeon

Harold Reid, singer

Tim Reid, actor/director

Matthew Ridgway, army chief of staff

Joseph Jenkins Roberts, first president of Liberia

Bill "Bojangles" Robinson, dancer/actor

George C. Scott, actor

Willard Scott, TV weatherman

Kate Smith, singer

Sam Snead, golfer

Statler Brothers, singing group

James "Jeb" Stuart, Confederate army officer

Thomas Sumter, army officer

Zachary Taylor, US president

Nat Turner, leader of slave uprising

John Tyler, US president

Blair Underwood, actor

Booker T. Washington, educator

George Washington, US president

James E. West, inventor

Thomas Woodrow Wilson, US president

Tom Wolfe, journalist

Coastal Virginia– Hampton Roads

We're starting in the Coastal Virginia area. Old-timers may recall it as Tidewater or Hampton Roads. When Virginia tourism changed to ten regions, the area became Coastal Virginia, but you'll still see references to Tidewater and Hampton. Don't be confused; just realize it's a difference without a distinction. In any case, we're at the confluence of the Chesapeake Bay, Nansemond River, Chuckatuck Creek, James River, Elizabeth River, Mill Creek, and other tributaries.

Charles City County

You've no doubt heard that Virginia is the Mother of Presidents, and John Tyler, 10th president of the United States, lived at *Sherwood Forest Plantation* in *Charles City* (14501 John Tyler Memorial Hwy.; 804-829-5377; sherwoodforest .org) from 1842 until his death in 1862. This classic example of Virginia Tidewater design has been elegantly restored and furnished with Tyler's possessions and shows the lifestyle of this mid-19th-century family. The home is situated on 25 acres of terraced gardens and lawns, woods, and landscape and surrounded by six original outbuildings. At more than 300 feet

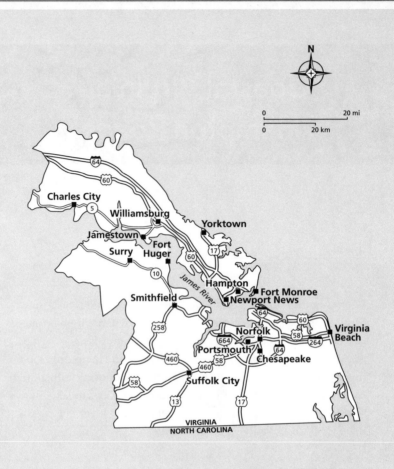

N

0   20 mi
0   20 km

Charles City

Williamsburg

Yorktown

Jamestown

Fort Huger

Surry

James River

Hampton

Fort Monroe

Newport News

Smithfield

Norfolk

Virginia Beach

Portsmouth

Chesapeake

Suffolk City

VIRGINIA
NORTH CAROLINA

long, this is reported to be the longest frame house in America. President Tyler added a 68-foot ballroom in 1845 to accommodate the popular dance of his time, the Virginia reel.

Today, the home is still owned by the Tyler family and maintained through the Sherwood Forest Plantation Foundation. The former president's great-grandson, who resides at the plantation with his wife, oversaw the important restoration in the mid-1970s. Their children and grandchildren frequently are seen at the plantation. The house and grounds are open for self-guided tours for $10 per adult, with children 15 and under admitted free. The house tour is available by appointment, for $35 per person.

funfacts

John Tyler was the first vice president to ascend to the presidency when he assumed the office after the death of William Henry Harrison, ninth president of the United States.

Hampton

When most Americans think of our space program, they think of the centers at Houston and Cape Canaveral. The original seven Mercury astronauts, however, trained right here, thus the street name **Mercury Boulevard** (formerly Military Boulevard).

You can also find Commander Shepard Boulevard (named for Alan B. Shepard) and bridges named for M. Scott Carpenter, L. Gordon Cooper, John H. Glenn, Virgil I. Grissom, Walter M. Schirra, and Donald K. Slayton. One of these days when you have nothing better to do, spend some time wandering around **Hampton** or poring over a map to find these historic spots. When you give up, try the **Hampton Visitors Center** (120 Old Hampton Ln., Hampton 23669; 757-727-1102; visithampton.com). They've compiled a list for me and promised to keep it handy for you.

The **Virginia Air and Space Center** (600 Settlers Landing Rd.; 757-727-0900; vasc.org) is a blast (off?). It isn't as large as the Smithsonian's Air and Space Museum in Washington, DC, but it isn't nearly as crowded either. Shaped like a huge wing ready for takeoff, it features walls of windows and light and space that set your creative mind in motion and your quest for adventure throbbing. Taking the Hampton city theme "From the sea to the stars," the displays are informative, interactive, touchable, and unusual.

Imagine being an astronaut. Space suit cutouts are here for photo-ops to fulfill, temporarily, your space age dreams. For a moon relic take a look at the 3-billion-year-old moon rock. Check out the 10 air- and spacecraft suspended from the center's 94-foot ceiling, and take a serious gander at the *Apollo 12* command capsule, which journeyed to the moon and back, in the middle of the gallery's floor. Within the center are more than 100 history, aeronautic, and space exhibits. Each end of the building is a glass wall that lets light cascade in and through the structure. The solid walls are painted a neutral color that seems to make them disappear into the horizon, so you feel as though you're standing in and among all the planes that are suspended above and around you.

You'll want to save some time for the Riverside 3D IMAX Theater, where you can view such films as *Hubble 3D,* or *Amazon Adventure 3D, America's Musical Journey 3D.* Visit on STEM Saturday when you can explore science, technology, engineering, and mathematics with interactive activities for all ages. Explore robotics, physics, chemistry, and more based on a theme of the day.

The Air and Space Center is open Tues through Sat 10 a.m. to 5 p.m. and Sun noon to 5 p.m. Admission prices are $19.50 for adults, $17.50 for seniors (65+), and $16 for students (3–18) and include the IMAX movie. For the IMAX film alone, it's $8.75 for adults, $7.75 for seniors, and $6.75 for children (3–18).

funfacts

Booker T. Washington received his degree from Hampton Institute (now Hampton University) in 1875.

To bring yourself gently down to Earth, walk out onto the plaza or *Carousel Park* (602 Settlers Landing Rd.; 757-727-1610; downtownhampton.com/go/carousel-park) to see the marvelously restored 1920 *Hampton Carousel,* moved from Buckroe Beach. Take the 4-minute ride Tues through Sun, 10 a.m. to 5 p.m. Apr through Dec. Tickets are $1 per person.

Aviation buffs should also catch the *Air Power Park* (413 W. Mercury Blvd.; hampton.gov/facilities/facility/details/airpowerpark-23), with its awesome 15-acre outdoor exhibit of missiles, rockets, and military aircraft from the country's various service branches, including a Nike surface-to-air missile, an F-105D Thunderchief, and an F-100D Super Sabre, the first Air Force fighter with supersonic performance. An indoor museum has rooms with more than 325 models of aircraft, spacecraft, and nautical vessels. A quiet observation deck lets you see Newmarket Creek with the visiting and resident herons, egrets, blackbirds, and other wildlife. A nature trail is scheduled to be added in 2019. The park is open daily from sunrise to sunset and the museum is open Mon through Fri from 9 a.m. to 4:30 p.m. There is no admission fee.

The *Hampton University Museum* (14 Frissell Ave., Huntington Building; 757-727-5308; museum.hamptonu.edu) is the oldest African-American museum in the country. The world-renowned American Indian Collection consists of more than 1,600 pieces from 93 tribes. The collection was established in 1878 when the US government began sending young Indians from

A Little Chapel

The **Little England Chapel** (4100 Kecoughtan Rd.; 757-660-8646), built around 1879 to introduce religion to post–Civil War blacks in Virginia, is the state's only known African-American missionary chapel. It contains a permanent exhibit explaining the religious lives of post–Civil War blacks in Virginia. There are handwritten Sunday school lessons, photographs, 19th-century religious books, and a 12-minute video. The chapel has been designated a State and National Historic Landmark.

western reservations to be educated at Hampton Institute. Now located in the Beaux Arts–style Huntington Building, the museum's galleries are devoted to traditional and contemporary African, American-Indian, African-American, and Pacific Island art. The Hampton Museum is open Mon through Fri, 8 a.m. to 5 p.m.; Sat noon to 4 p.m. There is no admission fee.

The **Casemate Museum** (20 Bernard Rd.; 757-788-3391; fortmonroe.org/ visit/casemate-museum), set in an impressive location—a cavern of rooms built within the thick walls of **Fort Monroe National Monument**—relates the battles of Hampton Roads, particularly during the Civil War, with large exhibits of the Contraband Decision made there by Major General Benjamin F. Butler in 1861 and the contraband camps that followed. A new visitor center opens in 2019.

The story of the *Monitor* and *Merrimac* battle is told here, and you can see the area where Confederate president Jefferson Davis was imprisoned after the war. When construction of Fort Monroe was completed in 1834, it was referred to as the "Gibraltar of the Chesapeake" because of the strength of its fortifications. You can walk through the fort, the third oldest in America, and take a look at the **Old Point Comfort Lighthouse**, built in 1802 and in continuous use since then. This is where the first Africans arrived in English North America 400 years ago in 1619.

From Little Acorns

In 1863 the members of the Virginia Peninsula's black community gathered around an oak tree on the grounds of what is now Hampton University to hear the first reading of President Lincoln's Emancipation Proclamation. Mrs. Mary Peake, daughter of a free black woman and a Frenchman, conducted the first lessons taught under that tree on the university's campus. The National Geographic Society designated the **Emancipation Oak** as one of the 10 Great Trees of the World.

Fort Algernoume was on this site from 1609 to 1667. Fort George was built in 1727 and destroyed by a hurricane in 1749. Weakened coastal defenses during the War of 1812 allowed the British to sack Hampton and attack and burn Washington by sailing up Chesapeake Bay.

Discussions about the future of the fort created a battle that lasted longer than the Civil War. It is now under joint control of the Fort Monroe Authority, a Commonwealth agency, and the National Park Service.

Fort Monroe was America's only active-duty fort that was completely surrounded by a moat and remains the largest stone fort ever constructed on this continent. A walking tour is available—note Quarters Number One, stop nine on the tour. The oldest building at the fort, it was built between 1819, shortly after the fort's construction began, and 1823 and has been in use ever since.

The museum is open daily from 10:30 a.m. to 4:30 p.m. There is no admission charge.

Newport News

Set on the grounds of **Christopher Newport University,** the **Ferguson Center for the Arts** (1 Ave. of the Arts; 757-594-7448; fergusoncenter.org) is a 1,700-seat concert hall where the Russian National Ballet, Sir James Galway, and Ralph Stanley and the Clinch Mountain Boys were among the performers during its 2006 inaugural season. Among the acts in the 2018–2019 season were performances of the *Nutcracker*, Shanghai Opera Symphony Orchestra, *Spamalot*, the Russian National Ballet Theatre, Graham Nash, and Joan Baez. That's a schedule to give you enough reason to move to Newport News. The concert hall joined a 440-seat music and theater hall, a 200-seat studio theater, and rehearsal space. The firm of Pei Cobb Freed and Partners (of I. M. Pei fame) designed the $54 million complex (incorporating part of the old Ferguson High School) with perfect acoustics and sight lines. Bruce Bronstein serves as executive director.

Underhanded?

At the entrance to Christopher Newport University, at Avenue of the Arts and Warwick Boulevard, stands a 24-foot **bronze statue of Captain Christopher Newport,** created by sculptor Jon Hair. His statue is heroic and shows the strength, determination, and courage of the man who was responsible for the success and survival of the English Settlement at Jamestown. It also shows him with two hands, even though he lost his right arm in battle many years before arriving in Virginia.

Raising the *Monitor*

During the summer of 2001, after years of planning and 28 days of around-the-clock work, the 30-ton steam engine of the shipwrecked Civil War ironclad **Monitor** was raised from its watery bed 240 feet below the surface, off the shore of Cape Hatteras, North Carolina. It was taken to the Newport News Shipbuilding yard on July 18, and then *The Mariners' Museum and Park* in Newport News started taking it through a multiyear conservation process. In the intervening years, the engine and the turret that was rescued have been the subject of extensive studies and restoration, and the projected completion date keeps moving onward and onward. The amount of concretion (the combination of sand, sediment, marine life, iron oxide—rust) that had bonded to the surface of the artifacts continues to amaze them. A blog lets you follow their progress: marinersmuseum.org/blog (then select the USS *Monitor* Center tab).

When people say you can discover some of the best craftsmanship on Earth at *The Mariners' Museum and Park* (100 Museum Dr.; 757-596-2222; mariner.org), believe them. Founded in 1930 by Archer M. Huntington, the museum contains one of the world's finest collections of figureheads and perhaps the largest figurehead of all time: the *Lancaster Eagle.*

Opened in Mar 2007, the *USS* **Monitor** *Center,* a $30 million, 63,500-square-foot facility, is filled with recovered artifacts, original documents, paintings, personal accounts, and interactive experiences that paint a dazzling portrait of the USS *Monitor* and the CSS *Virginia.* You can walk the deck of a full-scale replica of the USS *Monitor,* try your hand at maneuvering a sailing frigate in battle, visit the officers' living quarters, and go inside an archaeological re-creation of the *Monitor*'s revolutionary gun turret. You can be transported back in time to the famous Battle of Hampton Roads (Mar 8 and 9, 1862), and to the night of Dec 31, 1862, when the *Monitor,* the US Navy's first ironclad warship, sank 16 miles off the coast of Cape Hatteras, North Carolina. Sound and imagery combine to leave you amazed, entertained, and educated.

August F. Crabtree's collection of 16 miniature ships (at a scale of about a quarter inch to the foot) follows the evolution of the sailing ship. Born in 1905 in Oregon, Crabtree was the grandson of a Glasgow shipbuilder. It took Crabtree and his wife, Winnifred (they met when he was building model ships for Hollywood movies and she was painting them), more than 27 years to complete this world-famous collection. The ships are enclosed in glass cases with mirrors underneath so you can see completely around them. Some boards are not in place so you can see inside, and there's a magnifying glass on some so you can appreciate the exacting detail work. This display is worth the visit, all by itself.

Guided tours are available, during which you might hear how Admiral Lord Nelson was shipped home in a wine cask or learn some other interesting military information.

There are 12 galleries featuring decorative arts, ship models, small crafts from workboats to pleasure craft, with 100 fascinating full-size boats from around the world, ships' carvings, and sea power, as well as a gallery for changing exhibits.

Guarded by the 10-foot, 4-inch statue (and it seems much taller) of Leif Eriksson, the **Age of Exploration Gallery** display shows how scientific and technological developments in shipbuilding, ocean navigation, and cartography led to the explorations of the 15th and early 16th centuries. Exhibited in the gallery, which opened in conjunction with the quincentenary celebration of Columbus's voyage to the New World, are ship models, rare books, illustrations, maps, navigational instruments, shipbuilding tools, and other maritime artifacts. Fifteen short videos that bring the Age of Exploration to life feature footage filmed in Spain, India, and other countries. The hands-on Discovery Library features reproductions of navigational instruments and facsimiles of charts and books used by early mariners. Do you have an explorer growing up in your family? It's all sensational and can be found here.

Be sure to stop by the museum shop, which contains a large selection of maritime books, educational toys, gifts, and prints.

The Mariners' Museum is open Mon through Sat, 9 a.m. to 5 p.m.; Sun 11 a.m. to 5 p.m. It is closed on Thanksgiving and Dec 25. Admission is $1 for everyone, except it's free for members and those who are 3 and under. The Park and Trail are free. There's a fee for the 3D movie.

The **Virginia Living Museum** (524 J. Clyde Morris Blvd.; 757-595-1900; thevlm.org) combines the best and most enjoyable elements of a native wildlife park, science museum, botanical garden, aquarium, and planetarium. They are all in one inspiring, beautiful setting. Hundreds of Native American eastern coastal creatures—including mammals, birds, marine life, reptiles, and insects—go about their daily routines as you discover the secrets of life in the wild. C'mon—have you ever seen pine voles, ghost crabs, or moon jellyfish? You can here. Indoors, you will find a 60-foot living panorama of the James River, beginning with life in a mountain stream and ending in the amazing depths of the Atlantic.

There's an ever-popular touch tank for a safe approach to the up-close feel. Outdoors you can stroll amid the natural beauty of the lakeside forest as a picturesque boardwalk leads you on an up-close safari into the lives of native water animals. The walk is less than ⅗ mile, and there are benches along the way. You are asked to stay on the paths and not to touch the animals, enclosures, or electric fences. An amphitheater overlooking Deer Park Lake opened in spring 2008 for animal programs and special events.

If you've ever wondered how things work (I'm not sure I've ever seen this information on those TV shows about how things work), then take the museum's Behind the Scenes Tours. You'll learn how the animals and fish are acquired, how their diets are prepared, how the water matches the oceans and

OTHER ATTRACTIONS IN COASTAL VIRGINIA— HAMPTON ROADS

Bea Arthur Dog Park
Norfolk
(757) 622-7382
virginia.org/listings/OutdoorsAndSports/
BeaArthurDogParkNorfolk/

Busch Gardens Williamsburg
Williamsburg
(757) 229-4386
buschgardens.com/williamsburg/

Ingleside Plantation Vineyards and Winery
Oak Grove
(804) 224-8687
inglesidevineyards.com/

Military Aviation Museum
Virginia Beach
(757) 721-7767
militaryaviationmuseum.org/

Norfolk Tides Baseball Club
Norfolk
(757) 622-2222
milb.com/Norfolk

Shirley Plantation
Charles City
(804) 829-5121
shirleyplantation.com

US Army Transportation Museum
Fort Eustis
(757) 878-1115
transportation.army.mil/museum/index
.html

Water Country USA
Williamsburg
(757) 229-4386
buschgardens.com/williamsburg/
water-country-usa/

rivers, what happens when critters get sick or injured, and what a herpetologist and an aquarist do. You can even watch trout being fed and see where coyotes sleep at night. The list might be endless. I've not counted.

The museum is open daily 9 a.m. to 5 p.m. Admission is $20 for adults and $15 for children (3–12); ages 2 and under are free. Behind-the-scenes tour ticket is $14 plus the general admission. They do not participate in the AZA (Association of Zoos and Aquariums) reciprocal admission program.

My first visit to the **Downing Gross Cultural Arts Center** (2410 Wickham Ave.; 757-247-8950; downinggross.org) was a serious WOW! This is the building that held the 1918 Walter Reed Elementary School that my mother and some of her siblings attended. Now, it's a performing and visual arts center with the Ella Fitzgerald Theater, a permanent exhibit of folk artist Anderson Johnson, mirror-lined dance rooms, meeting facilities, and so much more.

Norfolk

Norfolk's appeal starts at its international airport. In other airports you're almost held captive between flights. At Norfolk you can take a 15-minute walk and arrive at the enchanting paradise of the **Norfolk Botanical Garden** (6700 Azalea Garden Rd.; 757-441-5830; norfolkbotanicalgarden.org) with its 175 acres of azaleas, camellias, dogwoods, roses, and other flora nestled among tall pines and placid waters, where something always is in bloom. The garden was started in 1938, with 200 African-American women and 20 men planting 4,000 azaleas as a WPA (Works Progress Administration) project, and is now the largest in the state. It now boasts one of the largest collections of azaleas, camellias, roses, and rhododendrons on the East Coast. Norfolk's unique climate allows the coexistence of botanical species that are usually found widely separated geographically. The presence of California redwoods in the garden's collections is a perfect example. Start in the Baker Hall visitor center with its state-of-the-art audiovisual program that will help orient you to the garden's lush landscapes. A changing educational exhibit area will have programs on plant groups and other horticultural topics. Thirty-minute narrated tours are offered on trams and canal boats (spring through fall, $8).

The World of Wonders (WOW) exhibit is designed especially for children. Set in 3 acres, it aims to foster a connection between children and environment by encouraging them to utilize their natural curiosity to explore the garden. The WOW is open daily from 9:30 a.m. to 6:30 p.m.

In the 2 acres of the **Bristow Butterfly Garden** and **Butterfly House** are butterflies and moths, from swallowtail to monarchs, in various stages of their life cycles. Come by to see what you need in your garden to attract and support their visits.

Bike Nights (approximately late Apr through mid-Oct) are a great way for families to explore the beautiful landscape and authentic gravel paths surrounding the garden. Guests are invited to grab bikes and head to the garden for 3 hours of bike riding bliss! Families will also be thrilled by the Family Overnight package, where sleeping under the stars inside the garden proves to be the experience of a lifetime. If flowers aren't your primary interest, you can spend your between-flight time—or whenever—joining others as they do their daily walking and jogging exercises along 12 miles of meandering pathways surrounded by more than 20 theme gardens, including the Renaissance, Japanese, camellia, and holly gardens.

When you're through with the viewing or the exercising, stop by the gift shop for garden books, tools, and gifts, or visit the teahouse for lunch, snacks, and refreshments.

The grounds are the site of more than 100 weddings a year and the annual *April International Azalea Festival.*

The gardens are open daily 9 a.m. to 7 p.m. Apr through Oct, and 9 a.m. to 5 p.m. the rest of the year (check hours for WOW, etc.). Adult entry fee is $12, seniors and military $10, and children (3–17) $10. Canal boat tours are $5 for adults. Look for the sign at the airport, or follow the road signs from I-64.

Beautifully landscaped MacArthur Square in downtown Norfolk is the site of the four buildings that make up the *Douglas MacArthur Memorial* (198 Bank St., MacArthur Square; 757-441-2965; macarthurmemorial.org), honoring the life of General Douglas MacArthur.

Inside the memorial is a theater with a continuously running 27-minute film on the life and times of the general, one of the most colorful and controversial men in American history. The *Jean MacArthur Research Center* (named after the general's late wife) houses the library and archives, an education wing, and the administrative offices for the MacArthur Memorial and the General Douglas MacArthur Foundation. The gift shop displays General MacArthur's 1950 Chrysler Imperial limousine, which he used from 1950 to the end of his life. Nine galleries on two floors circle the rotunda, where the general and his wife are buried. There is no admission fee to the memorial, which is open Tues through Sat 10 a.m. to 5 p.m., and Sun 11 a.m. to 5 p.m.

Early Jewish immigrants played an important part in Norfolk history, and their traditions and contributions are interpreted at the *Moses Myers House* (323 E. Freemason St.; 757-333-1087; chrysler.org/about-the-museum/historic -houses/the-moses-myers-house). The original part of the house was constructed in 1792, then expanded in 1797 to include a commodious dining room for entertaining and two bedrooms for Moses and Eliza Myers's nine children. Five generations of descendants of the Myers family lived in this home until it was sold to a preservation group in 1931. In the early 1950s, the city of Norfolk bought the residence, and the property is administered by the Chrysler Museum of Art. Nearly 70 percent of the furnishings are original.

You know the famed Gilbert Stuart painting of George Washington; well, there's a matched set of portraits of the senior Myers by Stuart hanging in the drawing room. Other noted American artists are also represented.

The house is open Sat and Sun noon to 5 p.m.

The *Chrysler Museum of Art* (1 Memorial Pl.; 757-664-6200; chrysler.org) was named for Walter Chrysler Jr. in 1970, when Norfolk offered to add a wing and rename its museum for him if he would move his art collection from Provincetown, Massachusetts, to Norfolk. The city also named a concert hall at Scope Arena for him.

Long considered one of the finest galleries in the country, the Chrysler suffered a potentially severe setback when Chrysler, the museum's chief benefactor, died and left 751 of his works to a nephew. They had been on loan to the museum, and the loss could have been devastating. The museum, however, retains more than 10,000 works (all gifts of Chrysler) in the permanent collection, valued at more than $100 million. After a $13.5 million renovation and new wing project that increased the museum's space by half, the gallery had a reopening in 2014. There is no admission fee, although contributions are always welcome. A free glassmaking demonstration is presented daily at noon. The museum is open Tues through Sat 10 a.m. to 5 p.m., and Sun noon to 5 p.m.

Anyone who's spent any time in Norfolk is sure to mention *Doumar's* (1919 Monticello Ave.; 757-627-4163; doumars.com). Abe Doumar created the ice-cream cone at the 1904 St. Louis Exposition. He originally called his rolled-up wafer that contained ice cream the "ice-cream cornucopia." After that he

Naval Station Norfolk

Naval Station Norfolk occupies about 8,000 acres in the Hampton Roads area and includes the naval base, port services, and air operations. It's home to more than 78 ships from the Atlantic Fleet. Check the website for the 45-minute guided bus tour to see aircraft carriers, destroyers, amphibious assault ships, historic homes from the 1907 Jamestown Exposition, and one of the busiest airfields in the country. Depending on the season, there may be as few as one tour a day to nine tours a day. The fee is $10 for adults and $5 for children (3–11) and seniors. A photo ID is required for everyone 18 and older. Buses are not wheelchair accessible. Tours depart from the Naval Tour and Information Center, 9079 Hampton Blvd., next to gate 5; (757) 444-7955; cnic.navy.mil.

opened a concession at Coney Island in 1905 and visited state fairs (President Teddy Roosevelt had a cone in Raleigh, North Carolina). In 1907 a shop was opened in Ocean View, Virginia, where in 1925 his brother George and crew sold 22,600 cones in a single day. After the 1933 hurricane destroyed much of Ocean View Park, George opened the Doumar Drive-In at 19th and Monticello Streets in Norfolk. It was the first and is now one of the last curbside restaurants in Virginia.

Although many people claim the credit for making the first ice-cream cone, Doumar's story stands up the best. The Smithsonian Institution has collected some of his pictures and memorabilia to add to an exhibit in the Museum of American History in Washington, DC. Barbecue is the main menu item, after the interest in the cones. Waffle-cone making is scheduled Mon through Sat from 10 to 11:30 a.m. However, they will take the machine out for demonstrations periodically, so call to determine whether it will be operational on the day and at the time you want to visit. Doumar's is open Mon through Thurs 8 a.m. to 11 p.m., Fri and Sat 8 a.m. to 12:30 a.m.

Oh, yes, Guy Fieri did visit and feature Doumar's on his Food Network show *Diners, Drive-Ins & Dives* in 2008.

In 1912 a grand lady, the Wells Theatre, now the ***Virginia Stage Company at the Wells Theatre*** (108 E. Tazewell St.; 757-627-6988 or 757-627-1234; vastage.org) opened to a capacity house with the musical *The Merry Countess*. The theater was converted into a movie house in 1935 after such stars as Billie Burke, Douglas Fairbanks, Fred and Adele Astaire, Will Rogers, and others had trod her boards. As at other theaters of the time, the '60s brought the garish light of X-rated flicks, and a bar was built where the stage had been. The fair damsel was saved from much distress when the Virginia Stage Company took over in Oct 1979, and the bar was removed. The thrust stage was built, and the lobby was returned to its approximate original size. The interior and exterior were scrubbed clean, paint was applied, seats were reupholstered, new carpet was laid, and productions once again were mounted.

The Virginia Stage Company presents a handful of plays each year that are worth seeing, but the amazing artistry that went into this steel-reinforced concrete structure of the pre–Beaux Arts period is a command performance.

The 53-acre ***Virginia Zoological Park*** (3500 Granby St.; 757-441-2374; virginiazoo.org) has been established to accurately reflect an entire habitat for its more than 350 animals and birds, so when you visit you will find plants in the animal exhibits and animals in the plant exhibits. With the monkeys are vines and assorted habitat plants; with the cats are jungle flora. This is such an important part of the operation that visitors receive a *Botanical Conservatory Guide* to help you through the zoo.

Cannonball Run

Well, actually it's the **Cannonball Trail** winding its way along historic sites in downtown Norfolk. The walk-it-yourself tour is a storytelling stage for interpreting 400 years of Norfolk's history with 25 stops along the way. Begin your sojourn at the Freemason Street Reception Center, 401 E. Freemason St.; (757) 664-6620 or (800) 368–3097; visitnorfolk.com/things-to-do/self-guided-tours/cannonball-trail-tour.

The conservatory was built in 1907, and there are more than 3,000 blooming annuals and 150 hanging baskets. The rose garden has beds of floribunda, hybrid tea, and climbing varieties.

Behind-the-scenes tours teach you about animal care, behavior, and conservation. Meet the rhinos, try to go eye-to-eye with the giraffes, and roar with the lions. Twelve different tours are offered, depending on which animals (e.g., sun bear, Malayan tapir, reptiles, etc.) interest you. Reservations must be made at least 2 weeks in advance. Tour fee includes admission to the zoo.

The zoo is open daily 10 a.m. to 5 p.m. except on major winter holidays. Admission is $17.95 for adults, $15.95 for seniors 62 and older, and $14.95 for children (2–11). Zoo members and children under 2 are free. Discounts are available for military, first responders, and others. The zoo train schedule depends on the season and definitely only runs on days when the temperature is 50 degrees Fahrenheit or above. Train tickets are $2 each and, for a fee, you can be a train engineer for a day.

Rowena's Bakery (243 W. Bute St., Ste. B; 757-627-8699; rowenas.com) started in 1983 when Rowena Fullinwider took a flying leap into the cake

Home Porting

Home porting is the phrase used by the cruise industry as cruise ships are based in various ports around the country, eliminating the need for travelers to fly to somewhere to get somewhere. In Virginia, it's the **Decker Half Moone Center** (757-664-1000; nauticus.org/cruise-virginia), a cruise port that's within walking distance of 2,000 hotel rooms, shopping, and museums. It's an 80,000-square-foot, 2-story terminal, located between Nauticus and Town Point Park. It's made of corrugated steel and glass that gives it a smooth, nautical look. It was the first cruise terminal in the nation to fully comply with Homeland Security standards. Norfolk certainly knows its starboard from its port. As Norfolk is so close to the Atlantic Ocean, most casinos and duty-free shops are open within an hour of sailing. Carnival (*Triumph*), Aida, Princess, and Silversea are among the cruise lines calling at Norfolk during 2019.

business. Her fame grew as people tasted her almond pound cake, made from an old family recipe. However, you should try the chocolate and lemon cakes before you decide which is your favorite. Rowena died in July 2013, but the bakery continues. The store is open Tues through Fri, 10 a.m. to 4 p.m.

Not everything is old in Virginia, although it may cover historic material. ***Nauticus, the National Maritime Center*** is a hands-on entertainment and education center with scores of interesting exhibits about the exploration of the world's oceans. This is a wonderful place to learn how vast the influences of water are on our lives, for it encompasses marine biology and oceanography, commercial shipping, naval technology, shipbuilding, and energy exploration. Whether your fascination is with science, technology, commerce, or the siren call of the deep, you'll see how the sea connects to our existence—and it's fun.

What does all this mean? Simply that you can sit in the captain's chair in the Navy pilothouse and observe the harbor from the bridge. You can plot ships in the harbor on the live Nauticus radar. How would you like to land your plane (F14 or prop) on an aircraft carrier (video game) or be a weatherman and conduct your own television show? One of my favorites in any marine exhibit is the touch pool, where you can feel the creatures of the sea, and Nauticus has one. Kids of various ages love periscopes, so they can check this one out and target in on a ship in the harbor.

This $52 million project is set on three levels at Norfolk's Waterside complex, at the west end of the waterfront, adjacent to Town Point Park. There's docking space on the water for research ships and active Navy ships, which you may visit.

Exhibits have been assembled with the assistance of the Coast Guard, Navy, Old Dominion University, Norfolk State University, the College of William and Mary's Institute of Marine Science, and the National Oceanic and Atmospheric Administration. Nauticus is open daily 10 a.m. to 5 p.m. from Memorial Day through Labor Day. It's open Tues through Sat from 10 a.m. to 5 p.m., and Sun from noon to 5 p.m. the rest of the year.

As part of the US Navy's 225th anniversary in late fall 2000, the battleship ***USS* Wisconsin** (nauticus.org/exhibits/battleship-wisconsin) was located adjacent to Nauticus. Launched Dec 7, 1943, the warship—at 888 feet one of the longest ever built—was one of the last four battleships built by the United States for service in World War II. It also saw action during the Korean conflict and the Persian Gulf action. Norfolk was the home port of the *Wisconsin* during most of its active-duty career. Included in locating the ship here was the building of a berth and a connecting walkway to the museum. The ship is open daily 10 a.m. to 5 p.m. from Memorial Day through Labor Day; Tues through Sat 10 a.m. to 5 p.m., and Sun noon to 5 p.m. the rest of the year.

Basic admission to Nauticus is $15.95 for adults, $11.50 for children (4–12), and $12.95 for active duty military and includes Nauticus and a self-guided tour of the battleship *Wisconsin*. A gold admission ($35.95 for adults, $31.50 for children, and $32.95 for active military) includes Nauticus and a guided tour of the *Wisconsin* interior and 3D movies.

Portsmouth

From its antiques and specialty stores to its shade-drenched streets, **Historic Olde Towne Portsmouth** is much more than one of the region's most pleasant places to take a stroll. It's a history-lover's dream come true. In a single square mile, the Olde Towne Historic District contains one of America's largest collections of architecturally noteworthy 18th- and 19th-century homes and churches.

Portsmouth was founded in 1716 by Colonel William Crawford, a merchant and ship owner who named the new town after Portsmouth, England. A walk through Olde Towne today reveals homes built in varied architectural styles, including Federal, Greek Revival, Classical Renaissance, Gothic, and Romanesque. While the homes are privately owned, Olde Towne is in fact a tourism attraction, renowned as one of the largest collections of historic homes in America.

Legend has it that Benedict Arnold was held captive in one of the homes. Another was used by Union forces to issue travel passes to citizens during the Civil War, while yet another concealed medicine for Confederate soldiers. Other homes hosted visits by four US presidents.

You can explore this national treasure through the *Path of History* brochure, a self-guided tour that directs you to 45 homes, monuments, and churches. This free brochure is available at the Portsmouth Visitor Information Center located at 6 Crawford Pkwy. (757-393-5111; portsvacation.com).

Since the founding of the Gosport Shipyard in 1767, the history of Portsmouth has been closely intertwined with the shipyard. Later renamed the Norfolk Navy Yard and finally the **Norfolk Naval Shipyard**, many historic ships have been built here. They include the CSS *Virginia* (originally Merrimac), the first ironclad to engage in battle; the nation's first battleship, the Texas; and the world's first aircraft carrier, the Langley. During the Revolutionary War, the shipyard was described by the British as "the most considerable one in America."

The new **Portsmouth Colored Community Library Museum** (904 Elm Ave.; 757-393-8983 ext. 20; portsvaafricanamericanheritage.com) is an important artifact, resource, and memorial to African Americans throughout the Hampton Roads region and Virginia. The library began serving black patrons in 1945, during the height of the Jim Crow laws, and closed when the city's main library was integrated in 1963. Today the restored library is a museum that is home to important photographs, oral histories, and exhibits. The museum is open Fri and Sat noon to 5 p.m. and by appointment.

The **Children's Museum of Virginia** (221 High St.; 757-393-5238; childrensmuseumva.com) is more than 74,000 square feet of foot-stomping, bubble-blowing, music-making, educational fun. Located in Olde Towne Portsmouth, the museum is based on the philosophy that children learn by doing. With more than 90 interactive exhibits (making it the largest interactive children's museum in Virginia) dedicated to enhancing the cultural, educational, and recreational development of children, the museum encourages a lifelong love of learning.

See the stars in the planetarium. Find out how much power it takes to run household appliances. Learn how sound travels in waves. Blow some bubbles. Make music. Climb a rock wall. Discover that bits, bytes, and chips aren't just in chocolate chip cookies. And be sure to marvel at the $1 million Lancaster Antique Toy and Model Train Collection, an amazing collection

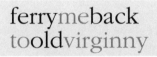

ferrymeback tooldvirginny

The first ferry service in America was established in 1636 on the Elizabeth River between Portsmouth and Norfolk. The *Gosport,* the first steam-powered ferry, was christened in 1832 and crossed the Elizabeth River in 5 minutes.

of antique toys and one of the most incredible train collections in the world! Check the museum schedule for classes and workshops (gingerbread houses in Dec, STEM club, Girl Scout badges, etc.), camps, and other special events.

The museum is open Tues through Sat 9 a.m. to 5 p.m., Sun 11 a.m. to 5 p.m. It's also open on Mon during the summer. Admission is $11 for adults, $10 for children (2–17), military, and seniors.

Isle of Wight County

Smithfield is the self-proclaimed "Ham Capital of the World." P. D. Gwaltney Sr. started his curing process in 1870, and the Smithfield curing process is protected by law. Only a ham cured within the Smithfield town limits can bear the name. You can smell the delicious aroma for miles around. The **Isle of Wight County Museum** (103 Main St.; 757-356-1223; smithfield-virginia.com) offers a display about ham history and exhibits on the Civil War and Indian artifacts. There's also a reproduction of an old country store. The museum is open Mon through Sat from 10 a.m. to 4 p.m., and Sun from noon to 5 p.m.

Pick up the brochure for the scenic Smithfield **Historic Old Town Walking Tour** and proceed past buildings dating from the mid- to late 1750s (the completely restored Old Courthouse and Clerk's Office at 130 Main St., the Old Jail at 106 N. Mason, the Eason-Whitley House at 220 S. Church, and others) up to pre–Civil War times. The mix of housing styles is almost eclectic. Early residents either tore down or updated their homes to make way for the newest styles (keeping up with the Smiths rather than the Joneses, if you will). Therefore, as you stroll around, you'll see Colonial, Federal, and Victorian styles. Fifteen homes and four buildings, 14 of which predate the Revolutionary War, are authentically 18th century. You can also view the four identical Victorian houses on Main Street and the Gingerbread Cottage on Grace Street.

You can spend at least 90 minutes on this walk and expand it to 3 hours. For information call (757) 357-5182 or (800) 365-9339.

funfacts

When you stop by the *Isle of Wight County Museum,* take a look at the interactive exhibit of a one-ton-plus ham biscuit. A Guinness World Record was awarded for this supersize edible created in honor of Smithfield's 250th anniversary. You can also see Smithfield Ham's oldest ham—more than 100 years old—protected in a glass case.

Guided walking tours are offered by the Tourism Bureau, and iPod tours (iPods provided) are available at the Isle of Wight County Museum. Group tours should be scheduled in advance. Agricultural tours also are available in season at **Darden's Country Store and Smokehouse** (16249 Bowling Green Rd.; 757-357-6791) to see peanuts from seeds to shelling and grading, cotton from plants to ginning, and the Darden family's popular smokehouse tour. The hours are Mon through Sat 7 a.m. to 6 p.m.

The **Schoolhouse Museum** (516 Main St.; 757-357-5182; theschoolhouse museum.org) is an African-American History Museum of Public Education. The two-room building was constructed in 1932 and features period desks and books. Oral histories have been given by those who attended the school.

Gracious lodging is available at the **Smithfield Inn and Tavern Bed and Breakfast** (112 Main St.; 757-357-1752; smithfieldinn.com), said to be one of the town's most enduring landmarks. It's been providing lodging in its 5 rooms (some with fireplaces) and serving meals since 1752, with slight interruptions when it was used as a rectory for the Christ Episcopal Church and for a period after the Civil War when it was uninhabitable.

Fort Huger (5080 Talcott Terr.; 757-357-2291; historicisleofwight.com/fort-huger.html), the "gateway to the Confederate capital," is the newest old attraction in the area. From here you can see the Ghost Fleet on the James River, take a walk through the trails, and see cannons mounted along the edges of the fort. Guided walking tours are scheduled periodically or by appointment (757) 356-1223. The fort is open daily from 8 a.m. to dusk. (The Ghost Fleet, or the James River Reserve Fleet, is one of three National Defense Reserve Fleets remaining in the country. This operational fleet of wood- and steel-hulled ships started in World War I, and there were nearly 300 mothballed ships by the start of World War II and nearly 800 ships by 1950. Many of the ships can be readied for service in as few as 20 days and used as emergency transportation for either government or other needs.)

Those who love to wander the waters around the James River and find their way to Pagan River have been delighted with **Smithfield Station Waterfront Inn and Marina** (415 S. Church St.; 757-357-7700; smithfieldstation .com), at the junction of the two creeks that form the river. Run by Ron and Tina Pack, it's a carefree place dedicated to those who want to pull up to a dock, be greeted by the owners, and not have to worry about "dressing" for dinner. The specialties at the restaurant are, naturally enough, seafood and pork, and you should definitely try the sweet potato–encrusted rockfish. Entertainment and special events are held on the boardwalk adjacent to the restaurant. Newlyweds and anniversary celebrants might enjoy the Cape Chesapeake Bay–style lighthouse building with honeymoon suites.

Stay a day or two and rent a bicycle or canoe to really "sit back" and relax. Then head out and go crabbing or look for osprey and eagles, deer, and muskrat.

Just across the street from the Station is the **Windsor Castle Park** (301 Jericho Rd.; 75742-3109; windsorcastlepark.com), a 208-acre riverside facility in the heart of downtown Smithfield. From here you have 4 miles of wooded walking trails, a dog park, state-of-the-art canoe/kayak launch, fruit orchards, fishing pier, scenic overlooks, picnic areas, and the Windsor Castle Historic Site. The Windsor Castle Farm was part of a 1,450-acre parcel patented in 1537 by Arthur Smith, an ancestor of the town's founder, Arthur Smith IV. It's open daily from dawn until dusk, and there's no admission charge.

About 2 miles south of Smithfield on Route 10 is historic **St. Luke's Church & Museum** (14477 Benn's Church Blvd.; 757-357-3367; historicstlukes .org). The 17th-century brick church is Virginia's oldest church building and the oldest surviving Anglican church building in North America. Architectural influences incorporate several "artisan mannerism" design elements, including Gothic, Romanesque, and Jacobean. Today, the 43-acre historic site and museum provides hourly, 45-minute guided tours that highlight the period artifacts and the oldest (1630s) English chamber organ in the world.

The National Historic Landmark and Patriotic Shrine hosts several special events throughout the year. The site is open Feb 1 through Dec 31, Tues through Sat, 9:30 a.m. to 5 p.m. Admission is $8 for adult; $46 for seniors (52+), AAA, and military; and $5 for educators and students.

Fort Boykin Historic Park (7410 Ft. Boykin Trail; 757-357-5182; genuine smithfieldva.com/attractions.html), on the high cliffs over the James River (which is navigable to Richmond), has been around since 1623 and has been involved in every military campaign fought on American soil. It first protected the colonists against the "Spaniards by sea and the Indians by land" and then was refortified during the Revolutionary War. It is named in honor of Major Francis Boykin, a member of General George Washington's staff. Its current seven-pointed star shape was created during the War of 1812, but much of the property was destroyed by a Union landing party. While the American poet Sidney Lanier was stationed here during the Civil War, he wrote "Hoe Cakes" and "Beautiful Ladies" and started his novel *Tiger Lilies*. The property had pretty much returned to nature until 1908, when Mr. and Mrs. Herbert Greer bought it and started landscaping the grounds. Picnickers are welcome, and the grounds are open daily from 8 a.m. to dusk.

Suffolk

Just the name of the *Great Dismal Swamp National Wildlife Refuge* (3100 Desert Rd.; 757-986-3705; fws.gov/refuge/great_dismal_swamp) in Suffolk sounds depressing, but nature lovers should jump for joy. Wander along the 140 miles of hiking and biking trails in this 111,000-acre swamp and you'll see bald cypress, shady creeks, and maybe barred owls, otters, bats, raccoons, and bears. Canoe and kayak access to Lake Drummond is via the feeder ditch near Chesapeake. All vehicles must pay a $5 daily fee for entry to the Wildlife Drive for touring or boating. The headquarters is open Mon through Fri from 7:30 a.m. to 4 p.m.

The *Suffolk Visitor Center* (524 N. Main St.; 866-SEE-SUFK or 757-923-3880; visitsuffolkva.com) is located in the historic Nansemond County Courthouse. It is open daily from 9 a.m. to 5 p.m. Narrated bus tours of the Great Dismal Swamp National Wildlife Refuge depart from the center.

In 1837 Mills Riddick built an impressive Greek Revival house, a style fairly common in the Midwest but rarely seen this far south, and it was immediately labeled *Riddick's Folly* (510 N. Main St.; 757-934-0822; riddicksfolly.org). As with most follies that still stand, he was proven right over the years. The carved cypress woodwork survives, as do the decorative medallions that crown the 14-foot ceilings. The rooms that housed five generations of his descendants are now home to gallery space for changing and semi-permanent exhibits, lectures, and art workshops; a gift shop where local artists and crafters sell their work; and the archives of the Suffolk Nansemond Historical Society.

Riddick's Folly is open Wed through Fri 10 a.m. to 5 p.m., Sat 10 a.m. to 4 p.m., and Sun 1 to 5 p.m. Ninety-minute guided tours are available. Admission is $7 for adults; $6 for seniors (55+) and active military; and $3 for students (6–18). It is partially wheelchair accessible.

Surry County

The free **Scotland-Jamestown Ferry** (16289 Rolfe Hwy. from the "Surry Side" or 2110 Jamestown Rd. from Jamestown; 800-823-3779; virginiadot.org/travel/ferry-jamestown.asp) or the Jamestown-Scotland Ferry (height clearance 12 feet, 6 inches) connects Route 31 over the James River and is the only 24-hour state-run ferry operation in Virginia. Four ferries can transport between 28 and 70 cars (depending on which ferry) across the scenic James River. Scotland has a population of 203 as of 2018, so Surry may not be your destination. You'd be missing some fun and interesting things, though (see below). However, the 15- to 20-minute trip is great for views of pelicans, ospreys, eagles, gulls, and other fauna. Going from Scotland to Jamestown lets you see the historic village much as the first residents and visitors might have seen it from the river. The four ferries are the *Pocahontas* (built in 1995), *Surry, Williamsburg,* and *Virginia* (built in 1936).

Should you be traveling the ferry on Fri afternoon between 4 and 7 p.m. during May and Oct, stop by the **Surry Farmers Market** (surrycountytourism .com/Farmers_Market.htm). You'll find prepared foods, locally grown produce, meat, dairy, baked goods, crafts, fun for children, and live entertainment.

Another stop "South of the James" is **Bacon's Castle** (465 Bacon's Castle Trail; 757-357-5976; surrycountytourism.com/Bacons_Castle.htm), a building that admittedly doesn't look like a castle and that Nathaniel Bacon (for whom it's named) probably never visited. The 1665 high Jacobean-style structure is said to be the oldest known brick dwelling in North America and has given its name to the area. Built by Arthur Allen, it was seized and occupied for three months in 1676 by troops who supported the rebel Nathaniel Bacon in an event known as **Bacon's Rebellion**. Two rooms are furnished from the original inventory, and there are archaeological and architectural exhibits offered. Guided tours are available. The castle is open Fri through Mon (June through Dec) and Fri through Sun (Feb to May). Admission is $10 for adults; $9 for seniors and military; and $6 for children (6–18).

Virginia Beach

There's more to **Virginia Beach** than the beach and ocean (obviously major attractions). Residents and vacationers have a lot of options for their leisure time, with visiting Mount Trashmore, catching rays, or traveling back and forth across the Chesapeake Bay Bridge-Tunnel, the 17-mile route connecting Cape Charles on the DelMarVa Peninsula to the western shore.

The *Norwegian Lady Statue* (25th Street and Oceanfront; thenorwegian lady.wordpress.com/about-2) is a 9-foot bronze replica of the wooden figure-head of the Norwegian barque *Dictator* that ran aground on a sandbar 300 yards offshore on March 28, 1891. Today, that would be 37th Street in Virginia Beach. Locals and visitors from a nearby hotel and men from two United States Lifesaving Services (now the Coast Guard) fought the storm to try to rescue the crew and passengers. Eight of the 17 people on board were rescued. Seven crew members are buried at Elmwood Cemetery in Norfolk. The figurehead later washed ashore and stood as a memorial on the oceanfront for 60 years until Hurricane Barbara damaged it in 1953. Funds were raised to create two new statues. The residents of Moss, Norway, commissioned this statue and gave it to Virginia Beach in 1962 with a duplicate erected in Moss to link the sister cities. An annual wreath laying is held every year in commemoration of the event.

The Virginia Beach Surf & Rescue Museum (24th Street on the Board-walk; 757-422-1587; vbsurfrescuemuseum.org/visit-us), housed in the former Life Saving Station (which became the Coast Guard), is the only station in Vir-ginia that's open to the public. It was built in 1903, when the men who risked their lives to save others worked for little more than a dollar a day. It was decommissioned in 1969. There's now a gift shop inside as well as the historical memorabilia of shipwrecks, lives saved, and other items related to the construc-tion of the Virginia Beach boardwalk and Virginia's connection to the water. The museum is open Tues through Sat 10 a.m. to 5 p.m., and Sun noon to 5 p.m. Admission to the station is $6 for adults; $5 for senior and military; free for children under 18. However, there's no charge to go into the museum store.

Two-thirds of the 9,250-plus acres of the *Back Bay National Wildlife Refuge* (4005 Sandpiper Rd.; 757-301-7329; fws.gov/refuge/back_bay) are marshlands while the rest is beach, dunes, woodland, and farm fields. The ref-uge is home to waterfowl, loggerhead sea turtles, and ghost crabs. Some 10,000 snow geese and a large variety of ducks stop by the refuge during Dec, the peak of the fall migration. You can take a self-guided walking or biking tour, or enjoy fishing to your heart's content. The outdoor areas are open daily from dawn to dusk. Stop by the Visitor Contact Station for information and a bird list. Pets are not allowed on the refuge, and swimming, sunbathing, surfing, and "other non-wildlife-dependent activities are prohibited." What you can do is hike, photograph, fish, observe, and educate or be educated. Please stay on the trails and roadways and do not enter the dunes.

Outdoor facilities are open daily from 30 minutes before sunrise to 30 minutes after sunset. The Visitor Contact Station is open Tues through Fri 8 a.m. to 4 p.m., and weekends 9 a.m. to 4 p.m. Memorial Day through Labor Day, and Fri 8 a.m. to 4 p.m. and Sat 9 a.m. to 4 p.m. the rest of the year. Fees vary by season and whether you enter by foot or vehicle, although from Nov through Mar there is no admission charge.

Virginia Beach is noted for *Mount Trashmore* (310 Edwin Dr.; 757-385-2995; vbgov.com/government/departments/parks-recreation), which solved two major problems in this community. First, it provided a place for a solid-waste landfill. Instead of filling shallow holes (impossible because of the high water table), the city built a mountain. Second, it provided a large recreational facility. Mount Trashmore spans 165 acres with one "peak" that is 60 feet in height and more than 800 feet long, and a second, smaller mountain. It was the first overground landfill created especially as a municipal park.

Kite flying is a trip in the spring, and on a brisk March day the air is filled with colorful boxes and other flights of fancy. You can also enjoy picnic shelters, playgrounds, volleyball courts, a 7-foot-deep bowl, 13.5-foot vertical ramp, and a 1.45 mile walking trail. After more than four decades, the park received some much-needed updates and refurbishments in 2018. Without fear of contradiction, I will say that Mount Trashmore inspired dozens of other cities in this country and abroad to seek similar solutions for solid waste and recreational problems. The park is open daily from 7:30 a.m. to sunset.

The historic *Cavalier Hotel* (4200 Atlantic Ave.; 757-425-8555; cavalier hotel.com) could be called a phoenix for all the lives it's lived. After a massive four-year, $85,000,000 renovation, the hotel opened its doors on March 7, 2018. The first time it did that was in 1927 and the glorious architectural elements and design from the past have met the modern-day luxuries you want

Virginia Beach Trivia

The *Virginia Beach Boardwalk* (actually concrete) is 40 blocks long and open for in-line skating, jogging, or strolling. A bikes-only strip of asphalt with lane markings runs next to the boardwalk.

No, you're not suddenly transported to the Hollywood Walk of Fame in La-La Land, but you are seeing plaques honoring such famous Virginians as Arthur Ashe, Patsy Cline, Katie Couric, Thomas Jefferson, Pocahontas, former Virginia governor Doug Wilder, and Edgar Allan Poe along the *Virginia Legends Walk* at Virginia Beach's 13th Street Park. Look for the Virginia Legends archway at 1300 Atlantic Ave. (757-463-4500; virginiabeach.com/listing/attractions-history/legends-walk).

to create a new perfection. You can join the list of presidents and celebrities (including F. Scott Fitzgerald and Judy Garland) who have stayed here. You can almost hear the lyrical notes from the Big Bands that played here. Enjoy the Seahill Spa, dine at venues with exquisite farm-to-fork cuisine, relax at the exclusive beach club, and savor the offerings from the on-site distillery and tasting room.

"Is there gold in seawater?" "How do waves change our coastline?" "What is it like beneath the surface of Chesapeake Bay?" The answers to these questions and more are waiting to be discovered at the *Virginia Aquarium and Marine Science Center* (717 General Booth Blvd.; 757-385-3474; virginia aquarium.com).

A visit to the center is two journeys: a journey across water that focuses on the diverse natural habitats across Virginia today and a journey through the habitats of Virginia's past. A 12,000-square-foot gallery is titled the Restless Planet: A Journey Across the Planet that Brings You Closer to Home. Its immersive habitats will look, feel, sound, and smell like a Malaysian peat swamp, a coastal desert, the Red Sea, and an active volcano. Save time and energy for the Adventure Park, an eco-friendly zip line and aerial adventure experience for children, teens, and adults. Behind-the-scenes tours are available so you can learn more about sea turtles, and how the staff cares for the fish and other marine animals.

The 800,000+ gallon facility is one of the best aquariums and animal habitats in the country. It's an enjoyable, hands-on educational operation from just about the moment you enter. Food is available at three dining options, from fast casual to grab 'n' go.

The aquarium is open daily 9 a.m. to 5 p.m. and closed on Thanksgiving and Dec 25. Combined admission for the aquarium and movie is $29.95 for adults (12–61), $24.95 for children (3–11), and $27.95 for seniors (62+). Tickets are also available for the aquarium only, movie only, Dolphin Discoveries boat trip, and Ocean Collections boat trip.

The *Old Cape Henry Lighthouse* is special because from here you can see the lighthouse that replaced it in 1881, offering you the option of taking a photo of a lighthouse from a lighthouse or taking a picture of two lighthouses in one shot.

Authorized and funded by America's first Congress, the lighthouse was built in 1791 and was the first public building authorized by that body. This lighthouse, near the entrance to the Chesapeake Bay, was used for almost 90 years, until 1881. The stones were mined in the Aquia Quarries, which also provided stone for the US Capitol, the White House, and Mount Vernon. It's open daily 10 a.m. to 5 p.m. mid-Mar to Nov 1, and 10 a.m. to 4 p.m. the rest of the year. It is closed on Thanksgiving, Dec 24, 25, and 31, Jan 1, and during some events such as the Shamrock Marathon around St. Patrick's Day. The last visitors are admitted 15 minutes prior to closing. *Note:* The lighthouse is located on the grounds of Fort Story military base, so you must clear security, and everyone 16 and over must have photo identification. Admission fees are $5 for adults (13+), $3 for children (3–12), and free for younger children and APVA (Association for the Preservation of Virginia Antiquities) members. There is a height requirement of 42 inches to enter the lighthouse. Enter through the Fort Story gate, off Route 60; 583 Atlantic Ave. (757-422-9421; nps.gov/came/cape-henry-lighthouses.htm).

Historic Triangle

This is the historical triangle area of Williamsburg, Jamestown, and Yorktown.

As a child, my visits to *Jamestown Settlement,* previously Jamestown Festival Park, were at least an annual treat. It's amazing how much things have changed over the years as historians have learned more about what happened here and how people lived centuries ago. Stockades used to be a feature; they aren't now because historians determined that stockades weren't used in Colonial Jamestown. Costumed guides no longer talk in first person because they found it off-putting for some people who didn't know how to ask questions and difficult to stay in character when confronted with a question about cameras, for example. The guides still wear what was worn, to some extent, but you'll also find guys with earrings, and one would suspect that the early settlers didn't do that.

Obviously, history buffs love this area, and at *Historic Jamestowne* (historicjamestowne.org) you can see the first permanent English settlement (1607) in North America. Of particular interest is the *Nathalie P. and Alan M. Voorhees Archaearium,* where objects belonging to the colonists 400 years ago and unearthed from the James Fort site are on display. The objects exhibit a new understanding of the settlers and their relationship with the Virginia Indians. Learn how the archaeologists found the fort and see arms and armor, medical instruments, and much more. Yes, dead men do tell tales, and you can see the remains believed to be of Captain Bartholomew Gosnold, a Jamestown founding father.

Historic Jamestowne is open daily from 9 a.m. to 5 p.m. It is closed on major winter holidays. Tickets are $20 for adults (16+) and free for children 15 and under. They're good for 7 consecutive days and include admission to Yorktown Battlefield. Holders of many National Park passes are admitted for $5 per person (including up to 3 additional adults with the pass holder). Active military pass holders and access pass holders are free. For more information, visit the Jamestown Visitor Center at 1368 Colonial Pkwy., or call (757) 856-1250.

The Jamestown Settlement is located adjacent to the entrance of Historic Jamestowne. The Settlement area features Powhatan Village, a Riverfront Discovery Area, and the depictions of the lives of the settlers through film, gallery exhibits, and living history. You can see and board replicas of the three ships—the *Susan Constant, Godspeed,* and *Discovery*—that sailed for 4½ months from England in 1607. A visit to the 'tween deck of the *Susan Constant* lets you see how tight the quarters were during the voyage. Guided tours of the museum's living-history areas are offered several times daily. *Tenacity: Women in Jamestown and Early Virginia,* a new exhibit on display from Nov 2018 through Jan 2020, explores little-known personal stories of the women and their impact on our new country. The Settlement is open daily from 9 a.m. to 5 p.m., and until 6 p.m. from June 15 through Aug 15.

Basic Jamestown Settlement tickets are $17 for adults and $8 for children (6–12). However, there are combinations tickets and web specials that also include the *American Revolution Museum* at Yorktown, Colonial Williamsburg, and Yorktown Battlefield. For more information call (757) 253-4838 or visit historyisfun.org.

I promote repeat visits to **Colonial Williamsburg** because displays change, seasons change, and your perspective changes.

Some differences are more subtle than others. During winter some furniture may wear slipcovers or some pieces may be displayed that wouldn't be displayed in the summer heat. During fall you can watch or even participate in grape stomping, something you won't find in spring or summer. In recent years more emphasis has been placed on making the colonial experience accessible to those with hearing, vision, or maneuverability limitations. Some places are accessible, some places have portable wheelchair ramps available, and slide programs about inaccessible areas of some of the buildings are being created. On the other hand, there are few curbs in the restored city, and automobiles are not permitted on the main streets during the day. An escorted walking tour is available for the visually impaired, and a special tour of the Powell-Waller House can be arranged. Free publications for the hearing impaired are available, as are discount tickets for some programs. For a copy of the *Colonial Williamsburg Guide for the Handicapped,* write to PO Box C, Williamsburg 23187, or call (757) 229-1000.

The Governor's Palace shows the lifestyle of Lord Dunmore, the last royal governor of Virginia, and his family. The Lord issued a proclamation in 1775 calling for all able-bodied men to assist him in defense of the British colony, including slaves who were promised their freedom in exchange for service in the King's Army. This was controversial at the time, especially among slaveholders, who feared a mass slave rebellion. But the proclamation proved successful, and within a month Dunmore had more than 800 soldiers. Some of these African Americans, both slave and free, were cooks, maids, footmen, and drivers; others were skilled carpenters, blacksmiths, coopers, wheelwrights, and spinners. Take the African American Contributions tour, or pick up a brochure to learn how they influenced life in Colonial Williamsburg.

Whether you're in the area for relaxation, shopping, or sightseeing (from which you'll need relaxation), you'll want a place to rest your head and fill your tummy. It happens at the ***Williamsburg Sampler Bed & Breakfast*** (922 Jamestown Rd.; 757-220-8011 or 800-422-8011; williamsburgsampler.com), where they serve their "Skip Lunch" breakfast. It started years ago when a former Penn State football player stayed over, and Ike Sisane decided the guy needed a little extra food for breakfast. The former football player described it as a "skip lunch meal," and the name stuck. A typical meal includes orange juice, fruit platter, eggs, meat and potatoes, muffins, and beverage. The inn is a stately 3-story, 18th-century plantation-style building with 4 guest rooms, including a 2-room suite.

moorepeace, please

The ***Moore House,*** at Yorktown, is the site where the terms of surrender for the British army were negotiated on Oct 17, 1781. The house is restored and decorated with 18th-century-style furnishings. It is open as staffing permits, so contact the office for current hours: (757) 898-2410; nps.gov/york/learn/historyculture/moore-house.htm.

As a marker of time passing, when this book was first published, the ***DeWitt Wallace Decorative Art Museum*** had just opened. It's now been

Sign on the Dotted Line . . .

The ***Nelson House*** (501 Main St.; 757-898-2410; visitingyorktown.com/nelson-house.html) in Yorktown was the home of Thomas Nelson Jr., a signer of the Declaration of Independence, a governor of Virginia, and commander of the Virginia Militia during the Siege of Yorktown. The Georgian mansion has been restored, and you can tour it depending on staffing availability. The Nelson House today is managed by the National Park Service and is open to the public during irregular hours. If you want to see the interior, contact the National Park Service at the Yorktown National Park Museum.

around long enough that it's been redone and once again is open for your enjoyment and astonishment at the beautiful things housed there. You'll find finely crafted 17th- to 19th-century household items here. The ***Abby Aldrich Rockefeller Folk Art Museum,*** in its expanded facility, features America's premier collection of works created by unschooled American artists, so this is the place to visit if you like rough-hewn toys, weather vanes, and painted furniture.

The area's evening programs have expanded as well, so you don't have to stay in your hotel room watching the television as if you weren't even on vacation. Family tours, shows, and concerts explore Colonial Williamsburg at night, and topics might include what frightened people out of their breeches and how they explained the unexplainable. The area is so pet friendly that GoPetFriendly.com calls Colonial Williamsburg the #1 pet-friendly attraction in Virginia and featured it in their Ultimate Pet Friendly Road Trip. Among other things, they note that "there are shady benches scattered all over town for one person to wait with your pet while the other(s) step into the shops or enjoy a tour."

There are a handful of ticketing options for Colonial Williamsburg, including a good neighbor (Williamsburg residents), Art Museum, Sampler, multiday, and Historic Triangle Area. Go through the options to see which is best for you. An adult one-day ticket is $40.99, and for children it's $20.49. An annual pass is $66.99 for adults and $33.49 for children. Contact the Williamsburg Visitor Center at (800) HISTORY (447-8679) or colonialwilliamsburg.com for pricing and information.

For a slightly more secluded attraction, stop by the 2,705-acre ***Waller Mill Park*** (901 Airport Rd.; 757-259-3778; williamsburgva.gov/government/ department-i-z/parks-recreation/waller-mill-park). It has a 360-acre lake where you can go fishing, pedal boating, canoeing, kayaking, biking, and hiking on 6.25 miles of wooded and water views, and then enjoy a picnic, a round of disc golf, and playing ball. A dog park means you can bring your fur baby (on a leash). Admission is $2 a vehicle.

History takes a while to happen, to interpret, and to understand. Such is the case with the Yorktown Victory Center, which after a decade of transformation is now (as of April 1, 2017) known as ***The American Revolution Museum at Yorktown*** (200 Water St.; 888-593-4682 or 757-253-4838). The permanent exhibits include dioramas, interactive exhibits, costumed interpreters, and short films, including *The Siege of Yorktown* and *Liberty Fever*, the museum's introductory film. A living history component includes a Continental Army encampment and a Revolution-era farm. For a few dollars more (starting at $115 plus admission), you can have a private guided tour of Jamestown

JANUARY

Hampton Monster Jam
Hampton Coliseum, Hampton
(866) 248-8740 (group sales)
monsterjam.com

Coastal Virginia Wine Festival
Virginia Beach Convention Center,
Virginia Beach
(757) 422-8979 ext. 130
coastalvirginiawinefest.com

Newport News Restaurant Week
Various restaurants, Newport News
newportnewsrestaurantweek.com

Winter Wildlife Festival
Princess Anne Recreation Center,
Virginia Beach
(757) 385-2990
vbgov.com/government/departments/
parks-recreation/special-events/Pages/
winter-wildlife-festival.aspx

APRIL

Virginia International Tattoo
Scope Arena, Norfolk
(757) 282-2822
vafest.org/tattoo

Great Dismal Swamp Birding Festival
Great Dismal Swamp, Suffolk
(757) 986-3705

Historic Garden Week
Statewide event includes James River
Plantation, Virginia Beach, Newport
News, Norfolk, and Williamsburg
(804) 644-7776
vagardenweek.org

Norfolk NATO Festival
Norfolk
vafest.org/norfolk-nato-festival

MAY

Virginia Beer Festival
Town Point Park Waterside, Norfolk
beerfestva.com

Bodacious Bazaar & Wine Festival
Fort Monroe National Monument,
Hampton
bodaciousbazaar.com/spring/

Annual Newport News Greek Festival
Newport News
(757) 596-6151
newportnewsgreekfestival.org

JUNE

Blackbeard Pirate Festival
Hampton
hampton.gov/2008/
Blackbeard-Pirate-Festival

JULY

Hampton Jazz Festival
Hampton Coliseum, Hampton
(757) 838-4203
hamptonjazzfestival.com

OCTOBER

Yorktown Wine Festival
Yorktown
(757) 877-2933
villageevents.org

Yorktown Victory Celebration
American Revolution Museum at
Yorktown
historyisfun.org/events/

NOVEMBER

Busch Gardens Christmas Town
Busch Gardens
Williamsburg, mid-Nov through Dec

DECEMBER

Lighted Boat Parade
Riverwalk Landing, Yorktown
(757) 890-4970
visityorktown.org/211/Boat-Parade

Settlement or the American Revolution Museum at Yorktown, or you can have a special-theme tour (food, military, historic clothing, gardens, arts, etc.) for an additional $60. Advance reservations are strongly suggested. A gift shop has books, jewelry, educational toys, and other items geared toward the museum's 17th- and 18th-century themes.

Admission is $15 for adults, $7.50 for youth (6–12), and a combination ticket with Jamestown Settlement is $26 and $12.50, respectively. The combination ticket may be used on separate days, so you don't have to try to do both in the same day. Open daily 9 a.m. to 5 p.m. (until 6 p.m. June 15 through Aug 15), closed Dec 25 and Jan 1.

Places to Stay in Coastal Virginia— Hampton Roads

HAMPTON

Crowne Plaza
700 Settlers Landing Rd.
(757) 727-8915 or
(866) 727-9990
ihg.com/crowneplaza/
hotels/us/en/hampton/
orfhv/hoteldetail

Magnolia House Bed and Breakfast
232 S. Armistead Ave.
(757) 722-2888
maghousehampton.com

NEWPORT NEWS

Boxwood Inn
10 Elmhurst St.
(757) 888-8854
historicboxwoodinn.com

Lodge at Kiln Creek
1003 Brick Kiln Blvd.
(757) 874-2600
thelodgeatkilncreek.com

NORFOLK

Bed and Breakfast at the Page House Inn
323 Fairfax Ave.
(757) 625-5033
pagehouseinn.com

Marriott, Norfolk Waterside
235 E. Main St.
(757) 627-4200 or
(800) 228-9290
marriott.com/hotels/travel/
orfws-norfolk-waterside
-marriott

PORTSMOUTH

Glencoe Inn
222 North St.
(757) 397-8128
glencoeinn.com

VIRGINIA BEACH

Barclay Cottage
400 16th St.
(757) 422-1956 or
(866) INN-1895 (466-1895)
barclaycottage.com

Schooner Inn
215 Atlantic Ave.
(800) 283-7263
schoonerinnvb.com

Hilton Virginia Beach Oceanfront
3001 Atlantic Ave.
(757) 213-3000
hiltonvb.com

WILLIAMSBURG

Fife & Drum Inn
441 Prince George St.
(888) 838-1783
fifeanddruminn.com

Great Wolf Lodge
549 E. Rochambeau Dr.
(800) 551-9653
greatwolf.com/
williamsburg/waterpark

Newport House
710 S. Henry St.
(757) 229-1775 or
(877) 565-1775
newporthousebb.com

Places to Eat in Coastal Virginia— Hampton Road

CHESAPEAKE

Pop's Diner Co.
1432 Greenbrier Pkwy.
(757) 502-8220
popsdinerco.com

JAMESTOWN

Jamestown Settlement Cafe
1760 Jamestown Rd.
(757) 253-2571
jamestowncafe.com

HAMPTON

Grey Goose
101-A W. Queens Way
(757) 723-7978
greygooserestaurant.com

NEWPORT NEWS

Jefferson Restaurant & Eatery
11831 Jefferson Ave.
(757) 591-8800
schlotzskys.com/virginia/
newport-news/2660

Sal and Mimma's Italian Restaurant
15400 Warwick Blvd.
(757) 243-2802
salandmimmava.com

NORFOLK

219 American Bistro
219 Granby St.
(757) 416-6219
219bistro.com

PORTSMOUTH

Bier Garden
438 High St.
(757) 393-6022
biergarden.com

Lobscouser
337 High St.
(757) 397-2728
lobscouser.com

VIRGINIA BEACH

Captain George's Seafood
1956 Laskin Rd.
(757) 428-3494
captaingeorges.com

Doc Taylor's
207 23rd St.
(757) 425-1960
facebook.com/
DocTaylorsSeasideMarket
Lounge

Nona's Italian Kitchen
1060 Lynnhaven Pkwy,
Ste. 106
(757) 368-0924
nonasitaliankitchen.com

The Jewish Mother
600 Nevan Rd.
(757) 478-9989
jewishmotherhilltop.com

Leapin' Lizard Cafe
4408 Shore Dr.
(757) 460-5327
facebook.com/
LeapingLizardCafe

Rick's Café
1612 Virginia Beach Blvd.
(757) 425-1625
rickscafevb.com

WILLIAMSBURG

Berrets Seafood
199 S. Boundary St.
(757) 253-1847
berrets.com

Cheese Shop
410 W. Duke of Gloucester
St.
(757) 220-0298
cheeseshopwilliamsburg
.com

Corey's Country Kitchen
5242 Olde Towne Rd.
(757) 645-2978

Dot's Back Inn
4030 MacArthur Ave.
(804) 266-3167
dotsbackrichmond.com

Edward's Virginia Ham Shoppe of Surry
5541C Richmond Rd.
(757) 220-6618
edwardsvaham.com

Five Forks Cafe
4456 John Tyler Memorial
Hwy.
(757) 221-0484
fiveforkscafe.com

Giuseppe's Italian Cafe
5525 Olde Towne Rd.
(757) 565-1977
giuseppes.com

Old Chickahominy House
1211 Jamestown Rd.
(757) 229-4689
oldchickahominy.com

Shorty's Diner
627 Merrimac Trail
(757) 603-6675
shortysdinerva.com

Trellis
403 Duke of Gloucester St.
(757) 229-8610
thetrellis.com

YORKTOWN

Cinco de Mayo
121 Grafton Station Ln.,
Ste. A
(757) 872-0061
cincodemayo-yorktown
-mexicanrestaurant
.business.site

Ginny's
1900 George Washington
Memorial Hwy.
(757) 592-9036
facebook.com/
ginnysrestaurant

Coastal Virginia–
Eastern Shore

The Eastern Shore section of Virginia includes Accomack and Northampton Counties at the southern part of what is known as the **DelMarVa** (Delaware, Maryland, Virginia) Peninsula. They're across the Chesapeake Bay from the rest of the state. You fly here, boat here, take the Chesapeake Bay Bridge to the north and drive south, or the Chesapeake Bay Bridge-Tunnel and drive north. Accomack is the northern county, and Northampton is the southern one. Almost all directions are given as "off Route 13," for that is the main north–south highway through this area. There are several "sea roads," which basically parallel the highway, such as Route 316 on the bay (Chesapeake) side and Routes 600 and 604 on the sea (Atlantic Ocean) side. It's along these roads that you'll find some of the unique Eastern Shore architecture, including homes with four different roof levels referred to as "big house, little house, colonnade, and kitchen."

Many people come for the most popular draw, or at least the best-known: the pony roundup and penning at Chincoteague. Others want sun and sand or the antiques and the duck decoys. They're all available here. My advice on buying decoys is to look at quite a few first so that you can compare them and

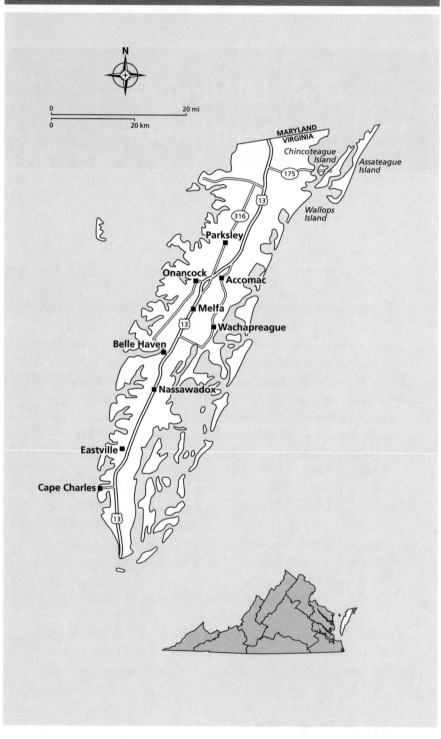

then decide what you want. There are decorative decoys (they look pretty) and working decoys (those that were hollowed out and had weights placed on the bottom for balance in the water and were used to lure ducks to the blinds). Some are brand-new and machine turned (you can even assemble and paint them yourself), some have intricately carved feather structures, and some are old and drab looking. You can expect to pay from $50 to $700 or more.

Normally, thousands of people just drive north or south on US 13 and never bother to see what's on either side of them. Fortunately, for those who like to get off that beaten path, there's a lot happening here. The region invites visitors and locals to "discover the undiscovered on Virginia's Eastern Shore" with a plethora of activities. These include where to watch a rocket launch, an explanation of how such places as Machipongo and Wachapreague were named, dog-friendly places to stay and play, the ghost ships of the Eastern Shore, a hunt for treasure, the Eastern Shore for rat lovers, wild barrier islands to explore, traditional and quirky holidays, glamping, food trucks, wilderness hikes, annual fests, and so much more. Though much has changed since the first edition of this book was written in 1985, the wide expanses of relatively flat countryside remain the same.

The most logical ways to cross the Chesapeake Bay, unless you have a boat, is to use the *Chesapeake Bay Bridge-Tunnel* (757-331-2960; cbbt .com), officially called the Lucius J. Kelkew Jr. Bridge-Tunnel, at the mouth of Chesapeake or the Chesapeake Bay Bridge, officially called the Gov. William Preston Lane Jr. Memorial Bridge in mid-Bay. On the eastern side of the bay is the DelMarVa Peninsula.

The bridge-tunnel, at 20 miles, is the world's longest bridge-tunnel complex. There are 2 mile-long tunnels, more than 12 miles of trestled railway, 2 bridges, nearly 2 miles of causeway, 4 man-made islands, and 5.5 miles of approach roads.

Take a minute or two to watch the ships coming into and going out of the harbor. Due to construction, fishing is curtailed until about 2023. However, once you can again drown a line for bluefish, trout, croaker, flounder, shark, and other species from the 625-foot fishing pier, take heart that Leo Olivarez, a utility contractor company supervisor, gave proof to the bounty of the sea when he was fishing around the rocks of the third island on June 22, 2008. Although he was fishing for small bluefish to use for flounder bait, he ended up with a world-record-setting 9-pound, 13-ounce spadefish (on 6-pound test line), which earned him an award from the Virginia Saltwater Fishing Tournament. Try your luck catching amberjack; Atlantic, Spanish, and king mackerel; black and red drum; blue and white marlin; bluefin and yellowfin tuna; bluefish; croaker; dolphin; flounder; gray trout; sea bass; spot; striped bass; tautog; and wahoo.

Whether you stop to visit or go from one side to the other, it's a marvelous way to see the magnificent confluence of the Chesapeake Bay and the Atlantic Ocean. A 45-minute film about the bridge-tunnel is available for viewing by appointment.

The toll is $18 (for automobiles) each way during peak hours and $14 off-peak with a $6 charge (or $2, depending on the day/time) if you return within 24 hours and show your receipt; if, however, you tell the toll taker that you're going out to the island and will be returning without going all the way across the bay, you will be charged only once. If you don't do this ahead of time, you will be charged a second toll for coming back the other direction. Peak season pricing is Fri through Sun from May 15 through Sept 15. E-ZPass is now accepted.

Just before you travel the bridge-tunnel (or in case you really don't want to travel it), the western tunnel entrance is great for watching the bay shipping traffic navigate the waterways. You might see a submarine booming out of the water (they can't traverse the bay submerged) or an aircraft carrier, but you're almost certain to see something interesting. So, grab a cup of coffee and sit a few minutes; perhaps you'll have a tale to tell your friends and family for years to come.

Some of the "happenings" are very today and tomorrow. Sometimes the FedEx pickup and delivery depends on the winds across the Bridge Tunnel, and if they're too stiff, then trucks aren't allowed across the bridge. Some things tell their old tales. For instance, the two counties have the oldest consecutive court records in the entire United States of America.

For those who participate in the annual Christmas bird count, you'll gladly have your pinfeathers pulled when you learn that more than 150 species have been spotted. That's one of the highest counts north of Florida. Monarch butterflies migrate through here, and birders have been known to band everything from bald eagles to hummingbirds.

Could any place be more idyllic?

Accomack County

In addition to the weirdly spelled (to outsiders) town names, another thing you'll notice here is that the county is Accomack and the town is **Accomac** (meaning "on the other side"). It's thought to be the second-largest restored town after Williamsburg—or maybe it's the second-largest colonial-period city after Annapolis. In any case it certainly shouldn't be mistaken for the tourist attraction that either Williamsburg or Annapolis has become. It does, however, have a lot of colonial-period buildings.

At the southern tip of the DelMarVa Peninsula is the **Eastern Shore of Virginia National Wildlife Refuge** (32205 Seaside Rd.; 757-331-3425; fws .gov/refuge/eastern_shore_of_virginia). It features a variety of habitats ideal for millions of migrant birds including warblers, tree swallows, and other songbirds and thousands of raptors as they travel on their journey south, starting in late Aug and peaking around mid-Nov. Before that, the monarch butterfly migration goes through Oct. They come to stage (gather in large groups) until the winds and weather are favorable for an easy flight over the Bay.

According to the US Fish and Wildlife Service, this land was known as Fort John Custis, and during World War II there were radar towers and large bunkers housing 16-inch guns to protect the naval bases and shipyards of Virginia Beach and Norfolk.

Within the 1,123 acres of maritime forest, myrtle and bayberry thickets, grasslands, croplands, and fresh and brackish ponds, there's even a place for you—there are trails and a photo blind. On Sat afternoons from Oct through Mar, the service offers free tours (4-mile walking tours) to Fisherman Island, an area otherwise closed to the public. There is no entrance fee. Stop by the welcome station for detailed information. The Wise Point Boat Ramp is now open with passes to launch and/or park at the ramp set at $10 for a one-day pass and $120 for an annual pass. The ramp is open daily from 5 a.m. to 10 p.m. Oct through Jan. Overnight use is not permitted. The visitor center is open Fri through Sun 10 a.m. to 2 p.m.

Wander around **Cape Charles** and see one of the largest concentrations of late-Victorian and turn-of-the-century buildings on the East Coast. The homes were built for the expanding merchant class and the executives of the Pennsylvania Railroad, for Cape Charles was established as the railroad's southern terminus, from which steamships carried passengers and freight to Norfolk. The town received Historic District designation in 1989 and was placed on the National Register of Historic Places in 1991.

Coffee has been filling the air since the opening of the **Cape Charles Coffee House** (241 Mason Ave.; 757-331-1880; capecharlescoffeehouse.com) located in a 1910 bank building. Paneled wood walls and chandeliers are the setting for espressos, lattes, and the signature Cafe Cape Charles (coffee, hazelnut, caramel, and melted chocolate). Food's available. The cafe is open daily (except Tues) from 8 a.m. to 5 p.m. for breakfast, lunch, and then coffee and desserts.

Many years ago, my family and about a half dozen other families went camping at **Cherrystone Family Camping Resort** (1511 Townfield Dr.; 757-331-3063; cherrystone.com/virginia-campgrounds), just north of Cape Charles on the Chesapeake Bay, for a week. We raked oysters off the campground coastline and went to Oyster (on the Atlantic side of the peninsula) to get clams. We found a guy there who was seriously upset because his crab trap was filled with blowfish (probably the one creature that really scares crabs), so we took them off his hands and carefully filleted them and understood why they're called the "chicken of the sea." My (late) uncle Joe Smith had a boat in Hampton Roads, and Sunday morning was "guys' day," so he took all the guys out fishing and they came back with a bunch of palm-size spots that were perfect for breakfast cooked over the fire. One of the guys had brought some venison, so we did have a little variety in our meals, but basically, except for some prepackaged cereal to keep the children happy, we lived off the land for the entire week. Of course, the mosquitoes lived off us, so maybe that was Mother Nature's way of evening the score.

Should you not want to spend time foraging for your food, rest assured the campground has plenty of activities, with a craft shop, horseshoes, mini golf, arcade, splash park, swimming pools, and much more. They have 700 campsites, cottages, camping cabins, and rental trailers in case you don't care to bring your own accommodations.

Chincoteague ("beautiful land across the water") and nearby *Assateague Island* are probably the best-known towns on the peninsula. Once in Chincoteague you'll find lots of places to shop, eat, and attend a variety of other activities, including a decoy festival, concerts, blessing of the fleet, and other events. The *Chincoteague Cultural Alliance* (Center for the Arts, 6309 Church St.; 757-381-7733; chincoteagueca.org) alone presents more than 100 events a year, including musical performances, live theater, farmers' and artisan markets, classes, shows, exhibits, workshops, and more.

Chincoteague National Wildlife Refuge and *Assateague Island National Seashore* are definitely the main attractions, and for good reason.

Almost the first thing you see on the US Fish and Wildlife Service web page for Chincoteague is warnings about tick and mosquito bites, poison ivy, raccoons and other mammals that may carry rabies, and unpredictable wild ponies. Listen to the advice, take care, and then enjoy yourself. It's well worth the precautions. Park and head to the *Herbert H. Bateman Educational and Administrative Center* (8231 Beach Rd.; 757-336-6122; fws.gov/refuge/ Chincoteague/visit/plan_your_visit.html). Enjoy the exhibits, displays, and wildlife-oriented programs. The staff will answer your questions and start the videos in the auditorium. There's also a gift shop with lots of books, clothing, and other souvenirs. The center is open daily from 9 a.m. until 5 p.m. in the summer and 4 p.m. the rest of the year.

Throughout the refuge you can take hikes, ride bikes, sit in the sun, and enjoy yourself. There's a 3½-mile bicycle/hiking loop open dawn to dusk for pedestrians and bikes (no mopeds allowed) and on which autos are allowed from 3 p.m. to dusk. Some 250 different birds fly by, and snow geese can be seen most of fall and winter. The refuge is a major resting and feeding area for the endangered peregrine falcon. Forest underbrush has been cleared in some areas, and nesting boxes have been constructed for the endangered DelMarVa fox squirrel. Scattered throughout the refuge are the sika (an oriental elk), Virginia white-tailed deer, and, of course, small bands of wild ponies.

This place is the genesis of the book and movie *Misty of Chincoteague*, Marguerite Henry's famed horse. Yes, the miniature horses still exist, and every year since 1925, there's an ***Annual Pony Swim and Auction*** held to sell off some of the horses to keep the herd at a manageable size. Thousands attend this event at the carnival grounds, held the last Wed and Thurs of July. Actually, there are other activities leading up to the penning and sale, so you can plan to spend a lot of time here. The wild ponies, which are assumed to be descended from mustangs that swam ashore from a wrecked Spanish ship in the 16th century, are auctioned by members of the volunteer fire department on Chincoteague. The members dress up in cowboy garb and corral the ponies, then carefully supervise them as the horses swim to Chincoteague, where they can sell for more than $2,000 each. How nice to be able to visit Misty's relatives and stroll alongside them as they munch the grass of this seashore wildlife refuge that is their home. Be warned: As many as 40,000 people come to see ponies swim for about 3 minutes. It is generally hot and humid, and there are no restrooms nearby. Unless you really want to see the auction, come another day. For more information about the event, contact the local Chamber of Commerce (PO Box 258, Chincoteague Island 23336; 757-336-6161; assateague.com or chincoteague.com/pony_swim_guide.html).

The first ***Assateague Lighthouse*** (757-336-3696; piping-plover.org) was built in 1833 and replaced with a taller one in 1867. It's 22 feet above mean high water and stands 142 feet high, and the 800,000 candlepower light can be seen for 19 nautical miles. The old oil storage building is an art gallery during the summer. Restoration work started in 2008, so you can climb to the top for a spectacular view. The lighthouse is open from spring through fall, but closed during inclement weather and when the temperature is more than 95 degrees. Climbs of the 198 steps are available from 9 a.m. to noon and 12:30 to 3 p.m. Call before you head there to make sure the lighthouse is open.

The ***Museum of Chincoteague Island*** (7125 Maddox Blvd.; 757-336-6117; chincoteaguemuseum.com) started life in 1965 as the Oyster Museum and was renovated in 2011 with a change to its name to more accurately reflect what's inside. Walk around and you'll see exhibits reflecting life on the islands from prehistorical to more recent times. The first order Fresnel lens (made in

Paris in 1866) that was used in the Assateague Lighthouse greets you at the entrance. Miles Hancock (1887–1974) was a noted duck decoy carver, and in 2017 his workshop was moved here from his former home about a mile away. It's been restored and is available for inspection. The museum is open Fri through Sun 11 a.m. to 5 p.m. Admission is $4 for adults.

After a day of sightseeing, surfing, sunning, and exploring (or even doing nothing), it's time to look for the lighthouse atop the *Island Creamery* (6243 Maddox Blvd.; 757-336-6236; islandcreamery.net), the only homemade ice cream on the island. It's only 20 minutes off Route 13, so it's an easy drive even if you haven't been exploring the island. The number one favorite flavor is Marsh Mud (really chocolate ice cream) in a homemade waffle cone. As much as I like chocolate, I'm also partial to their pineapple upside-down flavor. Bob and Nancy Conklin started the creamery in 1975 as a candy store and then progressed to the cold treats. Second-generation Kelly and Robin Conklin are now in charge of the operation, with Drew, Cole, and Courtney Conklin representing the third generation. It's open daily except Thanksgiving and Dec 25.

The *Refuge Inn* (7058 Maddox Blvd.; 757-336-5511 or 888-257-0038; refuge inn.com) is definitely where you'll want to rest your head. It's surrounded by trees, and you'll even find the occasional pony wandering by. The east side faces the parking lot, the pony pasture, and, of course, the morning sunrise. The west side faces the pine trees, picnic areas, the pool, and the sunset (sort of peeking through the trees). Which side is better? Depends on what you want and whether you want the pool or the ponies. In a Facebook poll, 63 percent favored the pony side. Friendly staff and comfortable rooms at the family-owned property make you feel welcome. Each room has a private patio or balcony with slider doors, free high-speed Wi-Fi, indoor/outdoor heated pool, lending library, board games, and more. The inn has a Tesla charger and a universal EV charger available free of charge. The continental breakfast has

No Tokens Needed

In July or Aug 2008, 84 subway cars were added to the *Blackfish Banks Artificial Reef* (daybreakfishing.com/blackfish-reef.html), located less than 10 miles from Chincoteague Inlet. They join 100 New York City subway cars that were "dumped" there in late 2002. No, they didn't come by rail, but by barges from the 207th Street Overhaul Shop on the banks of the Harlem River. Yes, they were stripped of all toxins and somehow made alluring to small sea bass, flounder, trout, amberjacks, jack crevelle, and some sharks.

Kiptopeke State Park

At the southern tip of the DelMarVa Peninsula is **Kiptopeke State Park** (3540 Kiptopeke Dr.; 757-331-2267; dcr.virginia.gov/state-parks/kiptopeke#general_information); its 536 acres offer a variety of outdoor recreational and conservation activities. There's a charge, but this is a great area for camping, boating, swimming, picnicking, and fishing. They have 2- and 3-bedroom cabins, 6-bedroom lodges, RV and tent camping, a yurt, and a bunkhouse. There's a boat ramp, lighted fishing pier, picnic areas, playground, beach bathhouse and swimming beach, 5.1 miles of hiking and biking trails, and seasonal interpretive programs. They request that you do not bring firewood into the park. Kiptopeke is a Native American word for "big water." The site was named in honor of the younger brother of a king of the Accawmack Indians who befriended early settlers in the area.

to be one of the top five on the Eastern Shore. As they say, "The Refuge Inn is like slipping into something memorably comfortable."

The *Locustville Academy Museum* (on Route 605 in the Academy Building; 757-709-9746; esvatourism.org) is the only remaining antebellum school of higher learning of about a dozen that existed on the Eastern Shore during the 1800s, and the weatherboarding, brick foundations, and interior are intact. The school provided advanced studies for college-bound students (boys and girls) or those entering business at a far lower cost than boarding schools. Advanced courses included Latin, Greek, and French, and in 1862 tuition did not exceed $20 for a semester. The school operated from the fall of 1859 until 1879 (except for brief periods during the Civil War) and apparently looks much as it did when it was in operation, although the original entrance road has been closed. Inside are an old teacher's desk and student's desk, old textbooks, photographs, documents, and historical artifacts including quilts made by a family member of one of the academy's founders. It's open by appointment.

Northampton County

North of Cape Charles is *Eastville,* the Northampton County seat where a time capsule was buried with a legend on it that says EASTVILLE COURT RECORDS TIME CAPSULE COMMEMORATING 365 YEARS OF THE OLDEST CONTINUOUS COURT RECORDS IN THE UNITED STATES. DEDICATED SEPTEMBER 20, 1997. TO BE OPENED EVERY 25 YEARS. So mark your calendar for a return visit in 2022.

The town has a population of about 200 people, depending on the season and who's counting. Take time to stroll around the town, see the old courthouse (1731), the new courthouse, the prison (1814), Christ Episcopal Church (1741), and the attractive homes that line the streets of this quiet town.

With this much country and so much water, you have to know there's an outstanding seafood restaurant somewhere. That somewhere is the *Island House Restaurant* (17 Atlantic Ave.; 757-787-4242; theislandhouserestaurant .com/Home). The 200-seat restaurant overlooks the Wachapreague harbor and specializes in fresh seafood, as one would hope and expect, and clams, oysters, and Angus beef burgers and prime rib. Save room for the chocolate bread pudding, or if you missed the Island Creamery in Chincoteague, they serve it here. Besides great views and good food, you can climb the spiral staircase for a view of the barrier islands from the lookout tower.

The *Blue Crab Bay Co.* (29368 Atlantic Dr.; 757-787-3602 or 800-221-2722) in *Melfa* has been providing "Classic Coastal Cuisine Since 1985" with Pamela Barefoot at the helm. In December 2016 she sold it to Eastern Shore native Elizabeth Lankford, who continues to improve and expand the company's reach. Stop by for beverage mixes (Sting Ray spicy bloody Mary mixer with ocean clam juice), Virginia peanuts and snack mixes, soups and seafood, coastal gifts, Eastern Shore wine, and more. When you need an Eastern Shore gift, this is the place. The shop is open 9 a.m. to 5 p.m. Mon through Fri, 10 a.m. to 4 p.m. on Sat, Sun hours in the summer and Thanksgiving weekend through mid-Dec noon to 4 p.m.

The picturesque harbor town of *Onancock*, on Chesapeake Bay 2 miles west of US 13 via Highway 179, is delightfully typical of Eastern Shore towns.

Elvis Ate Here, Sorta

The *Exmore Diner* (4264 Main St.; 757-442-2313; exmoredinerva.com) originally in New Jersey, has been in Exmore since P. C. Kellam had it trucked to town in 1953. In the trucking business, he'd gone to see a Yankees game in New York, stopped by the diner for a bite to eat, and saw the For Sale sign. He realized he had 100 truckers a day coming to his place, and there was no restaurant in town. He had his wife wire the $5,000 to him, and he owned a diner.

According to early legend, Elvis Presley ate in the diner when it was in New Jersey, but no one knew where he sat or what he ordered.

A bright neon clock highlights the stainless-steel exterior; the interior has 4 tables and 24 stools. Historians and historic preservationists think it's one of the most delicious-looking diners in the state. Regulars go for the chicken and dumplings, chipped beef, butterfly shrimp, and hamburger steak. The diner also specializes in Eastern Shore seafood and fresh made-when-ordered burgers. The diner is open Mon through Sat 6 a.m. to 8 p.m., Sun 6 a.m. to 6 p.m.

A short walking tour of more than a dozen historical homes and churches begins at **Ker Place** (69 Market St.; 757-787-8012; shorehistory.org/ker-place), the 1799 home of the Eastern Shore Historical Society. Be impressed with an exhibit of how an ancient boat-carving technique changed five large logs into a boat used for oystering, crabbing, and fishing. It's open Tues through Sat 11 a.m. to 3 p.m. Mar through mid-Dec and by appointment. Admission is by donation. Ker Place is closed Jan and Feb except for special events.

The **Railroad Museum** (18468 Dunne Ave.; 757-665-RAIL; facebook.com/Eastern-Shore-Railway-Museum-642326862627001/) in **Parksley** explores railroading history along the Eastern shore. Among the exhibits is a Richmond, Fredericksburg and Richmond Railroad post-office car that was built in the 1920s. The Eastern Shore Model Railroad Society operates a layout in HO scale. You can see it during the festivals and events or by appointment. Another car is a Seaboard Air Line #8011 diner, a 1947 stainless-steel car that was used by Amtrak on its Washington, DC, to Miami route. Purchased in 2000, plans are under way to operate it once again as a restaurant. A Wabash caboose is undergoing restoration. The museum is open daily (except Mon from Nov through Mar) from noon to 4 p.m. Admission is $2 per person 12 and older.

Wallops Island is occupied by the **National Aeronautics and Space Administration's (NASA) Visitor Center** (NASA Wallops Visitor Center, Building J-17; 757-824-2298 or 757-824-1344; https://www.nasa.gov/content/nasa-wallops-visitor-center-2). This was the nation's first rocket-firing and testing station, and 19 satellites have been launched from Wallops Island, 16 of which remain in orbit. It's possible that the flight center could be used for commercial satellite launches in the future. The site is geared toward small launchings, making it less expensive and easier for private firms to use than the Kennedy Space Center in Florida. Patented to John Wallop in 1672, Wallops Island became a National Advisory Committee for Aeronautics (NACA) site for aerodynamic research, while part of it was leased to the Navy for aviation ordnance testing. The NACA eventually became NASA, which took over the site when the nearby Chincoteague Naval Air Station closed at the end of World War II.

funfacts

Wallops Island is named after John Wallop, a 17-century surveyor and original owner of the island.

You're invited inside the NASA museum for a self-guided tour that can last from 15 minutes to several hours. Groups of more than 20 are asked to make advance reservations. There's an *Apollo 17* moon-rock sample collected by astronaut Jack Schmitt from near the landing site in the Taurus–Littrow Valley region of the moon. Films, one on the 40-year history of Wallops Island and one on space highlights, are shown on a regular basis. Unlike at some other space and government areas, cameras are encouraged at this facility. The gift shop sells postcards, plates, cups, mugs, books, T-shirts, patches, and other space flight souvenirs. There are 100 to 150 space launches a year from Wallops, but there's little to no advance schedule; you have to stay several miles away, and some of them go up so fast that they're off the ground and out of sight before you've blinked your eyes. Call (757) 824-2050 for launch information. Model rocket launches are held the first Sat of every month.

The visitor center is open daily from July 1 through Aug 31, and Tues through Sat Labor Day through Jun 10 a.m. to 4 p.m. There is no charge. To get to Wallops Island, Chincoteague, and Assateague Island, turn east off US 13 at T's Corner, onto Route 175. It has no physical street address, so the GPS coordinates are N 37-56.359, W-75-27-398.

Wachapreague bills itself as *The Little City by the Sea*, and this fishing resort is said to have the state's largest charter boat marina, with all the

ANNUAL EVENTS IN COASTAL VIRGINIA— EASTERN SHORE

APRIL

Historic Garden Week
69 Market St.
Onancock
(804) 644-7776
vagardenweek.org

MAY

World Migratory Bird Day Celebration
Chincoteague National Wildlife Refuge
Chincoteague Island
(757) 336-6122
fws.gov/refuge/chincoteague/

Annual Chincoteague Seafood Festival
Tom's Cove Park
8128 Beebe Rd.
Chincoteague
(757) 336-6161
chincoteaguechamber.com/events/51st
-annual-chincoteague-seafood-festival/

JULY

Volunteer Fireman's Carnival and Annual Pony Penning and Auction
Chincoteague
(757) 336-6161
chincoteaguechamber.com

OCTOBER

Annual Chincoteague Island Oyster Festival
Tom's Cove Park
Chincoteague Island
(757) 336-6161
virginia.org/listings/Events/
AnnualChincoteagueIslandOysterFestival/

NOVEMBER–DECEMBER

Christmas Manor Comes to Life
7150 Piney Island Rd.
Chincoteague Island
(757) 336-6161
chincoteaguechristmas.com

OTHER ATTRACTIONS IN COASTAL VIRGINIA— EASTERN SHORE

Cape Charles Beach
Cape Charles
(757) 331-3259
capecharlesbythebay.com

Historic Palace Theatre
Cape Charles
(757) 331-2787
capecharlesbythebay.com/business/
historic-palace-theatre

Tangier History Museum
Tangier
(757) 891-2374
tangierisland-va.com/history

Tangier Onancock Ferry
Onancock Marina
Onancock
(757) 891-2505
tangierferry.com

wonderful fishing tournaments that accompany so many people involved in such a delightful sport. The area is great for bird watching, particularly during the spring and fall migration. Flat terrain means biking is relaxing and enjoyable. Call the town hall, (757) 787-7117, for details or visit wachapreague.org.

Places to Stay in Coastal Virginia— Eastern Shore

BELLE HAVEN

Bay View Waterfront
35350 Copes Dr.
(757) 442-6963 or
(800) 442-6966
bayviewwaterfrontbedand
breakfast.com

CAPE CHARLES

Cape Charles House Bed-and-Breakfast
645 Tazewell Ave.
(757) 331-4920
capecharleshouse.com

Cape Charles/ Chesapeake Bay KOA Campground (seasonal)
32246 Lankford Hwy.
(800) 562-4207
koa.com/campgrounds/
chesapeake-bay

CHINCOTEAGUE

Channel Bass Inn & Tea Room
6228 Church St.
(757) 336-6148 or
(800) 249-0818
channelbassinn.com

1848 Island Manor House
4160 Main St.
(757) 336-5436 or
(800) 852-1505
islandmanor.com

Refuge Inn
7058 Maddox Blvd.
(757) 336-5511 or
(888) 257-0038
refugeinn.com

ONANCOCK

Charlotte Hotel & Restaurant
7 North St.
(757) 787-7400
thecharlottehotel.com

Places to Eat in Coastal Virginia— Eastern Shore

CAPE CHARLES

Brown Dog Ice Cream (seasonal)
203 Mason Ave.
(757) 695-3868
browndogicecream.com

Chesapeake
307 Mason Ave.
(757) 331-3123

Dead Rise Pies
425 Mason Ave.
(757) 331-6232

The Local
21229 S. Bayside Rd.
(757) 607-2035

The Shanty
33 Marina Rd.
(757) 695-3853

CHINCOTEAGUE

Don's Seafood Market & Restaurant
4113 Main St.
(757) 336-5715
donsseafood.com

Island Creamery
6243 Maddox Blvd.
(757) 336-6236
islandcreamery.net

The Village Restaurant
6576 Maddox Blvd.
(757) 336-5120
chincoteague.com/
thevillage

NASSAWADOX

Great Machipongo Clam Shack
6468 Lankford Hwy.
(757) 442-3800
greatclams.com

ONANCOCK

Bizzotto's Gallery
41 Market St.
(757) 787-3103
bizzottos.esva.net

Blarney Stone Pub & Restaurant
10 North St.
(757) 302-0300
blarneystonepubonancock
.com

WACHAPREAGUE

Island House
17 Atlantic Ave.
(757) 787-4242
wachapreague.com

Chesapeake Bay

Essex County

The small town of **Tappahannock** was founded in 1680, the same year as Philadelphia. It had seen several name changes before settling on this Indian name meaning "rise and fall of water." Thirteen buildings are on the National Register of Historic Places, and you can walk the streets (which still carry their original names) to view the buildings, including the **Old Debtors' Prison** on Prince Street between Church and Cross Streets. The Confederate soldier statue on Prince Street in Tappahannock, a common memorial in many Virginia cities, lists all the local men who fought in the war. Look for a booklet entitled *Essex County Virginia—Its Historic Homes, Landmarks and Traditions* at the **Essex County Museum** (218 Water Ln.; 804-443-4690; essexmuseum.org). The museum is open daily from 10 a.m. to 3 p.m., except Wed and Sun.

Gloucester County

Gloucester County is the home of the annual **Daffodil Festival** (6467 Main St.; 804-693-2355; daffodilfestivalva.org), held

CHESAPEAKE BAY

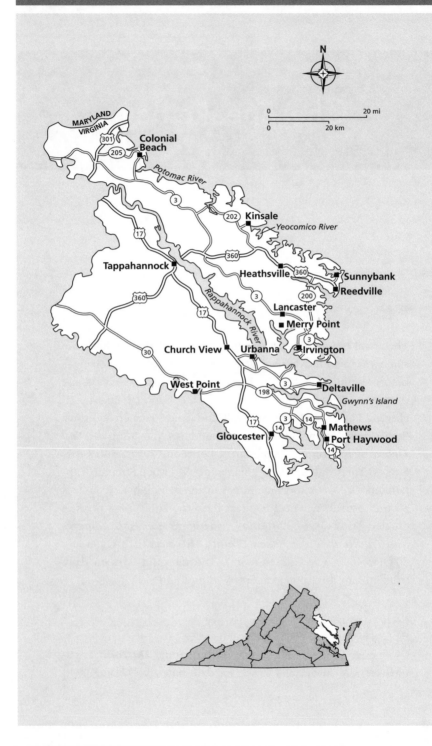

N

0   20 mi
0   20 km

MARYLAND
VIRGINIA

301

Colonial
Beach

205

Potomac River

3

202   Kinsale

Yeocomico River

17

360

Heathsville   360   Sunnybank

Tappahannock

3   200   Reedville

360

Lancaster

17

Merry Point

Rappahannock River

30   Church View   Urbanna   Irvington

3

West Point

198   3   Deltaville

Gwynn's Island

17   3   14   14   Mathews

Gloucester   Port Haywood

14

the last weekend in Mar or the first weekend in Apr. Enjoy the parade, entertainment, 5K and fun races, and children's events when the fields are abloom with these gorgeous messengers of spring.

When Hurricane Isabel "visited" the area in late 2003, it damaged the upriver landing of the **Gloucester Point Beach Park** (1255 Greate Rd.; 804-642-9474 or 804-693-0014; virginia.org/Listings/OutdoorsAndSports/Gloucester PointBeachPark) so badly it had to be closed. It reopened in May 2006, and now you can enjoy the Point Walk, picnic areas, swimming, volleyball, a sandy beach, and a wheelchair-accessible Beach House that is open seasonally.

Gloucester is the birthplace of **Dr. Walter Reed** (1851–1902), the US Army physician who, in 1901, led the team that determined that yellow fever was spread by mosquito, information that allowed the completion of the Panama Canal. His home at the intersection of Routes 616 and 614 is one of the buildings maintained by the Gloucester Preservation Foundation (4021 Hickory Fork Rd.; 804-693-7452). The 1-story gable-roofed frame dwelling was built around 1825 and has a rear shed addition. The grounds are open to visitors daily, and the building is open on special occasions or by appointment.

Drive off Route 17, following the signs for the **Virginia Institute of Marine Science** (VIMS), but for just a moment keep on driving down to the water. **Gloucester Point** is a great place for a view of the **Yorktown River Bridge** (have your camera ready). VIMS (N 37.25, W-76.50; 804-684-7061 or 804-684-7000; vims.edu), which is part of the **College of William and Mary,** has a free aquarium with more than 50 species of marine organisms from throughout Virginia's waters. There are 8 tanks, containing from 50 to 3,000 gallons of water, and a special 200-gallon touch tank, so you may, as they say, get up almost close and personal. VIMS is open Mon through Fri from 9 a.m. to 4:30 p.m. Be sure to ask for a complete set of some great seafood recipe brochures, at no charge. A 1-acre **Teaching Marsh,** an area restored both for practical and educational purposes, provides a demonstration area for regulated wetland plant species (the educational side) and an area to naturally remove contaminants from the Coleman Bridge storm water runoff, thus improving the water quality in the York River (the practical side). The VIMS Waterman's Hall is open daily from 9 a.m. to 4:30 p.m. Ninety-minute public walking tours (best suited for adults and older children) are available and can include the Teaching Marsh. They are offered on Fri from late May through Aug and require reservations. Tours start in Watermen's Hall. Other activities, including a monthly after-hours lecture series, provide other information about our environment. There's a gift shop on the premises, too. When you can't be there in person, check the website for the osprey cam and watch the nesting and the chicks as they hatch and mature.

King William County

Back toward Richmond is the **Pamunkey Indian Museum,** which has several nice displays and a videotape about the Pamunkey people and their way of life, from the Ice Age to the present. These people were members of the tribe under the leadership of Chief Powhatan (the name he told the settlers), who was the father of Pocahontas. Some of the items in the 15 display windows are original; some are as it's assumed they were. Of special interest is Pamunkey pottery, including a new form, which is glazed and burned, as well as the older coil method. If you time your visit right, you might see a demonstration.

The museum is open Fri and Sat 10 a.m. to 4 p.m. and Sun 1 to 5 p.m. (closed on major holidays). The museum may not open exactly on time, but stay around a few minutes and someone will come by. Admission is $2.50 for adults, $1.25 for children (6–13), and $1.75 for seniors. Picnic tables are available. It's located about 10 miles off Route 30 (off I-95) on Route 633 and then Route 673, past the Lanesville cemetery and over the railroad tracks. The road turns, but the signs are easy to follow. For more information call (804) 843-4792 or visit baylink.org/Pamunkey.

Not far away, in **West Point,** is the **Mattaponi Museum** (804-769-3854; uppermattaponi.org) with historical presentations, a fish hatchery, a church, a museum, and a nature trail. Webster "Little Eagle" Custalow is the chief, and Carl "Lone Eagle" Custalow is the assistant chief of this tribe that has had this reservation since 1658. The reservation is approximately 150 acres, with much of it dedicated to wetlands and approximately 60 of the 450 Mattaponi Indians living on this property.

When you visit both reservations, you'll notice that the Pamunkey property is mostly agricultural, with lots of cornfields and homes scattered throughout the land. The Mattaponis have houses in clusters, with most of their efforts spent on shad fishing. A hatchery and marine science facility feature such programs as fish tagging, water quality monitoring, and the development of educational materials for schools and communities about protecting water resources.

Lancaster County

For those who like old churches, there's a dandy one in **Irvington**. The **Historic Christ Church** (420 Christ Church Rd.; 804-438-6855; christchurch1735 .org) was finished about 1735 and is an excellent example of a colonial American church that has remained practically unchanged since that time. Built in cruciform design, the church has 3-foot-deep walls. A marvelous three-decker pulpit lets you know immediately where your attention should be focused (whether you were there for services or serenity). The individually enclosed high-backed pews seem to offer privacy for your spiritual thoughts. Stop at the reception center for a slide presentation about the church and then browse through the museum. Services are held on Sun at 8 a.m. from Memorial Day to Labor Day.

The church grounds are open daily. The church building is open Mon through Fri 8:30 a.m. to 4:30 p.m. all year. From Apr through Nov, it is also open on Sat 10 a.m. to 4 p.m. and Sun 2 to 5 p.m. They ask a suggested donation of $5 a person.

The *Hope and Glory Inn*, a boutique inn, has another attraction: the 6-plus acres of the *Dog and Oyster Vineyard* (170 White Fences Dr.; 804-438-9463; hopeandglory.com/the-dog-oyster-vineyard) just 0.3 mile up the road. You know you've reached it when you see the two 40-foot corkscrews (the world's largest?) at the driveway entrance. The vineyard's name is in honor of the resident rescue dog that protects the grapes from deer and other critters and the oysters that are a local delicacy. The vineyard has four varieties of grapes: Chardonel, Vidal Blanc, Chambourcin, and Merlot. It's open weekends during winter and daily in the summer.

The *Mary Ball Washington Museum* (8346 Mary Ball Rd.; 804-462-7280; mbwm.org) in *Lancaster* has a marvelous collection of local memorabilia, Civil War artifacts (including two battle flags used by troops from Lancaster County), and displays on Northern Neck Indians and life on the water. The genealogical library, said to be one of the best on the East Coast, includes families from southern Maryland and Virginia and the migratory paths they took through Virginia into Kentucky. There's also a historical lending library, programs, workshops, and films. Organized to honor the Lancaster County–born mother of George Washington, it's located in the *Lancaster House* (ca. 1800), which was lovingly restored by the Lancaster Women's Club. The museum is open Wed through Fri 10 a.m. to 4 p.m., and the library is open Wed and Thurs 10 a.m. to 4 p.m., Fri and Sat 11 a.m. to 3 p.m., and by appointment. Closed from mid-Dec through Jan. Admission is $3 for the museum house and grounds and $5 to work at the library.

Merry Point Ferry, one of four remaining free state-run historic river ferries in Virginia (in operation since 1668), crosses the western branch of the Corrotoman River. For years the *Arminta* had plied these waters, carrying three small cars or two regular-size cars and taking about 10 or 15 minutes to cross, but the *Lancaster,* an all-in-one steel boat and scow, is now in service. The *Lancaster* carried 16,378 vehicles and 26,097 passengers in the hurricane-shortened summer of 2003. Taking the ferry from Corrotoman to Ottoman will land you in the town of Lively. The ferry runs "on demand" Tues through Fri from 7 a.m. to 5:30 p.m. and Sat from 9 a.m. to 5:30 p.m. In other words, no service on Sun and Mon and it probably won't be running at times of extreme tides or adverse weather. It also doesn't run for 30 minutes at noon so the operator can take a lunch break. Take Route 604 off either Route 3 or Route 354 to Ottoman Ferry and Merry Point Roads in Merry Point. For more information call (800) 367-7623 or 511 from any phone in Virginia, or visit virginiadot .org/travel/merry_point_ferry.asp.

Mathews County

For a delightful escape, head over to *Gwynn's Island,* a 2-by-1.5-mile piece of land off the coast of Mathews County, where the Piankatank River flows into the Chesapeake Bay. It's named for Hugh Gwynn, who purchased the island in 1642. Archeological finds indicate the island was inhabited as much as 10,000 years ago. Stop by the *Gwynn's Island Museum* (Route 633; 804-725-5022; gwynnsislandmuseum.org) that's dedicated to preserving the history of Gwynn's Island and Mathews County and to honoring men lost at sea and all who served their country. Housed in a 100+-year-old building that was an Odd Fellows Lodge and then the island's first public school, a general store, and a barbershop, it contains school memorabilia, prehistoric fossils, a humpback whale skull, Indian and colonial artifacts, and other displays from the Civil War to the present in its two floors of exhibits. It's open Fri, Sat, and Sun from 1 to 5 p.m. from Apr through Oct, or by appointment.

Middlesex County

Urbanna, one of America's original harbor towns (established in 1673), enjoys a marvelously picturesque setting and is the home of the *Urbanna Oyster Festival* (804-758-0368; urbannaoysterfestival.com). Thousands (perhaps 75,000) come to the little harbor on Urbanna Creek the first weekend in Nov to enjoy the harvest of the famous oyster beds in the Rappahannock River. During the festival there are 125 craft and food booths where you can find oysters fried, stewed, on the half shell, roasted, ready to shuck yourself, or in chowder. During oyster season, oysters are sold by the bushel, processed, packed, frozen, and shipped all over.

If you're traveling in a recreational vehicle and looking for a base of operations, you need look no farther than *Bethpage Camp-Resort* (679 Brown's Ln.; 804-758-4349; bethpagecamp.com) in Urbanna. In fact, you may enjoy Connie McGuire's hospitality so much that you decide to spend all your days there. Bethpage has been awarded the "National Park of the Year" for a third time by the National Association of RV Parks and Campgrounds (ARVC), which lets you know their amenities and recreational opportunities are exceptional. Set along the southern reach of the Rappahannock River, there are plenty of water activities, including a swimming lake with sandy beach, swimming pools with lifeguards, waterpark, boat ramp, fresh- and saltwater fishing, crabbing, and charter boat fishing. There's a lake pier with a band gazebo, 2 recreation centers (2,000 square feet and 12,000 square feet), catering facilities, camp store, laundry rooms, basketball and tennis courts, horseshoe pits, children's playground, activities, and game room. The 700-plus sites are level and either in the open or in the naturally wooded and beautifully landscaped setting with water, electric (30 and 50 amp service), and sewage hookup.

The season, from Apr 1 through mid-Nov, offers plenty of organized activities, from a Cinco de Mayo weekend with Mexican crafts and piñatas through Halloween and the expected costume contest.

Daily, weekly, and monthly rates are available. They've added another facility, Greys Point Camp, in Topping. For more information call (804) 758-2485 or visit greyspointcamp.com.

Down the road from Urbanna is **Deltaville,** "the Boatbuilding Capital of the Chesapeake." At one time there were more than 20 boatbuilders in this area, many of them second and third generation, creating craft that still are used today. Some of the finest houses along the Northern Neck can be found in this area.

The **Deltaville Maritime Museum & Holly Point Nature Park** (287 Jackson Creek Rd.; 804-776-7200; deltavillemuseum.com) is located on 30 acres of property donated to Middlesex County by Ms. Pette Clark and includes 2 houses, numerous outbuildings, 3 docks, and a small boat launching area. Within the museum you may see an exhibit about the area's involvement in the Civil War, the museum's part in the John Smith Historic Water Trail (America's first national park on the water), or the changing of the town's name from Sandy Bottom to Deltaville. You may stroll the 36 acres of grounds, which include a Living Shoreline, Woodland, Lindsey Camellia, everlasting Immortals, Willis Wilson, and Community Gardens. There's also a Wildflower Meadow and a Children's Garden (with pickable flowers and vegetables). Join them for **Family Boatbuilding Week,** when families build a Wright skiff, very much like the small utility boats John Wright built here around the 1930s. Call for operating hours. Admission is $5 for adults and free for those 18 and under.

Northumberland County

According to Lee Langston-Hughes, who became the director of the Reedville Fishermen's Museum in January 2017, the village of **Reedville** has a population of 400 in the winter and 402 in the summer. There are two restaurants and a terrific ice cream parlor that are open spring through late fall, four bed-and-breakfast establishments, and only two traffic lights in all of Northumberland County; neither light is in Reedville. Reedville was established by Captain Elijah Reed in 1867 and prospered from the menhaden fishing industry. The millionaires' row of Victorian mansions lining Main Street indicates that it may well have been the richest town per capita in the United States at the turn of the 20th century. It is still one of the most active fishing ports in the country. The oldest house now standing is part of the **Reedville Fishermen's Museum** (504 Main St.; 804-453-6529; rfmuseum.org), located on the banks of Cockrell's Creek. The museum contains artifacts and historical items relating to the menhaden fishing industry. Here you'll see unique models of boats and tools used in constructing and maintaining the fleet, and information about oystering, crabbers, and pound fishermen. Rotating exhibits and educational programs are scheduled regularly.

Part of the museum is the **William Walker House,** built in 1875. It has been refurbished and refurnished and represents a waterman's home at the turn of the 20th century.

The museum is open Apr through Oct, Tues through Sat 10:30 a.m. to 4:30 p.m., and Sun 1 to 4 p.m. During Nov and Dec it is open Fri and Sat from 10:30 a.m. to 4:30 p.m. and Sun 1 to 4 p.m. It's closed Jan through mid-Mar. Admission is $5 for adults, $4 for groups, and $3 for seniors. For museum members and children under 12, it's free.

funfacts

The American social novelist, and a major figure in post–World War I literature, **John Dos Passos** (b. Chicago, Jan 14, 1896, d. Sept 28, 1970) is buried in the Yeocomico Church graveyard, near Hague. He and his wife, Elizabeth Dos Passos (b. New York City Feb 22, 1909, d. Warsaw, VA Mar 29, 1998), retired to Westmoreland County.

The **Sunnybank Ferry** (virginiadot.org/travel/sunnybank_ferry.asp) crosses the Little Wicomico River on Route 644 between Kayan and Sunnybank, just as it has done since 1903. It started as a hand-pulled cable, and it's now a motorized one, transporting cars, bicycles, and pedestrians. The boat, the *Northumberland,* was built in nearby Deltaville in 2010. It is free, operated by Virginia Department of Transportation (VDOT), and generally runs on demand Mon through Fri from 8 a.m.

to 4:30 p.m. and Sat from 8 a.m. to noon except during inclement weather and unusual water levels (either too high or too low). It's also closed for 30 minutes at noon so the operator can take a lunch break. Call 511 from any phone in Virginia.

Among the historic places in **Heathsville,** mostly hidden from view behind the old Northumberland County Courthouse, is the **Tavern Café.** It's run entirely by volunteers of the Tavern's Culinary Guild. They serve "scrumptiously-delicious, made-from-scratch" soups, quiches, salads, sandwiches, breads, scones, and sweet treats. The menu changes weekly, depending on what the volunteers want to make. A Heritage Arts Center gift shoppe sells locally made handcrafts and is home to several in-residence artisans (think jewelry, weaving, spinning, etc.). The **Historic Rice's Hotel/Hughlett's Tavern** (73 Monument Pl.; 804-580-3377; rhhtfoundationinc.org) is home to four artisan guilds including blacksmiths, woodworkers, spinners and weavers, and quilters. The Carriage House has a collection of antique carriages. Stop by on the third Sat of the month, Apr through Oct, for the Heathsville Farmers Market. Oh, it's so off the beaten path, and so many locals don't even know it exists that they've erected a colorful COLONIAL COUPLE sign next to the CAFÉ sign, and it appears they're pointing to the Tavern and walking toward it. Open Thurs through Sat 10 a.m. to 2 p.m.

Westmoreland County

Westmoreland State Park (State Park Road and Kings Highway; 804-493-8821; dcr.virginia.gov/state-parks/) was built in 1936 by the Civilian Conservation Corps, one of the original six in the state system. Call (800) 933-PARK (7275) for camping or cabin reservations. Within its 1,321 acres they offer camping, boating, fishing, 6 miles of trails, and an Olympic-size swimming pool, and it's open from dawn to dusk. Cell phone service is limited, but there is Wi-Fi in the camp store.

Fossil hunters have the opportunity to find items that could be millions of years old in the park. Thousands of fossils of Miocene-era sharks, whales, porpoises, clams, shells, coral, and plants are contained in these rocks, but check

funfacts

The site of James Monroe's birthplace, Monrovia (4460 James Monroe Hwy., Colonial Beach; monroefoundation.org), has been swallowed up by the modern but old-time resort town of Colonial Beach. This land was first settled by James Monroe's great-great-grandfather Andrew, a Scot, in 1647. A replica of the home of our fifth president is being reconstructed to the tune of about $650,000 and is scheduled to open in Apr 2019.

with the ranger about where you're allowed, and not allowed, to look for them. You can find remnants of rays, fish, birds, and other animals, with sharks' teeth the most common fossil found in the area. You might, though, find the remains of the scallop *Chesapecten jeffersonius,* the state's fossil, which could date back 5 million years. At the edge of the Potomac River, the soft shale and sandstone ***Horsehead Cliffs*** rise about 200 feet above the water and stretch 300 to 400 feet along the shore. The formations occurred 5 million to 15 million years ago, when a shallow subtropical sea stretched all the way to the fall line. A ranger-guided fossil walk is available.

funfacts

George Washington and Robert E. Lee were both born in Westmoreland County.

Kinsale, a quaint maritime village founded in 1706 on the Yeocomico River, is still considered one of the best deepwater ports in the lower Potomac. It thrived until the early 20th century when steamboat traffic died. The ***Kinsale Museum On-the-Green*** (449 Kinsale Rd.; 804-472-3001; kinsalefoundation .org), in a restored 18th-century pub, chronicles this period with changing exhibits and artifacts of those times. A walking tour of the historic village is available at the museum. It's open Fri and Sat from 10 a.m. to 5 p.m.

OTHER ATTRACTIONS IN CHESAPEAKE BAY

Beaverdam Park
Gloucester
(804) 693-2355
gloucesterva.info/facilities/facility/details/
beaverdampark-3

Good Luck Cellars
Kilmarnock
(804) 435-1416
goodluckcellars.com

Menokin
Warsaw
(804) 333-1776
menokin.org

Northern Neck Bottling Plant
Montross
(804) 333-3600
glassbottlesoda.org/bottlers/
northernneck.shtml

Steamboat Era Museum
Irvington
(804) 438-6888
steamboateramuseum.org

Voorhees Nature Preserve
Oak Grove
colonial-beach-virginia-attractions.com/
westmoreland-berry-farm.html

Westmoreland Berry Farm (seasonal)
Oak Grove
colonial-beach-virginia-attractions.com/
westmoreland-berry-farm.html

ANNUAL EVENTS IN CHESAPEAKE BAY

JANUARY

Lee Family Birthday Commemoration
Stratford Hall
Stratford
(804) 493-8058
stratfordhall.org

APRIL

Daffodil Festival
Historic Court Circle
Gloucester
(804) 693-2355
daffodilfestivalva.org

Historic Garden Week
Statewide event includes Colonial Beach,
Dunnsville, and White Marsh
(804) 644-7776
vagardenweek.org

JUNE

**Potomac River Festival and Boat
Parade**
Colonial Beach Boardwalk
(804) 214-6880
colonial-beach-virginia-attractions.com/
potomac-river-festival.html

JULY

Fourth of July
Colonial Beach Boardwalk
(804) 214-6880
colonial-beach-virginia-attractions
.com/4th-of-july.html

SEPTEMBER

Chickahominy Pow-Wow/Fall Festival
Chickahominy Tribal Grounds
Providence Forge
(804) 557-3775
chickahominytribe.org

Virginia Oyster Academy
Tides Inn
Irvington
(480) 264-3012
virginia.org/listings/Events/
VirginiaOysterAcademy

NOVEMBER

Urbanna Oyster Festival
Urbanna
(804) 758-0368
urbannaoysterfestival.com

Places to Stay in Chesapeake Bay

CHURCH VIEW

Dragon Run Inn
35 Wares Bridge Rd.
(804) 758-5719
dragon-run-inn.com

GLOUCESTER

Inn at Warner Hall
4750 Warner Hall Rd.
(804) 695-9565 or
(800) 331-2720
warnerhall.com

MATHEWS

The Callis House Inn
345 Main St.
(804) 413-1804
callishouseinn.com

PORT HAYWOOD

Inn at Tabbs Creek
384 Turpin Ln.
(804) 725-5136
innattabbscreek.com

REEDVILLE

**Ma Margaret's House
Bed and Breakfast**
249 Greenfield Rd.
(804) 577-1110
mamargaretshouse.com

The Gables
859 Main St.
(866) 599-6674
thegablesbb.com

TAPPAHANNOCK

Essex Inn Bed and Breakfast
203 Duke St.
(804) 443-9900 or
(866) 377-3982
essexinnva.com

Places to Eat in Chesapeake Bay

COLONIAL BEACH

Dockside Restaurant and Blue Heron Pub
1787 Castlewood Dr.
(804) 224-7230
docksiderestaurantand
blueheronpub.com

GLOUCESTER

Ann's Family Dining
6545 Market Dr.
(840) 693-1764

Bangkok Noi Thai Cuisine
6724 Main St.
(804) 695-1177
bangkoknoithaicuisine.com

Courthouse Restaurant
6714 Main St.
(804) 210-1506
thecourthouserestaurant
.com

Olivia's in the Village
6597 Main St.
(804) 694-0057
oliviasinthevillage.com

REEDVILLE

Crazy Crab Restaurant
(seasonal)
902 Main St.
(804) 453-6789
crazycrabreedville.com

Tommy's Steaks and Seafood (seasonal)
729 Main St.
(804) 453-4666
tommysfinedining.com

Chitter Chat's Ice Cream Parlor (seasonal)
846 Main St.
(804) 463-3335
chitterchatsicecream.com

WEST POINT

Tony and George's Seafood and Italian
2880 King William Ave.
(804) 843-4448
facebook.com/Tony-and-
Georges-Seafood-Italian-
Restaurant

Northern Virginia

Poor Northern Virginia. Other than those who follow Civil War history (and the new Amazon HQ2 employees), there probably aren't many visitors who say, "Oh, I'm going to Northern Virginia for my vacation." They say they're going to Washington, DC, and decide to stay in the neighboring state across the Potomac River and catch the Metro into DC, then return for eating and sleeping. That's all well and good for the restaurants and hotels—their managements love it. But it's not fair to the visitor who could be missing a spectacular Virginia museum, an unusual spot to get away from it all for a few hours, or a significant link to history.

When you stay on this side of the river, you can visit an old gristmill, see where the George Washington cherry tree fable originated, or check out an apothecary that seems frozen in time.

City of Alexandria

The *Alexandria Visitors Center at Ramsay House* (Alexandria Convention & Visitors Bureau; 221 King St.; 703-838-5005 or 800-388-9119; visitalexandriava.com) is the place to

start your Alexandria touring. It's open daily 9 a.m. to 5 p.m. You can find a calendar of events, discount coupons, and special offers from Alexandria's shops and restaurants at visitalexandriava.com/holidays.

If you enjoy walking tours and ghost tales, call *Alexandria Colonial Tours* (703-519-1749; alexcolonialtours.com) for their "Ghosts & Graveyards" tour, where you'll hear legends, folklore, and twisted tales, starting with George Washington's time, and American experience and you'll end up in a cemetery! Tours are presented by colonial-clad guides. Other tours highlight the African-Alexandria's history. Group reservations are required. As you wander around the historic section of town, you'll notice cobblestone streets (the 100 block of Prince Street and the 600 block of Princess Street), brick sidewalks, and vintage streetlamps. You can see the narrowest houses in Alexandria in the 400 block of Prince Street and the 500 block of Queen Street. These were alley houses built between two other houses. Sometimes they were called *"spite houses"* or *"mother-in-law houses."*

phoningitin

Northern Virginia phones have been assigned to one of two area codes, 703 and 571 (703 being the original code). All telephone calls to and from Northern Virginia phones must include the area code (but not a "1"), even if you're calling across the street or next door.

Alexandria features an architectural style that may be unique, called a *Floun-der house.* A typical house was cut in half the long way, was usually much taller and narrower than normal, and was probably built to satisfy a provision of the sale of the lots that the property would be improved within two years. People who envisioned building something grander started with the Floun-der, which became a minor wing when the larger front part was constructed. The original section usually was built without windows because of taxes on glass. Besides the Flounder house, you can also find examples of Georgian (starting about 1700 and ending around the time of the Revolutionary War), Federal (late 18th century), Greek Revival (late 1840s), Victorian (1860–1900), Gothic Revival, Italianate (1820–1885), Second Empire (1885–1900), Richardson Romanesque (1880–1900), and Queen Anne (1880–1910) architecture.

After the exhausting sightseeing and shopping, stop by *Hank's Oyster Bar* (1026 King St.; 703-739-HANK [4265]; hanksoysterbar.com), a restaurant operated by chef-owner Jamie Leeds. In September 2010 Jamie announced a partnership with Bruce Wood and Kenny Hobar of Dragon Creek in Montrose, Virginia, whereby the guys would help develop an oyster in Nomini Creek that is unique to Hank's. They're also collecting the oyster shells to be returned to local waters to help repopulate the oyster crop. Because the creek has a low salinity factor, the oyster has a wonderfully sweet flavor, great for on the half shell, baked, or fried. There are other items on the menu, of course. Just as the oysters have flourished, so has the restaurant, and it now has four siblings in Washington—at Dupont Circle, Capitol Hill, the Wharf, and Nationals Park—and two cousins, Hank's Pasta Bar and Hank's Cocktail Bar.

A bar can be just a bar, and then it can be the ***Light Horse Restaurant and Bar*** (715 King St.; 703-549-0533; thelighthorserestaurant.com), an Old Town neighborhood place that welcomes the community and gives back to it. Oh, and it serves good, interesting food and a nice selection of beverages. Operating partners John Jarecki and Kevin Penn also throw in the occasional Taps for TAPS night where $1 from each pour of select beers is donated to TAPS. The Tragedy Assistance Program for Survivors is a non-profit organization that provides care and support to families grieving the loss of a member of the armed forces. Jarecki and Penn have been volunteers in the program for years and Penn, a retired Marine, was named the TAPS Mentor of the Year for 2019. The bar is upstairs (lots of TV sets, skeeball, shuffleboard, and other games); the restaurant, with a seasonal menu, is downstairs with dinner daily from 4 to 10 p.m. and a late-night menu after 10. Upstairs is open daily from 11 a.m. to 2 a.m.

One of the most widely imitated art forms is the transformation of an old factory into an arts center. One of the first was the ***Torpedo Factory Arts Center*** (a 1918 factory where torpedo shell cases were manufactured), housing more than 80 artists and 6 galleries on 3 floors of studio space. You can buy original artwork (weavings, paintings, musical instruments, pots, prints, sculptures, jewelry, glassworks, and photographs), talk with the artists, attend lectures, take art classes, and participate in a variety of other activities. You can also see an MK-14 torpedo on display on the first floor. An annual jury for

Public Art

Four Metro stations in Northern Virginia feature public arts projects. The ***Rosslyn station*** (Orange and Blue lines) has a Y. David Chung–painted mural, **Scenes of Rosslyn,** that's 88 feet by 4 feet and portrays stylized images of local architecture; it was installed in 2000. Elizabeth Ryland Mears created the stained and architectural glass panels titled **Tunnel of Light,** installed at the ***Franconia-Springfield station*** (Blue line) in 2004. Ray King's Solar Sails, on the south wall of the Tysons Corner station (Silver line) over Chain Bridge Road, is laminated glass panes on tension-pulled steel and was installed in 2015. In 2016, David Wilson's untitled creation of glass art opalescent panes was installed in the Wiehle-Reston East station (Silver line).

It's a Photo Moment

I'm always looking for that perfect or unusual photo, particularly when it comes to views of Washington. If you didn't see enough of the Washington skyline as you landed at Reagan National Airport (perhaps you came in from the south approach or you were on an inside seat, or maybe you drove), there are some great spots with amazing views of downtown Washington, with its marble monuments and greenery. Try *Freedom Park,* the *Iwo Jima Memorial, Arlington House at Arlington Cemetery,* and the *Vantage Point Restaurant and Lounge* on the 17th floor at the Holiday Inn Rosslyn. The *George Washington Masonic National Memorial,* the most visible sight in Alexandria, also provides a spectacular view of the city and of Washington, DC, which is 6 miles away. You'll want to bring your widest and longest camera lenses to shoot from the observation tower of this 333-foot-tall building.

---

studio space is held each Mar. All artists working in fine arts and fine crafts are eligible. The Torpedo Factory Arts Center (105 N. Union St.; 703-746-4570; torpedofactory.org) is open daily 10 a.m. to 6 p.m. and until 9 p.m. on Thurs, except major holidays. Studio and gallery hours vary.

The *Alexandria Archaeology Museum* (105 N. Union St., #327; 703-746-4399; alexandriava.gov/archaeology) and research lab are located on the third floor of the Torpedo Factory Arts Center. In addition to the rotating exhibits on the archaeological history of the area, they might have a Family Dig Day where children, their families, and friends enjoy a hands-on experience with the past while screening for artifacts on an excavation site. Two weeklong day camps are held in the summer for 12- to 15-year-olds. The museum is open Tues through Fri 10 a.m. to 3 p.m.; Sat 10 a.m. to 5 p.m.; and Sun 1 to 5 p.m. The museum is closed on Mon and Tues (Nov through Mar). There is no admission fee.

The *Alexandria Old Town Farmers' Market,* on the south plaza of City Hall at 301 King St., was established in the original lot sale of July 1749, when two lots were designated for the purpose. The farmers' market started in 1753 and is said to be the nation's oldest continually operating market. George Washington spent his young adult life in this area and is said to have sent produce here to be sold. The market moves indoors during winter to the lobby of City Hall. The farmers' market is open on Sat from 7 a.m. to 12 noon. There's free parking in the Market Square garage during market hours. For more information call (703) 746-3200 or visit alexandriava.gov/OldTownFarmersMarket.

Four other farmers' markets worth checking out include *Old Town North Farmers' Market*, 901 N. Royal St. (open Thurs afternoon); *Del Ray Farmers' Market,* E. Oxford and Mount Vernon Avenues (open Sat from 8 a.m. to noon); *Four Mile Run Farmers' and Artisans Market,* 4109 Mount Vernon Ave. (open Sun mornings); and the *West End Farmers' Market,* 4800 Brenman Park Dr. at Ben Brenman Park (open Sun mornings from May through Oct). For more information visit alexandriava.gov/FarmersMarkets.

John Gadsby was an Englishman who operated a tavern and an inn in the late 18th century. What is now *Gadsby's Tavern* was the center of all that was political, social, and commercial. Meetings, dances, and theatrical and musical presentations all found a home here. Dentists treated their patients here, and merchants sold their wares.

The buildings were used as a tavern and hotel until the late 19th century and then housed a variety of businesses, eventually falling into disrepair and near-demolition. Fortunately the American Legion Post 24 bought and saved the buildings in 1929, but it wasn't until 1972 that they were given to the city of Alexandria.

Both structures, restored to their late 18th-century splendor, are open for viewing, and an Early American–style restaurant serves visitors in three of the tavern rooms.

The *Gadsby's Tavern Museum* (134 N. Royal St.; 703-838-4242; oha .alexandriava.gov/gadsbystavern) is open Tues through Sat 10 a.m. to 5 p.m., and Sun and Mon 1 to 5 p.m. (Apr through Oct); Wed through Sat 11 a.m. to 4 p.m. and Sun 1 to 4 p.m. (Nov through Mar). Admission to the museum is $5 for adults; $3 for children (5–12); with discounts to AAA members, Gadsby's Tavern restaurant diners, and those who have coupons issued by other museums. Society members, AAM members, and Alexandria City employees are free.

funfacts

Gadsby's Tavern Museum was the site of George Washington's last two birthday celebrations.

Civil War history buffs will delight in visiting *Fort Ward Museum and Historic Site* (4301 W. Braddock Rd.; 703-746-4848; alexandriava.gov/historic/ fortward). Because Virginia was a Southern state, Union troops occupied Alexandria and Arlington Heights at the beginning of the war. They began construction of 162 earthen forts around Washington, with Fort Ward the fifth largest of the fortifications and supply bases. Named for Commander James Harmon Ward, the first Union naval officer to be killed in the war, the fort had 36 guns mounted in 5 bastions.

Major preservation work started on the fort in 1961 as part of a Civil War Centennial project. The Northwest Bastion was restored, with a reconstructed ceremonial gate marking the entrance to the fort. Young soldiers can let their imaginations go wild with the defense displayed here. A reconstructed Officers' Hut represents a typical fort dwelling of that time.

Exhibits on a number of Civil War subjects are in the museum, which was opened in 1964. Interpretive programs, tours, and lectures are offered throughout the year. Open Tues through Sat 10 a.m. to 5 p.m. and Sun noon to 5 p.m. The historic site is open daily 9 a.m. to sunset. There is no admission charge, but donations are accepted. It's closed on New Year's Day, Thanksgiving Day, and Dec 25.

The *George Washington Masonic National Memorial* (101 Callahan Dr.; 703-683-2007; gwmemorial.org) houses a collection about Washington's life from his days as a surveyor to his first inauguration. Over the front doors is a frieze of Washington in profile. The main lobby features two 46-by-18-foot murals by Allyn Cox, one depicting the laying of the cornerstone of the United States Capitol in Sept 1793, and one of General Washington at a religious service on St. John's Day 1778 in Christ Church, Philadelphia. There's a 17-foot, 3-inch bronze statue of George Washington in the Memorial Hall and a collection of Washington memorabilia, including the clock that stopped by itself when he died, the family Bible, and sabers used at his funeral. The auditorium is surrounded by granite columns and bronze medallions of the US presidents who have been Freemasons. The Parade Room contains an elaborate display of a mechanical parade of miniature uniformed Shrine Units. The memorial is open daily, 9 a.m. to 5 p.m., except on major holidays. Admission is $15 per adult. Guided 1-hour tours are offered daily at 9:30 and 11 a.m. and 1, 2:30, and 4 p.m. Photo ID is required. Groups should reserve at least two weeks in advance. There's plenty of free parking, and it's also within walking distance (uphill) of the King Street Metro station. Although it is not wheelchair accessible, Masons visiting the shrine will be helped by the brothers.

The Alexandria neighborhood of *Del Ray,* which celebrated its 100th anniversary in 2008, has been cited as an exceptional living community. One of its successful ventures is First Thursday, held from 6 to 9 p.m. from May through Sept, when Del Ray throws a community theme party. You should notice the red caboose on the grounds of the Mount Vernon Community School, a salute to the 1890s, when Del Ray became the home of the first interurban streetcar (and probably the first commuting suburb) in the United States. At the corner of Mount Vernon and Commonwealth avenues is where people want you to go when they say, "Meet me at the Egg" refers to the 12-foot-tall, 15-ton marble and limestone sculpture called *Three Eggs in Space,* created by Karen Bailey. Contact the Del Ray Citizens Association at delraycitizen.org.

Still another viewpoint of the area can be found along the *Mount Vernon Trail* (703-289-2500; nps.gov/gwmp/mtvernontrail.htm), which parallels

Designer Library

Virginia has a Michael Graves–designed library—quite a difference from the structured architecture of Old Town Alexandria, and one you're sure to remember. The *Charles E. Beatley Jr. Central Library* (named after the city's long-serving mayor, who died in Dec 2003) is located at the intersection of Duke and Pickett Streets, south of the Old Holmes Run Channel. At 60,200 square feet, it's more than twice as large as the Barrett Branch, which had been the central library. Special features include a full-service library for the blind, speaking computer terminals with OptiVoice artificial speech and enlarged type capabilities, and dataports at carrels for personal laptops. The precast stone clock on the south side, the Duke Street facade, weighs 5 tons. The library is open Mon through Thurs, 10 a.m. to 9 p.m., Fri, 10 a.m. to 6 p.m.; Sat, 10 a.m. to 5 p.m.; and Sun, 1 to 5 p.m., if you want to view the interior. The library is located at 5005 Duke St. Call (703) 746-1702 or visit alexlibraryva.org for more information.

the George Washington Memorial Parkway from Mount Vernon to Theodore Roosevelt Island in the Potomac River. Starting south at the *Arlington Memorial Bridge* (dedicated in 1932 to symbolize the union of the North and South following the Civil War and connecting the Lincoln Memorial to the Lee home), you'll go past the *Lyndon Baines Johnson Memorial Grove* in Lady Bird Johnson Park; the *Navy-Marine Memorial* (the Ernesto Begni del Platta statue honoring Americans who served at sea, dedicated in 1934); *Gravelly Point,* which is a terrific place to view the planes taking off and landings at Reagan National Airport; *Old Town Alexandria; Jones Point Lighthouse* (in service from 1836 to 1925); and *Dyke Marsh* (a 240-acre wetland where more than 250 species of birds have been sighted). You can catch a look at *Fort Washington* (on the Maryland side) and end at *Mount Vernon.* Volunteers patrol the trail on bike periodically, usually more frequently on the weekends and super gorgeous days. They can help with questions, remind you about the helmet laws, and assist with minor first aid situations.

You can walk, jog, or bike the length of this 18.5-mile trail or just parts of it. Three areas along the trail are quite steep and might be a little strenuous for new bikers. There are plenty of places to picnic and to enjoy nature and history, and a physical fitness course helps you vary the type of exercise you're doing. Check with *Big Wheel Bikes* in Old Town; call (703) 739-2300 or visit bigwheelbikes.com for information about renting a bike for an hour or a day.

Among the numerous Alexandria cemeteries is the *African-American Heritage Park* (902 Wythe St.; 703-746-4356; alexandriava.gov/historic/black history). There are 6 identified headstones of about 21 burials that took place here. The wetlands part of the cemetery is a home for mallards, painted turtles, beavers, and crayfish. ***Truths that Rise from the Roots Remembered,*** a bronze sculpture of trees by Jerome Meadows, is a tribute to the contribution of African Americans to Alexandria. A number of other statues are placed throughout the cemetery. The park is open during daylight hours. The museum is open Tues through Sat, 10 a.m. to 4 p.m., and admission is $2.

It isn't often that you can see what a Quaker pharmacy of 200 years ago looked like, but you can at the ***Stabler-Leadbeater Apothecary Shop*** (105–107 S. Fairfax St.; 703-746-3852; alexandriava.gov/Apothecary). Edward Stabler opened his shop in 1792, when Alexandria was a bustling port city with about 300 homes. The family operated the business through the War of 1812, an 1821 yellow fever epidemic, the Civil War, the Spanish-American War, and World War I, before succumbing to the Great Depression and closing the store in 1933.

Fortunately, Stabler was a master pack rat; miraculously, more than 8,000 herbs, potions, pill rollers, mortars and pestles, drug mills, medical glassware, documents, journals, letters, and paper labels are still around. Volunteers have gone through the boxes of deteriorating books and letters, finding a note from Martha Washington, a letter to Robert E. Lee, prescriptions for curing everything from gout to hams, and much more. Among the changes that took place over the lifetime of the apothecary are the introduction of prescription forms, the hypodermic needle, pills, and controlled-substance regulations. This is the only old apothecary museum in the country where the shop sold retail, wholesale, and manufactured products. Thirty-minute guided tours are offered at quarter past and quarter to the hour. The museum is open Tues through Sat from 10 a.m. to

Sealed with a Kiss

Postage stamp collectors probably are familiar with the work of *Howard Paine* of Delaplane, Virginia. Paine was involved in the design or as art director for such stamps as the one of Elvis Presley (issued in 1993), still the most popular commemorative stamp. He also designed the stamp dedicated to jazz (issued Mar 26, 2011), Kansas statehood (issued Jan 27, 2011), Raoul Wallenberg, Big Bands, and the Leonard Bernstein commemorative stamp issued on July 10, 2001. The first US postage stamp to honor the favorite pastime of cruciverbalists was issued in February 1998 as part of the Celebrate the Century series. The stamp was issued to commemorate the anniversary of the publication of the first crossword puzzle and is in the sheet for the decade of 1910 to 1919. Paine designed this stamp also. At the same time, he was a graphic artist and the art director at the National Geographic Society. Paine died in on Sept 13, 2014, at the age of 85.

5 p.m. and on Sun and Mon from 1 to 5 p.m. (Apr through Oct). It's open Wed through Sat from 11 a.m. to 4 p.m.; and Sun from 1 to 4 p.m. the rest of the year. The admission fee is $5 for adults and $3 for children (5–12); children under 5 are free, or buy a multisite pass if you'll be visiting other historic sites.

Gourmet and donuts may seem an oxymoron to you, but that might be because you've never tasted the offerings at *Eamonn's, A Dublin Chipper* (as in fish-and-chips). Yes, they serve super-tasty fried fish-and-chips, so it's difficult to save room for the fried dough balls, but you should try. If you're not a donut fan, you might want to try the fried Milky Way or fried bananas. They boast that they don't use any preservatives ("'cause it's just not good for yis"). It could be nothing stays around long enough to need them. They are located at 728 King St. Call (703) 299-8384 or visit eamonnsdublinchipper.com for more information.

Arlington County

At 26 square miles, Arlington is the smallest self-governing county in the United States. Established Mar 13, 1847, as Alexandria County, the name was changed to *Arlington* on Mar 16, 1920. The county is named for the estate where George Washington Parke Custis lived before he built the house currently known as Arlington House in Arlington National Cemetery. The estate had been named to honor England's Earl of Arlington.

For brochures and specific information, contact the *Arlington Convention and Visitors Services* (800-677-6267; stayarlington.com), or write them for information at 1100 N. Glebe Rd., Ste. 1500, Arlington 22201. They also have a Mobile Visitors Center that travels throughout the different communities. Now, on to touring and learning about Arlington.

The biggest news in Arlington in 2018 was the opening of the *CEB Tower observation deck* (1201 Wilson Blvd.; 703-423-0600; theviewofdc.com). It offers a 360-degree view of Maryland and Washington's skyline across the Potomac River and nearby Virginia through floor-to-ceiling windows. If you've never been to this area or don't know your Silver Spring and Georgetown from your National Harbor, and you don't mind dropping a few bucks ($22 for an adult ticket; less online) for this eye-dropping view, this is the place to start. The 12,000-square-foot deck takes up the 31st and 32nd floors and includes interactive displays and a cafe with wine, craft beer, and some food. Turn around and take a selfie of yourself with the Washington Monument and the National Mall in the background.

Near Arlington National Cemetery, the Iwo Jima Memorial, and the Netherlands Carillon is *Fort Myer,* home of the oldest military division in the United

Honoring the Last Full Measure

In 1992, Merrill Worcester, owner of Worcester Wreath Company of Harrington, Maine, donated several thousand surplus wreaths to decorate the headstones at Arlington National Cemetery for the winter holiday season. This continued until 2005, when a photo of the wreaths and snow covering the headstones went viral on the internet and people started requesting a wreath on a headstone at a particular cemetery or a cemetery-wide project. This became **Wreaths Across America,** and, in 2006, wreaths were placed at 150 cemeteries, and that grew to more than 300 in 2008 in every state, Puerto Rico, and foreign countries. More than 100,000 wreaths are placed at more than 1,400 cemeteries, in all 50 US states, at sea, and abroad. The program with the mission of "Remember, Honor and Teach" accepts donations and welcomes volunteers who will place the wreaths in mid-December. If you'd like to participate, either at Arlington or in another area, to donate, or to use this event as a teaching moment, check for information at wreathsacrossamerica.org.

States, the Third US Infantry Division. This is the ceremonial unit for Arlington National Cemetery.

The caissons, stables, and the **Old Guard Museum** (201 Lee Ave.) in the fort are often open to the public on weekdays. Blackjack, the riderless horse whose symbolism was so moving during the funerals of Presidents John F. Kennedy and Dwight D. Eisenhower as well as more than 150 other funerals, is buried on the marching grounds. Look for the plaque and flowering bushes marking his grave. A stable has been dedicated as a museum to him. The rest of the museum, which is the only US Army museum in the Washington, DC, area, is dedicated to the regiment that began its history in 1784. The museum is not open to the public at this time, but shares its history and archive holdings.

Restaurants in Virginia have been quick to jump on the farm-to-table or farm-to-fork program that helps support local farmers while providing that unmistakable taste of fresh-from-the-field food to appreciative diners. The **Lost Dog Cafe and Gourmet Pizza Deli** and the **Stray Cat Cafe** serve real milk shakes, gluten-free pizza for only $4 more than the regular, and have about a dozen beers on tap and maybe 200 more in bottles. That's all well and good, but there's another reason to visit the Lost Dog or Stray Cat—owners Ross Underwood and Pam McAlwee participate in another valuable community program: They have been rescuing stray dogs and cats and, through a nonprofit foundation they started, placing more than 2,000 abandoned and homeless critters every year. Each pet has been spayed or neutered before adoption. You can help their cause by dining at one of their five restaurants: 5876 Washington Blvd., Arlington, (703) 237-1552; 2920 Columbia Pike, Arlington, (703)

553-7770; 1690A Anderson Rd., McLean, (703) 356-5678; 2729A Merrilee Drive, Fairfax, (703) 205-9001; or 808 N. Henry St., Alexandria, (571) 970-6511. You can volunteer or donate to the foundation at lostdogcafe.com.

The Women in Military Service for America Memorial, located at the ceremonial entrance to Arlington National Cemetery (703-892-2606; womensmemorial.org), is the only major national memorial honoring all military women—past, present, and future. Just listening to the stories of the battles fought to create the memorial, particularly the architectural ones, is almost as impressive as learning about the battles these women fought for more than two centuries, from Revolutionary days to the present. You can search for women who have served, either in person or online. There's a gift shop; rotating exhibits of artifacts, photographs, documents, memorabilia, and uniforms; a film, *In Defense of a Nation;* a computerized register with the stories of some 250,000 military women (and accepting more); and a monthly children's program. The Women's Memorial is open daily from 8 a.m. to 5 p.m., closed Dec 25. Children are welcome, and it's wheelchair accessible.

It seems there's a museum for and about everything, and now there's one about drugs—not pharmaceuticals meant to save your life, but illegal drugs. It's the *Drug Enforcement Administration's Museum and Visitors Center* at DEA headquarters (700 Army Navy Dr.; 202-307-3463; deamuseum.org). On display are 150 years of drug- and alcohol-abuse paraphernalia, including bent spoons, bongs, hash pipes, hookahs, marijuana, photos, and old syringes. It also follows the DEA history and its predecessors, starting in 1906 when the government began regulating drugs. The display is fairly small, and there is a gift shop, run by the Association of Former Federal Narcotics Agents Foundation. Just as the US Mint doesn't give samples of the paper money it prints, the DEA museum doesn't offer drug samples. But you can pick up a DEA sweatshirt, coffee mug, miniature lapel badge, badges in Lucite, pens, key chains, or a Beanie bear with a DEA shirt. You also can drop off expired, unused, and unwanted prescription drugs during the annual take-back day in April (no questions asked about where, how, or why you obtained the drugs). The museum is open Tues through Sat from 10 a.m. to 4 p.m. in Pentagon City (across from the Pentagon City Metro stop).

When you stop by the 17-acre *Lyndon Baines Johnson Memorial Grove,* off the George Washington Memorial Parkway, you will find white

funfacts

Arlington National Cemetery covers 624 acres and conducts approximately 6,900 funerals a year, or 27 to 30 per weekday. Flags are lowered to half-staff 30 minutes before the first funeral until 30 minutes after the last funeral.

pine, dogwoods, numerous flowering bushes, and a tape recording of Lady Bird Johnson's remarks at the dedication ceremony in 1976. Her speech is played through an outdoor speaker installed at one end of the footbridge that connects the grove to the Pentagon parking lot. There is also a 43-ton obelisk that was brought in from Marble Falls Quarry, near the LBJ Ranch in Johnson City, Texas. It looks rough intentionally, just as Johnson was rough. There are no quotations or citations proclaiming Johnson's victories while in office. There is just peace, tranquility, and natural beauty that signifies the Johnsons' contribution to our national park system and the highway beautification program.

funfacts

The escalator at the Rosslyn Metro station is the fifth longest (194 feet, 8 inches) in the Washington, DC, Metro system and takes 140 seconds to ride. The two longest escalators are in Maryland at Wheaton (230 feet) and Bethesda (212 feet, 10 inches). The hockey-puck-looking disks placed on the metal surface between the escalators were installed so people would not try to slide down them.

There's no physical address, so the GPS coordinates are N 38.87, W-77.05 for the Boundary Channel Drive entrance and N 38.877, W-77.050 for the George Washington Memorial Parkway Entrance; open dawn to dusk. For more information call (703) 235-1530 or visit nps.gov/lyba/index.htm.

The *Upton Hill Regional Park Mini Golf Course* (6060 Wilson Blvd.; 703-534-3437; nvrpa.org/park/upton_hill) in Seven Corners is where you'll find one of the longest mini golf holes in the world. The 140-foot hole is part of

Five-Sided News

The *Pentagon* is 3,705,793 square feet large, or twice the size of the Merchandise Mart in Chicago. There are 131 stairways, 19 escalators, 13 elevators, 17.5 miles of corridors (the Pentagon says it takes only 7 minutes to walk between any two points), 691 water fountains, and 284 restrooms. Guided 1-hour walking tours (yes, the guides walk backward) are offered daily from 9 a.m. to 3 p.m. and start at the Pentagon Metro station entrance. Call (703) 697-1776 for more information. Reservations should be made from 8 to 90 days ahead of time.

The *Pentagon Memorial* (pentagonmemorial.org), dedicated to the 184 people who died from the attack on Sept 11, 2001, is open to the public every day, all day (restrooms are open from 7 a.m. to 10 p.m.). A 28-minute audio tour provides a sequential narrative of the events of 9/11. Call (202) 741-1004 at the entrance (or listen online) and the audio will take you to various points throughout the park. You can reach the memorial by following the marked path from the Pentagon Metro station.

the course designed by Jim Bryant, one of the world's foremost miniature golf course designers. These holes have more exotic themes than you find in your normal miniature golf course.

The course is open seasonally, and if that's not your favorite activity, you can enjoy the water park, bocce ball, horseshoes, hiking (3 trails), batting cages, playground, picnicking, or just being in a wooden oasis that's a donut hole inside a very heavily populated area. Fees are charged for admission and activities, often with residents receiving a discounted rate. The main park is open year-round.

To get away from museums and traffic, stop by Arlington's **Bon Air Memorial Rose Garden** (850 N. Lexington Ave.; 703-228-6525; parks.arlingtonva.us/locations/bon-air-park), with its selection of roses (more than 157 varieties, of which 32 have been awarded the American Rose Society's "E" award for Excellence), azaleas, ornamental tree garden, and wildflower area. The park isn't huge, but it's nice, and there are benches for sitting and enjoying the gardens. It is open from sunrise to sunset.

Clarendon—a small corner of North Arlington, which until 1846 was the rest of the diamond shape of the District of Columbia—was named in 1899 for the Earl of Clarendon (1609–1674). Catch the Metro (Orange line) to Clarendon Station under the intersection of Fairfax Drive, Washington Boulevard, and Wilson Boulevard. Wander out to see the **American Legion War Memorial** monument and to enjoy the variety of restaurants, pubs, coffeehouses, and shops reflecting the multiethnic (Japanese, Chinese, Korean, Moroccan, Indian, Cuban, Greek, Peruvian, Persian, Mexican, Irish, Salvadoran) population of the area.

Not far from the Virginia Square Station (Metro) is the **Arlington Arts Center** (3550 Wilson Blvd.; 703-248-6800; arlingtonartscenter.org) home of exhibits, classes, and live theater.

Precious Stones

The 15-foot pinkish granite archway monument at 540 S. Washington St. in Falls Church honors two African Americans, **Joseph Tinner** and **Edwin B. Henderson,** who started the fight for civil rights in 1915. They founded what was the first rural NAACP branch. Tinner worked in a quarry, and the stone excavated there was used for the foundations of many Falls Church buildings. As these buildings were demolished, local residents claimed the old stone and used it in their gardens. When the monument was approved, the residents gave up their stones to the tune of 16 tons from 26 different sites. For more information call (703) 241-4567 or visit tinnerhill.org.

Daisy, Daisy

At 100 feet wide, the **W&OD Trail** (Washington and Old Dominion Railroad) is one of the skinniest in all of Virginia. Measuring 45 miles of rails-to-trails path from Arlington to Purcellville for bikers, hikers, and others makes it one of the longest. It's accessible in Falls Church, Vienna, Reston, Herndon, and Leesburg. You may walk, hike, jog, bike, or in-line skate along the trail. Horseback riders may use a bridle path that parallels the trail for 32.5 miles from Vienna to Purcellville. Check the site (wodfriends .org) for tidbits about the railroad, towns along the trail, old houses within a long stone's throw of the trail, flora and fauna, and so much more.

The **Ball-Sellers House** (5620 3rd St. S; 703-577-7042; arlingtonhistorical society.org), a log house built around 1742, is Arlington's oldest residence and is believed to be typical of the way many early settlers lived in colonial Virginia. John Ball built the one-room house on a 166-acre land grant, along Four Mile Run, from Lord Thomas Fairfax. It has a loft and an attached lean-to room at the rear. Ball, his wife, and their five daughters lived here until Ball's death in 1766. It was donated to the Arlington Historical Society in 1975; it's open Sat from 1 to 4 p.m., Apr through Oct and by appointment. There's no admission charge, but donations are appreciated.

When is a used bookstore a boon? When people face downsizing, and they try to eliminate some or all of the books collected over a lifetime. Or, when you have to furnish your new home and want the books you never had room to shelve. Thank goodness for used bookstores, and in this case, thanks goes to the **Hole in the Wall** bookstore (905 W. Broad St.; 703-536-2511; holeintheweb .com). The selection includes new and used books, graphic novels, cookbooks, history, comic books, science fiction, adventure, and children's books. Open Mon through Fri 10 a.m. to 8 p.m. and weekends 10 a.m. to 6 p.m.

Culpeper County

Culpeper, originally called Fairfax, was founded in 1759 when George Washington (who was 17 at the time) was commissioned to survey and plot the town and county of Culpeper. Over the years it thrived and suffered. During the Civil War, there were more than 100 battles and skirmishes in the area, primarily because its central railroad was vital to both the North and the South. Homes became military lodging and hospitals, and over the years many farms, houses, historical artifacts, and, of course, lives were lost. About 100 years later, in the 1960s, the town was nearly devastated financially when a highway bypass was constructed, taking residential, commercial, and industrial growth away from the town center. A major Main Street project has strengthened and revitalized the historic core.

Stop by the depot, now the **Culpeper Visitors Center and Chamber of Commerce** (111 S. Commerce St.), for information about area activities and attractions. You can call (540) 727-0611 or (844) 490-2577 or visit the town's website at visitculpeperva.com.

More than 200,000 people visit the **Culpeper National Cemetery** (305 US Ave.; 540-825-0027; cem.va.gov/cems/nchp/culpeper.asp) every year as they follow Civil War events. Established on Apr 13, 1867, as a burial site for Union soldiers, the cemetery now is home to soldiers from all American wars and is listed on the National Register of Historic Places. Note the stone lodge/gatehouse near the entrance. Its mansard roof is unique in the Culpeper area but typical of cemetery architecture. Originally, the building was the residence and office of the cemetery's superintendent. The office is open weekdays from 8 a.m. to 4:30 p.m., and the grounds are open daily from dawn to dusk.

You may have heard that the Library of Congress has been working to save original movies that were shot on nitrate film and other formats that date from more than 100 years ago. They are doing more than that. Specialists acquire, preserve, and provide access to what is immodestly called "the world's largest and most comprehensive collection of films, television programs, radio broadcasts, and sound recordings" at this state-of-the-art facility. Stored on 90 miles of shelving, the films and television programs are presented to the public in a 204-seat Art Deco–style theater. There are usually 3 shows a week, on Thurs, Fri, and Sat at 7:30 p.m. and the occasional 2 p.m. Sat matinee. Typical programs might feature *The Miracle of Morgan's Creek,* a 1944 film from Paramount that starred Eddie Bracken, Betty Hutton, William Demarest, and Diana Lynn; a 1926 silent black-and-white film, with music accompaniment by Andrew Simpson, from MGM entitled *Flesh and the Devil* with John Gilbert and Greta Garbo; or *Mister Buddwing* with James Garner, Suzanne Pleshette, and Jean Simmons in an MGM film that was directed by Delbert Mann. These programs are presented at the **Packard Campus of the National Audio-Visual Conservation Center** (19053 Mount Pony Rd.; loc.gov/avconservation/Packard) on a 45-acre campus in Culpeper. The programs are free, but you must make reservations by calling (540) 827-1079, ext. 79994, or (202) 707-9994.

Many people think "old" when they think of Virginia. At the **Museum of Culpeper History** (113 S. Commerce St.; 540-829-1749; culpepermuseum .com) in the historic train depot, they're displaying "really old" with exhibits about dinosaur existence and activity, including tracks from a theropod, aetosaur, and phytosaur that were discovered and removed from the Culpeper

Stone Company Quarry. Also on display are artifacts from Native American life and the Civil War.

The museum is open Mon through Sat from 10 a.m. to 5 p.m. and on Sun from 1 to 5 p.m. Guided tours must be arranged by appointment. Admission is $5 for adults, $4 for seniors (65+) and military veterans.

From spring through fall, you can see a variety of equestrian events at **Commonwealth Park** (13256 Commonwealth Pkwy.; 540-825-7469; hitsshows .com/culpeper/hits-culpeper-series), including Grand Prix, Hunter, and Jumper events. These HITS (Horse Shows in the Sun) productions continue an equestrian history that started in 1897 and continued for the next 54 years. Show jumping returned to Culpeper in the 1980s, and some of the country's richest show jumping competitions have been held here. Children 12 and under are allowed in for free.

When it's time to eat, stop by **Baby Jim's Snack Bar** (701 N. Main St.; 540-825-9212; facebook.com/BabyJimsSnackBar), a diner known for its burgers and shakes. For a "local" experience, go to the window and order "two dogs with the works, an order o' fries, and an RC." Just make sure you go early and join commuters preparing for a hard day's work in Washington, DC. Baby Jim's is open Mon through Wed 6 a.m. to 9 p.m.; Fri and Sat 6 a.m. to 10 p.m.; closed Sun.

Fairfax County

The **Fairfax Museum and Visitor Center** (10209 Main St.; 703-385-8414; historicfairfax.org/monthly-events-programs) is housed in the former Fairfax Elementary School, built in 1873. It was the first 2-story school in Fairfax County and is listed on the National Register of Historic Places. This is where you can see fascinating exhibits on the area's history, sign up for walking tours of the historic district (spring and fall), and obtain information about places to visit and shop and where to eat and stay. The center is open daily from 9 a.m. to 5 p.m.

George Washington's Mount Vernon Estate and Gardens (3200 Mount Vernon Memorial Hwy.; 703-780-2000 or 703-799-8121; mountvernon.org) is one of the more popular "off the beaten path" sites in Northern Virginia. Frequent special events make a visit even more interesting and delightful. Check out the website for a list of events (historicfairfax.org/monthly-events -programs). Here are just a few:

In Feb you can have "breakfast with George" on the weekend around his birthday. His favorite breakfast is said to have been "hoecakes swimming in butter and honey," and you can sample this delicacy (while supplies last) and then participate in "America's Smallest Hometown Parade" in the afternoon. Admission is free if you're named George or if your birthday is Feb 22. Yes, if your name is Martha or you were born on June 2, you also receive free admission on that day. Mrs. Washington is available for photographs on Mother's Day in May and shares her thoughts on motherhood in the late 18th century.

July Fourth, as can be imagined, is a daylong celebration with patriotic music, a reading of the Declaration of Independence (by "George" himself), a band concert, and birthday cake (while supplies last).

By far, the annual 18th-century **Craft Fair,** held in mid-Sept, is one of the highlights of the year. You can watch colonial-attired crafters create baskets, leather goods, woodcarvings, paper cuttings, and other items from the period, and you can buy them for a most unusual souvenir.

If you saw Mount Vernon 10 or 20 years ago, you should consider visiting again because it is a constantly changing destination. Mount Vernon is now the only site in the country that shows how whiskey was made in the 18th century.

Mount Vernon is open daily from 8 a.m. to 5 p.m. (Apr through Aug); 9 a.m. to 5 p.m. (Mar, Sept, and Oct); and 9 a.m. to 4 p.m. (Nov through Feb). *Note:* That's at least an hour earlier than other attractions in the DC area, so if you're an early riser and want to cram as much as possible into your sightseeing day, start with Mount Vernon. Adult admission is $20; senior tickets (62+) are $19; and children (6–11) with an adult are $12. Discounts are available if you buy online.

Washington's Gristmill (mountvernon.org/the-estate-gardens/distillery) is a reconstruction of George Washington's 1772 stone mill on Dogue Creek, built when the creek was still navigable. Located in the George Washington's Gristmill Historic State Park, it's in a beautiful scenic setting just 3 miles from Mount Vernon. The mill has a 16-foot waterwheel and millstones that weigh 1,000 pounds each. The foundation cornerstone of Washington's mill is shown at the beginning of the tour. During the careful excavation, part of the wheel, bearings for the wheel, part of the trundlehead, complete wheel buckets, and other items were found. Open daily 10 a.m. to 5 p.m. Mar 31 through Oct 31, the mill is at 5514 Mount Vernon Memorial Hwy.

The **Fairfax Station Railroad Museum** (703-425-9225; fairfax-station .org) includes, naturally enough, a museum of railroad memorabilia, complete with a Norfolk & Western railroad line caboose. Clara Barton, founder of the Red Cross, nursed many Civil War wounded on a neighboring hill, and there's an exhibit area dedicated to her pioneering work. One of the most enjoyable parts of the museum is when a group of "N" gauge railroaders from the Northern Virginia NTRAK club come in at least one Sun a month to display their

It's the Truth, by George!

Did you know:

- George Washington's real birthday was Feb 21, not 22.

- The Father of Our Country had no children of his own, but when he married widow Martha Custis, he adopted her children, John, age 4, and Martha, age 2.

- Washington never wore a wig. Rather, he powdered his light auburn (not red) hair that had started turning gray by the end of the Revolutionary War, when he was in his early 50s. He was also losing his vision.

- He never chopped down a cherry tree or said, "I cannot tell a lie." That story was the fabrication of Parson Mason Locke Weems, a minister and Washington biographer. You can sometimes buy a copy of his book, *Life of Washington,* at the **Weems-Botts Museum** (703-221-3346 or 703-221-2218; dumfriesvirginia .org) in Dumfries.

- George Washington "Washy" Parke Custis, Washington's grandson, was demonstrating Washington's strength by saying that his grandfather could throw a piece of slate across the Rappahannock River, which is not now, and never has been, as wide as the Potomac.

- Washington didn't sleep everywhere.

- He didn't design the layout for the city of Alexandria, but he did assist during an early (1749) survey of the town when he was 17.

- Washington's signature is not on the Declaration of Independence; he was busy fighting the war.

- It's said that Washington stood 6 feet, 2½ inches, quite tall for that time, although it's also reported that when he was measured for a coffin, that figure was 6 feet, 3½ inches. Washington was 67 when he died in 1799, quite a long life for those days.

- General Washington had all his troops inoculated for small pox, despite the Continental Congress's refusal to pay for the shots.

trains from 1 to 4 p.m. Constructed in the 1850s, the museum opened in 1989 and is open Sun from 1 to 4 p.m. Admission is $4 for adults and $2 for children (5–15). The museum, which is wheelchair accessible, is located at 11200 Fairfax Station Rd. (look for the caboose in the front yard).

Combining beauty, conservation, education, and more, the 95-acres of **Meadowlark Botanical Gardens** (9750 Meadowlark Gardens Ct.; 703-255-3631; novaparks.com/parks/meadowlark-botanical-gardens) have large ornamental gardens, native plants (including wildflowers), walking trails, lakes,

Blast from the Past

Nostalgia buffs might want to visit the **29 Diner** (10536 Lee Hwy./Rte. 29; 703-352-0029) in Fairfax, built in 1947 and listed on the National Register of Historic Places. Clad in blue and silver porcelain enamel and stainless steel, the interior is complete with old photos, articles, awards, and notes of appreciation along with a marble counter and terrazzo floor. Blue Naugahyde seats, tile, and Formica highlight the decor. Favorites include the country fried steak and fried chicken. The diner is open 6 a.m. to midnight Mon through Thurs and 24 hours on Sat and Sun.

shade garden, gazebos, and so much more. Within the visitor center are displays about conservation and plant diversity with an indoor tropical garden in the atrium—great for meetings and events. The Korean bell garden, funded by the Korean American Cultural Committee (to the tune of about $1 million), has Korean trees, a meandering path, and, as you might imagine, a bell pavilion and bell. Check their schedule for gardening and horticulture workshops, field trips, and other activities, and plan to attend the Winter Walk of Lights with dozens of illuminated displays. Open daily at 10 a.m.; closing according to sunset. Admission is $5 for adults, $2.50 for children and seniors. Dogs are permitted on the Perimeter Trail.

As you head west toward Dulles International Airport, you travel past a lot of shopping centers (areas that were corner grocery stands just a few years ago) and brainy think tanks. But you can spend a day at **Colvin Run Mill Historic Site** and not begin to realize you're only moments away from the bedlam of the commercial area. The site is wooded and beautifully landscaped. Explore the 200-year-old working mill, see the general store, picnic, hike, and take advantage of special programs.

Originally near Natural Bridge and now home in **Centreville, Foamhenge** (15621 Braddock Rd.; 703-830-4121; coxfarms.com/about/contact.aspx) is a full-size replica of Stonehenge, only carved from Styrofoam. Mark Cline of the Enchanted Castle Studios created, or sculpted, this full-size replica of England's Stonehenge. Yes, it's made of foam and took about six weeks to build. The Styrofoam construction is astronomically correct. Foamhenge is open Sat noon to 2 p.m. from mid-Apr to late Aug (free) and daily from mid-Sept through Oct (fee).

Colvin Run Mill Historic Site is located off Leesburg Pike (Hwy. 7) at 10017 Colvin Run Rd., 5 miles west of Tysons Corner. It's open daily except Tues, 11 a.m. to 4 p.m. For more information call (703) 759-2771 or visit co.fairfax .va.us/parks/crm.

Okay, *Dulles International Airport* (metwashairports.com/dulles) isn't exactly off the beaten path (unless you live in Maryland, and then it's the other side of the world), and 22.7 million people flew into and out of this facility in 2017.

However, thousands travel almost to the airport to flock to the nearby Smithsonian Institution's National Air and Space Museum's facility for the display and preservation of its collection of historic aviation and space artifacts. Named the *Steven F. Udvar–Hazy Center* (14390 Air & Space Museum Pkwy.; 703-572-4118; airandspace.si.edu/udvar-hazy-center) for the museum's major donor, this new space provides display room for a lot of things that couldn't be included in the Smithsonian's National Air and Space Museum on the National Mall in Washington, DC. It opened in Dec 2003 in honor of the 100th anniversary of the Wright brothers' first powered flight.

There are more than 80 aircraft and dozens of space artifacts here, including an SR-71 Blackbird reconnaissance aircraft, the Dash 80 prototype of the Boeing 707, the Superfortress *Enola Gay,* and a de Havilland Chipmunk, which is an aerobatic plane.

A 2011 addition to the collection is the *Space Shuttle* Discovery. As the longest-serving orbiter in the shuttle fleet, it was delivered to the James S. McDonnell Space Hangar to replace the Space Shuttle *Enterprise,* which was moved to the Intrepid Sea, Air & Space Museum in New York City.

You can walk among the artifacts on the floor and look into space or stroll along skyways to see the hanging displays. Some of the airliners, engines, helicopters, rockets, satellites, ultralights, and experimental flying machines are on display for the first time in a museum setting. There's also the *Donald D. Engen Observation Tower* (164 feet high) for a view of the area and planes taking off and landing, and an IMAX theater. If you've contributed to this museum, you should be able to find your name on a permanent memorial at the entrance.

There is no admission fee to the museum, which is open daily from 10 a.m. to 5:30 p.m. except Dec 25. There is a fee for the IMAX films; tickets can be purchased online. Parking is available for $15 a car until 4 p.m.

A Town of Firsts

Clifton, a town of about 282 people (although other residential areas nearby have glommed onto the Clifton zip code for its cachet), located at the junction of the railroad tracks and Route 645, southwest of Fairfax, was the first community in the area to have electricity—from the Bull Run Power Company—in 1925. It also had the first high school whose students commuted by train from other parts of Fairfax County.

Fauquier County

Almost before you're out of earshot of the planes from Dulles International Airport, you're in the area of The Plains, and that's where you'll find the award-winning fantastic food of Chef Tom Kee at the ***Rail Stop Restaurant*** (6478 Main St.; 540-253-5644; railstoprestaurant.com) in a neat, old white building with random-width wooden floor boards. Join the rest of the regulars, and those who've been sightseeing nearby, in one of the two main dining rooms, or reserve the Red Room, which can accommodate between 2 and 6 people. It's beautifully decorated and showcases the outstanding wine selection. You can choose from a special menu. Advance reservations are requested; they're required for the Red Room. The Rail Stop is open Tues through Sat for dinner and Sun brunch.

Romanticism abounds at the ***Flying Circus Aerodrome & Airshow*** (5114 Ritchie Rd.; 540-439-8661; flyingcircusairshow.com) as those daring young (and not-so-young) men continue to entertain since 1972. John King, who keeps this operation flying, says his pilots like to fly. "They love airplanes and they love to share" that love with the public—and they do it without compensation. Not only can you watch the flights, but you can take a flight in a biplane before and after the show. Shows are presented in ***Bealeton*** on Sun, depending on the weather, from May to late Oct at 2:30 p.m. (pre-show starts at 2), but it's best to arrive between 11 a.m. and 1 p.m. as the line gets long. Shows last about 90 minutes, and after the show, you're allowed to go on the airfield to meet the pilots and other airshow performers for about 30 minutes. A snack bar has some food stuff (cash only), or you may bring lunch and sit at the picnic tables in a tree-shaded area. Pets are allowed if they're kept under control at all times and with the caveat that the planes are noisy so you shouldn't bring a skittish animal. A hot-air balloon festival is held in Aug, with rides, all weather permitting. Admission is $15 for adults; $13 for military with valid ID; $7 for children (5–12).

When you want apples, you want Fauquier County and the ***Apple House*** (4675 John Marshall Hwy.; 540-636-6329; theapplehouse.net) in ***Linden***. I dare you to resist the fragrant aroma and lure of the freshly baked apple-cinnamon or apple-butter donuts. I'm told the mountaintop orchards benefit from rare climatic conditions, and the high altitude produces apples "sweeter and more intensely flavored than valley-grown fruit." Take a taste of the nonalcoholic sparkling ciders (also no added sugar and no preservatives) they've named Alpenglow (a reddish glow seen near sunset or sunrise on the summit of mountains). They offer the original Alpenglow (red Delicious and Winesap apples); mulled sparkling cider (apple pie in a bottle, they call it); sparkling scuppernong cider (wild grape muscadine from North Carolina and cider); classic blush (Virginia-grown rougeon grapes, muscadine, and various species of apples); and sparkling juice. Sampling is encouraged, they say, because "taste tells all."

You may want to think about spending some time at the restaurant with its own pork barbecue, beef brisket, salads, sandwiches, and daily specials. If you see a food truck named Fork'd, you're looking at the Apple House truck, serving their pork barbecue, crazy fries, grilled cheese, and more.

They've added so many things to the gift shop selection that the shop has become an attraction of its own. The Apple House is open Mon 7 a.m. to 5 p.m. and Tues through Sun from 7 a.m. to 8 p.m.

Fredericksburg

In Fredericksburg, you're in an area that boasts that "George Washington slept in a lot of places, but he lived here." With 350 original buildings built before 1870, the area is steeped in history from colonial times and the Revolutionary and Civil Wars. It's possible to stay here several days without seeing everything. Be sure to get your free all-day parking pass at the *Fredericksburg Visitors Center* (706 Caroline St.; 540-373-1776; visitfred.com), see the audiovisual display, and obtain directions and operating hours for museums, the national parks, and other attractions.

A *Timeless Ticket,* at $32 for adults (one free student ages 6–18), provides discounted admission to several area attractions (the Fredericksburg Area Museum, Mary Washington House, Rising Sun Tavern, Hugh Mercer Apothecary Shop, Historic Kenmore, Belmont, the James Monroe Museum and Memorial Library, Ferry Farm, Gari Melchers home and studio at Belmont, and Fredericksburg and Spotsylvania National

funfacts

There are 15,206 victims of the Civil War buried in the Fredericksburg National Cemetery.

The Apocryphal Stone's Throw

George Washington inherited *Ferry Farm* (Rte. 3, 268 Kings Hwy.; 540-370-0732; kenmore.org) when he was 11 and spent his boyhood years on this property, 1 mile east of Fredericksburg and 38 miles south of Mount Vernon, on the banks of the Rappahannock River. Legend claims the cherry tree story ("I cannot tell a lie") and his powerful toss of a "silver dollar" across the Rappahannock took place here. George Washington's Ferry Farm is now a National Historic Landmark.

By Women for a Woman

President Grover Cleveland unveiled the *Mary Washington monument,* at Washington Avenue and Pitt Street in Fredericksburg, in 1894. Mary Washington (George Washington's mother), who died in 1789 at the age of 81, was buried at her favorite spot near her daughter's home. President Andrew Jackson laid a cornerstone for the monument in 1883, but it was never finished. A new monument was commissioned in 1893 thanks to the efforts of a group of women called the Mary Washington Monument Association. The new monument was dedicated in 1894. It is the first monument ever erected to a woman by women. Call (800) 678-4748 for more information.

Military Park) with no expiration date. So, if you only make it through three or four on this visit, bring the ticket with you on your next visit and you can see some more. The price represents a 40 percent discount over individual prices. If you have but a short time and you're a member of AAA, you will receive a 20 percent discount on admission. The Timeless Ticket is available at the visitor center and other selected sites. The visitor center is at 706 Caroline St., Fredericksburg, and can be reached by calling (540) 373-1776 or (800) 678-4748. Visit the website at visitfred.com.

Riverby Books (805 Caroline St.; 540-373-6148; riverbybooks.com) has three floors of used and rare books, with an emphasis on Civil War and Virginiana, in a pre–Civil War building. You'll also find philosophy, fiction, board books, and other topics within their 30,000 book selection. They're the largest of Fredericksburg's used book stores and will buy your unwanted books, whether it's one or an entire library. I love the bins of Scrabble tiles

funfacts

The Masonic Lodge into which George Washington was initiated in 1752 is in Fredericksburg.

and jewelry findings so you can make a necklace of initials or even buy the tile that your game is missing.

Fredericksburg is home to *Mary Washington College,* so you can feel a historic or a more modern atmosphere depending on where you travel. For great souvenirs and items to ship to your friends, stop by John and Kathryn Mitchell's *Made in Virginia* store (920 Caroline St.; 540-371-2030 or 800-635-3149; madeinva.com), where you can find wonderful edibles ranging from Brunswick stew to Graves' Mountain red raspberry preserves to Barboursville Cabernet Blanc wine. It's open 9:30 a.m. to 6 p.m. Mon through Sat and 10:30 a.m. to 6 p.m. on Sun.

An institution, even one that was started in 1947 by Carl Sponseller, doesn't have to be stodgy. It can be fun and tasty. Such is the case with *Carl's Frozen Custard* (2200 Princess Anne St.; 540-372-4457; carlsfrozencustard.com). *Note:* This is frozen custard, not ice cream! That means more eggs, less air, more taste. You'll see they have only three flavors—chocolate, vanilla, and strawberry—with sauces and syrups of other flavors to add to the custard. My favorite is the hot-fudge milk shake. It's not on the menu and they charge a few cents more to add the hot fudge to the milk shake. Well worth it. They do not have a cash register. Everyone's trained to do the math. No credit cards. Carl's is open Sun through Thurs 11 a.m. to 11 p.m., and Fri through Sat 11 a.m. to 11:30 p.m., from the Fri before Presidents' Day to the Sun before Thanksgiving Day.

funfacts

Goolrick's (901 Caroline St.; 540-373-3411; goolrickspharmacy.com) is a great place for a sandwich and a refreshing drink, and claims to be the oldest continuously operating soda fountain (since 1863) in the nation. It's open from 9 a.m. to 6 p.m. Mon through Fri and until 4 p.m. on Sat. It's closed on Sun.

Kenmore (1201 Washington Ave.; 540-373-3381; kenmore.org), a mid-Georgian structure, was built in 1752 by Colonel Fielding Lewis for his second wife, Betty, the only sister of George Washington. Kenmore contains the finest ornamental plasterwork in America and authentic (but not original) furnishings of the period. Lewis was providing munitions for the war but, not receiving payment, eventually was forced to auction the furnishings.

You'll love the hot, fresh gingerbread and spiced tea at the end of the tour (from Mary Washington's original recipe, which you can purchase in the gift shop), and you can have tea in the kitchen or on the lawn. Stroll through the boxwood gardens, restored by the *Garden Club of Virginia.* There's a marvelous 9½-foot Daniel Hadley diorama of Colonial Fredericksburg, done in

And they swam and they swam . . .

On the chilly morning of Feb 23, 2004, thousands of spectators watched as the *Embrey Dam* on the Rappahannock River at Fredericksburg was destroyed. The 770-foot-wide dam was constructed in 1854 to provide power and a drinking water reservoir to the growing community. By the 1960s, the power plant was no longer in service, and the movement was afoot to undo this insult to nature. Now the 184-mile Rappahannock is the longest free-flowing river leading into the Chesapeake Bay watershed, and the shad can swim upstream to spawn.

cooperation with the Hagley Museum in Delaware. If you've taken the walking tour, been to the Stone House, and paid attention to all the details, you'll realize that there are some errors in the depiction, such as the height of Sophia Street compared to the river, and that the Baptist church is the newer one, not the older one, but this is such a magnificent diorama that it shouldn't be missed. The Lewis family tree is on display, filling a matrix that is 29 1-inch squares across and 49 1-inch squares down.

Besides being known for some of the most beautiful rooms in the country, Kenmore is cited as one of the first victories in the fight against suburban development. In 1922 a developer bought Kenmore and planned to demolish the house or convert it into apartments and subdivide the remaining 2 acres of land. His plans were thwarted by local historical preservationists.

Kenmore is open 7 days a week, 10 a.m. to 5 p.m. Mar through Oct and from 10 a.m. to 4 p.m. Nov and Dec. It's closed Easter Sunday, Dec 24, 25, and 31, and Jan 1. Admission is $12 for adults; $6 for students, and combination tickets are available ($19 and $8.50) if you'll be visiting Ferry Farm, too. Discounts are available for seniors, AAA, active military, trolley passengers, and DAR members.

Fredericksburg is surrounded by battlefields and cemeteries, including Fredericksburg, Chancellorsville, Wilderness, and Spotsylvania Courthouse, each with programs run by the National Park Service. Descriptive audiotapes for driving tours are usually available at each headquarters building. Get directions from the Fredericksburg Visitors Center.

The **National Park Service Visitors Center,** the starting place for a self-guided tour through Fredericksburg and Spotsylvania Civil War battlefields, is open daily from 9 a.m. to 5 p.m. with extended hours during summer months. A small museum includes an orientation program and some exhibits. There is no admission charge. Guided tours of the Sunken Road are given three times daily in summer. You need permission from the National Park Service, but you can visit the place where Confederate general Thomas Jonathan "Stonewall" Jackson's arm was buried after it was amputated on May 3, 1863.

During the Battle of Chancellorsville, Jackson was shot by friendly fire, and his left arm was amputated in a field hospital. It was taken to the family home, Ellwood Plantation, and a marker notes the spot. Jackson died a few days later and was buried in Lexington, Virginia. Stop by the visitor center for a map. The visitor center is located at Lafayette Boulevard and Sunken Road. The Chancellorsville Battlefield Visitors Center is located off Route 3 West and is open from 9 a.m. to 5 p.m. daily. Write Fredericksburg and Spotsylvania National Military Park/Chatham Manor (headquarters for Civil War battlefields), 120 Chatham Ln.,

---

Oldie and Goodie

The Red Fox Inn and Tavern (2 E. Washington St.; 540-687-6301; redfox.com), in historic Middleburg, is the oldest restaurant in Virginia. Opened in 1728, the restaurant is in the middle of Hunt Country, with gorgeous views outside and photo-worthy cuisine. Large fireplaces, paintings that depict earlier days, and candles provide a warm and inviting ambiance. The menu offers selections from old-time peanut soup to modern dishes, all accompanied by the best of Virginia wine. Yes, they offer a variety of overnight accommodations.

Fredericksburg 22405, or call (540) 693-3200. Visit the website for more information (nps.gov/frsp).

Gari Melchers, one of America's finest impressionist painters, lived at **Belmont** (224 Washington St.; 540-654-1015; garimelchers.umw.edu/gari-melchers/belmont-estate) from 1916 until his death in 1932. His former home now houses the *Memorial Gallery,* where spacious rooms are filled with antiques and paintings by Melchers and others, including Jan Brueghel, Frans Snyders, Auguste Rodin, and Berthe Morisot.

> **fun**facts
>
> Gari Melchers painted the murals that adorn the walls of the Library of Congress in Washington, DC.

Belmont is open daily from 10 a.m. to 5 p.m. from Apr through Oct and 10 a.m. to 4 p.m. from Nov through Mar. Admission fees are $10 for adults, $9 for AAA members, and free for up to two students (ages 18 and younger) with a paying adult. Access to the grounds is free.

Loudoun County

Since 1833, ferryboats have been moving travelers across the Potomac River between **White's Ferry** (on the Maryland side: 24801 White's Ferry Rd.; 301-349-5200; poolesvillemd.gov/338/Whites-Ferry) and **Leesburg,** Virginia. There used to be 100 ferries crossing the Potomac; now there is only one left. It used to be known as Conrad's Ferry, but after the Civil War a Confederate officer, Colonel Elija V. White, bought and renamed it. For three decades the *Jubal Early* (named for the Confederate general) carried about six cars a trip, but the demand became so heavy that owner Malcolm Brown (who retired in 2016) installed a new 30-ton vessel in mid-1988 that can carry as many as 24 cars.

The ferry is propelled by a small diesel boat on the upriver side. When the ferry reaches the far side, the ferry pilot casts off a line, and the current carries the small boat around to point it in the right direction for the return trip. There is a general store on the Maryland side that is open only in summer.

The ferry charge is $5 for cars one-way or $8 round-trip ($1 for pedestrians, $2 for bicyclists, and $3 for motorcycles), and the ferry operates on call from 5 a.m. to 11 p.m. daily as water levels and flow permit. Call or check their Facebook page to be sure the ferry is in, unless you're just planning to take a pretty ride and you're not dependent upon the ferry taking you across the river. Take US 15 north out of Leesburg to the signs.

The renovated 3-story brick *Aldie Mill* (39401 John Mosby Hwy.; 703-327-9777; nvrpa.org/park/aldie_mill_historic_park) was built between 1807 and 1809 and was once the largest factory of its kind in the county. Now, every Sat and Sun from noon to 5 p.m. mid-Apr through mid-Nov and by appointment, tours are given through the mill, showing the early machinery that was used to grind wheat and corn. Further work has been and continues to be done, including clearing of the head and tail races, stabilizing the archaeological sites, and creating pedestrian trails and interpretive signs. The Aldie Mill, which was restored in Oct 2010 with help from the Loudoun Preservation Society, is Virginia's only known gristmill powered by twin overshot wheels (the water pours over the wheel, making the wheel turn forward, instead of "down" the wheel, which would make it turn backward).

Middleburg is the heart of horse country and other outdoor activities. It's where Ellen Crosby sets her Virginia wine country mystery novels, including her 2018 book, *Harvest of Secrets*. Head there to visit the fascinating *National Sporting Library & Museum* (102 The Plains Rd.; 540-687-6542; nationalsporting.org), which is dedicated to "preserving, promoting, and sharing the literature, art, and culture of equestrian, angling, and field sports." The 26,000-volume library holds historic collections, rare books, and fiction by Will

Who's Bluffing Now?

On Oct 21, 1861, troops from the North and the South met at *Ball's Bluff* (Ball's Bluff Road; 703-779-9372; novaparks.com/parks/balls-bluff-battlefield-regional-park), outside of Leesburg, for one of the first Union battle disasters of the war. There are 25 graves holding the remains of 53 unknowns and one known (grave 13) soldier. The Ball's Bluff Battlefield Regional Park is the smallest national cemetery in the nation and is open from dawn to dusk. Guided tours are offered on weekends from early May through Oct.

A Rustic Retreat

Despite the mini-skyscraper and multi-mall population of Tysons Corner, you have only to go to Loudoun County for a taste of the rustic and a wooded view of the Potomac River. In **Algonkian Park** (47001 Fairway Dr.; 703-450-4655; novaparks .com/parks/algonkian-regional-park), just 15 miles west of Tysons Corner, are a dozen furnished, air-conditioned cabins accommodating 4 to 10 people. There are decks for watching the scenery and fully equipped kitchens. Relax in a unit with a fireplace or one of the more elegant models, complete with hot tub. Can't unwind quite that much? Within the 838 acres, there's an 18-hole golf course, boat landing, waterpark, hiking, and miniature golf.

James, R. S. Surtees, and Irish writers Edith Somerville, Martin Ross, and others. Early copies of *Spirit of the Times* and the *American Turf Register and Sporting Magazine* are also there. Recent exhibitions have included *On Fly in the Salt* and *Sidesaddle 1690–1935*. The museum offers a public lecture series gallery tours, book signings, exhibition lectures, and more. Children can learn mathematical and scientific secrets in the museum's artwork. Students can be challenged to identify geography, plants, animals, and weather patterns from the sporting and landscape paintings. Sculptures turn into mathematical principles of ratio and proportion. The museum and library are open Wed through Sun 10 a.m. to 5 p.m. Library admission is free. Museum admission is $10 adults; $8 seniors (65+) and youth (13–18). Admission is free on Wed and the last Sun of the month.

Prince William County

From Occoquan on the east to Manassas on the west, from the storyteller of George Washington's life to the largest tourist attraction in the state (yes, **Potomac Mills Outlet Mall** attracts as many as 250,000 shoppers in a weekend) to Civil War battlefields, Prince William County has just about everything a traveler could want.

The wheelchair-accessible **Veterans Memorial Park** (14300 Featherstone Rd.; 703-491-2183; pwcgov.org/government/dept/park/vetspark) has a picnic area, lighted tennis and volleyball courts, ball fields, soccer fields, horseshoe pits, a playground area, a 50-meter outdoor pool and a water slide, hiking trails, and a community center where classes are offered. You'll see lots of four-wheeling here, but it's of the skateboard variety, at the largest skate park in Prince William County. At the **Scott D. Eagles Skatepark** (pwcgov.org/

Order in the Court

The old **Prince William County Courthouse** (12229 Bristow Rd.; 703-792-6600; pwcgov.org/government) in Brentsville started service in 1822 when there were 19 homes, 3 stores, 2 taverns, 1 house of entertainment, a church, and the clerk's office and jail located in this town, the geographic center of the county. At the time there were 130 people, including 3 attorneys and 3 physicians, residing in the area. The town served as the county seat from 1820 to 1894. During the Civil War the courthouse roof was destroyed and court records were burned for fuel. By 1894 the county seat had been moved to Manassas.

---

government/dept/park/vetspark/Pages/Vets-Skate-Park.aspx), dedicated to a man who died young but immensely enjoyed his skateboarding while he was here (no, he didn't die of a skateboard accident), there are 7,200 square feet of bowls, bumps, moguls, a half-pipe, and smooth surfaces with sidewalk and street features for urban skaters. For those who've always wanted to try skateboarding but were reluctant to invest, skateboards can be rented at the park.

Nature is another huge attraction here because the park is next to the beautiful Marumsco Creek, Featherstone National Wildlife Refuge, and Occoquan Bay National Water Reserve. The park is open daily year-round during daylight hours, except in bad weather. The ranger office is closed on federal holidays.

Occoquan is an Indian word meaning "at the end of the water," which is obvious once you visit the town. There are oodles of antiques and specialty stores, craft shops, and restaurants in the historic 4 blocks of town.

Start your visit at the Prince William County Visitor Center (200 Mill St.; 703-491-4045; occoquan.org) to pick up some information about Occoquan and Prince William County. It's open daily from 9 a.m. to 5 p.m. (closed for 30 minutes for lunch). Craft lovers (both contemporary and country) should be sure to visit during the spring craft show, usually the first weekend of June, and the fall show, usually the last weekend of Sept. Call (703) 491-2168 for more information.

At the end of Mill Street, the main drag of Occoquan, is the **Mill House Museum** (413 Mill St.; 703-491-7525). This was the site of the first automated gristmill in the nation. Ships and barges came to this mill along the Occoquan River with holds filled with grain, which was processed and then returned to the boats to be taken to Alexandria and the West Indies. The mill operated for 175 years, until fire destroyed it in 1924. The miller's office is now a museum operated by Historic Occoquan, with artifacts and displays about the town,

The Stone Age

The trim on the **Aquia Episcopal Church** (2938 Jefferson Davis Hwy./US 1; 540-659-4007; aquiachurch.com) is made of Aquia sandstone, or Aquia stone, also called freestone because it could be freely carved in any direction. Aquia sandstone was also used for the original US Capitol—the center section with the dome—Mount Vernon, Gunston Hall, the White House, and some Philadelphia bridges. Completed In 1757, services are still held in the church, which is on the National Historic Landmark register.

including photographs of the damage done by Hurricane Agnes in 1972. Open 11 a.m. to 4 p.m. daily, there's no admission charge.

History and beauty and recreation combine at 500-acre **Leesylvania State Park** (2001 Daniel K. Ludwig Dr.; 703-570-0372; dcr.virginia.gov/state-parks/leesylvania). It has 1/2 mile of sandy beach; a state-of-the-art boat launch into the Potomac that is one of the largest in the state; and fishing for bass, perch, catfish, and more. For landlubbers, there's hiking on miles of scenic trails through hardwood forests, wetlands, and coastal bluffs. It's also a residence for bald eagles, beaver, deer, and other birds and waterfowl. History buffs will appreciate the remains of a Civil War Confederate artillery battery built here to protect the Potomac River.

The Lee family plantation was built on this site in the mid-18th century, and it was home to Henry Lee II and his wife Lucy Grymes Lee. Eight Lee children were born and raised here, including General Robert E. Lee's father, Revolutionary War hero Henry "Light Horse Harry" Lee.

Stop by the visitor center that interprets the Potomac River environment and the history of the land that was the estate of Light Horse Harry and Robert E. Lee. There's a discovery room with touch tables, a weather station, children's activities, and a "legacy" room with historical and archaeological displays, area maps, and historical information.

There's also a 288-foot fishing pier; in addition to daytime fishing, the pier is available for night fishing Fri and Sat and holidays from mid-May to mid-Sept. Admission and some other fees are charged.

Dumfries, the oldest chartered town in Virginia, is another Scot-settled town that was a major seaport until the late 18th century. Now, pure-white whistling swans (perhaps as many as 200) return from Canada to Quantico Creek each year as early as mid-Oct and leave within 24 hours of March 19 (the same date as the Capistrano swallows out west). You can tell when they're getting ready to leave, for they gather in from the various creeks and noisily discuss things (the day's itinerary?), and then they all take off at the same time.

Just west of Quantico Creek is the **Weems-Botts Museum,** a four-room Colonial restoration. One half of the house was once the bookstore of Parson Mason Locke Weems, the biographer of George Washington who created the legend of the cherry tree. The museum docent tells many little-known facts about George. Benjamin Botts, who lived from 1776 to 1811, bought the home from Weems in 1802. He became a prominent lawyer in Prince William County and was on the defense team for Aaron Burr at his treason trial.

Books on the history of the area from colonial days to Civil War times are sold at the shop. A resource library is available for genealogical research. The museum is open (May through Oct) Thurs through Mon, 10 a.m. to 4 p.m., and by appointment at other times. The museum is open on Mon if it's a legal holiday. Admission is $5 for adults, $3 for seniors (55+) and for children (6–12). Start your tour at the Museum Annex (3944 Cameron St.; 703-221-2218; historic-dumfriesva.org/visit/tours).

All 7 blocks of **Quantico** constitute the only town in the United States completely surrounded by the US Marine Corps; the only land access is through the **Quantico Marine Base.** For years the town has been totally landlocked, and then the government deeded 4.5 acres of waterfront property to Quantico to build a park, so now it can be reached by the Potomac River, as well. The town has its own mayor, five council members, and its own police department. As an indication of the cooperation between the base and the town, Quantico is the only place in the world where Marines are allowed to wear their "utilities" (work uniforms) off base.

In the first year of operation, from Nov 2006 to Nov 2007, the **National Museum of the Marine Corps** (18900 Jefferson Davis Hwy.; 877-635-1775; usmcmuseum.com) had 650,000 visitors. Even if you aren't a Marine, you're likely to be intrigued by the building's design that's visible from I-95. The signature 210-foot stainless steel spire (designed by Fentress Bradburn Architects) soars over the tree line and is clearly visible day and night. To some it emulates the iconic image of the raising of the American flag over Iwo Jima, and to others it appears to be huge swords at salute, aircraft climbing to the heavens, or a howitzer at the ready. This privately operated facility features the history of the Marines from when they formed in 1775 through World War II, the Korean War, Vietnam, and the Global War on Terror, and a gallery of combat art. The museum has been so successful and so much more popular than the "experts" predicted that they had to add three more galleries. That addition provided more than 12,000 square feet of exhibit space that holds 250 new artifacts. In my view of awesome is the interactive exhibit about John Philip Sousa, director

Eyes Down

When you stop by the $1.9 million **Center for the Arts** (9419 Battle St.; 703-333-ARTS; center-for-the-arts.org) in Manassas, on the site of the former Hopkins Candy Factory, take a look at the open floor area to see an exposed French drain and an adjacent trench that gave up some souvenirs of a massive fire that consumed the town in 1905. An archaeological dig was conducted during the summer of 2001 in hopes of finding Civil War relics, but the railroad tracks used for the drain were as far as they could research. There were thoughts that this might have been a bakery for Union troops, established by General John Pope.

of the president's Own Marine Corps Band, because you can experience a concert of your choosing.

When a docent is available, guided tours are conducted daily at 10 a.m. and 2 p.m., and a free audio tour is available. The museum store carries a full line of Marine-themed merchandise, and food service is available. The museum is open daily from 9 a.m. to 5 p.m., except Dec 25. There is no admission fee.

The **Manassas Museum** (9101 Prince William St.; 703-368-1873; manassas museum.org) in **Manassas** is set in a Victorian Romanesque 1896 building (the community's first national bank). It has a museum and a classroom for children to experience some natural and American history.

In the exhibit area you can see why this area, halfway between Washington, DC, and the Shenandoah Valley and the core of train transportation, spurred the region's development and why two of the Civil War's most famous battles were fought nearby. Collections include period photographs from the Civil War, children's toys of a century ago, and a major exhibit about the 1911 Peace Jubilee, which celebrated the 50th anniversary of the battle at Manassas. There's a gift shop with history books and souvenirs. The museum is open daily from 10 a.m. to 5 p.m. from Memorial Day through Labor Day, and Tues through Sun the rest of the year. Admission is $5 for adults and $4 for seniors older than 60 and students (6–17).

The **Manassas Walking Tour,** which you can take at your leisure, includes the museum, the 1875 Presbyterian church, the world's first military railroad, the defenses of Manassas and the Railroad Depot, the Candy Factory, Conner Opera House, and the Old City Hall. A brochure is available from the museum for this tour and the driving tour, which warns about the possible lack of parking at the historical markers and the heavy traffic.

Manassas was the site of the first and second battles of Manassas, and many of the events are marked in the **Manassas National Battlefield Park.**

OTHER ATTRACTIONS IN NORTHERN VIRGINIA

Arlington National Cemetery
Arlington
(703) 607-8052
arlingtoncemetery.org

Children's Science Center Lab
Fairfax
(703) 648-3130
childsci.org

Fredericksburg Area Museum
Fredericksburg
(540) 371-3037
famva.org

Friendship Firehouse Museum
Alexandria
(703) 746-3891 (weekends only)
alexandriava.gov/FriendshipFirehouse

Great Falls National Park
Great Falls
(703) 285-2966
nps.gov/grfa/index.htm

Lee-Fendall House Museum & Gardens
Alexandria
(703) 548-1789
leefendallhouse.org

National 9/11 Pentagon Memorial
Pentagon Metro Station
(202) 741-1004 (24-minute audio tour of 9/11 events)
pentagonmemorial.org/explore/biographies/audio-tour

Pope-Leighey House
Alexandria
(703) 570-6902
woodlawnpopeleighey.org

US Marine Corps War Memorial
Arlington
(202) 289-2500
nps.gov/gwmp/learn/historyculture/usmcwarmemorial.htm

Wolf Trap Farm Park for the Performing Arts
Vienna
(703) 255-1900
wolftrap.org

Woodlawn Plantation
Mount Vernon
(703) 780-4000
woodlawnpopeleighey.org

To assist your historical tour, pick up a *Prince William County Historical Marker Guide* at the welcome center or one of the museums. This will be a nice companion to John S. Salmon's *Guidebook to Virginia's Historical Markers,* published for the Virginia Landmarks Commission by the University Press of Virginia, Charlottesville.

The Battle of Manassas (as the Confederacy referred to it), also known as the Battle of Bull Run (as known by the Union forces), was the first major battle of the Civil War. It's commemorated at the Manassas National Battlefield Park with electronic battle maps, equipment displays, battle memorabilia, and interpretative presentations of the battlefield's history.

Start at the Henry Hill Visitor Center (12521 Lee Hwy.; 703-361-1339; nps.gov/mana) to view the museum, slide program, a 3D map charting the strategies of the two battles, and a bulletin board listing the day's interpretive programs. The grounds are open daily from 8:30 a.m. to dusk. The center is open daily 8:30 a.m. to 5 p.m. except Thanksgiving and Dec 25. The Stone House, which served as a field hospital during the battles, is open from 10 a.m. to 4:30 p.m. on weekends Apr through Memorial Day and Labor Day weekend through Columbus Day weekend. Admission is free. The park is located north of I-66 in Manassas.

Rappahannock County

It's easy to see why people love this area with its forested mountains and bucolic countryside. You're surrounded by a picture postcard wherever you look. You shouldn't be surprised that more than 50 artisans, artists, and photographers live in the county. You can find their work in the galleries of Washington, Sperryville, and Flint Hill. Or, you can accomplish everything at one time by attending the annual Nov *Artists of Rappahannock Studio and Gallery Tour* sponsored by the Rappahannock Association for the Arts and the Community (10 Firehouse Ln.; 540-675-3193; raac.org). Check the site for a list of participating artists and work samples.

famousresidents

Among the famous people who live or have lived in the Rappahannock County area are painter Ned Bittinger, former columnist James Kilpatrick, music director of the New York Philharmonic Lorin Maazel, former senator Eugene McCarthy, and sculptor Frederick Hart.

You will be excused if you think Rappahannock County should be in the Northern Neck or eastern part of the state. The Rappahannock River does form the northeastern boundary and separates it from Fauquier County. I'm sure no one's bothered (nor should they), but with 921 students in grades pre-kindergarten through 12th and a 2000

History in Black and White

Emmy and Peabody Award–winning journalist Jack Ford came across a historic plaque commemorating the story of freed slave Kitty Payne on the lawn of the Rappahannock County Courthouse, where she was tried in 1846. The old jail in the background is where she and her three young children lived for several months until the kidnapping case was resolved. Ford tells this story in his 2018 book, **Chariot on the Mountain** (238 Gay St.; 540-675-5350; jackfordauthor.wordpress.com/about-the-book).

ANNUAL EVENTS IN NORTHERN VIRGINIA

JANUARY

Alexandria Restaurant Week
(703) 838-5005
visitalexandriava.com

Fredericksburg Restaurant Week
(540) 372-1216
fredericksburgrestaurantweek.com

FEBRUARY

Breakfast with George Washington
Mount Vernon
(703) 780-2000 or (800) 388-9119
mountvernon.org

George Washington Birthday Parade and Weekend Festivities
Alexandria
(703) 829-6640
washingtonbirthday.net/events-1

Chocolate Lovers Festival
Fairfax
(703) 385-1710
fairfaxva.gov/government/parks-recreation/
special-events/chocolate-lovers-festival

MARCH

Easter Sunrise Service
Arlington
(202) 685-2851
arlingtoncemetery.org

APRIL

Annual Beeping Egg Hunt
Gari Melchers Home and Studio
Falmouth
(540) 654-1015
garimelchers.umw.edu

Everything But the Garage Sale
Fredericksburg Expo Center
Fredericksburg
(540) 548-5555
everythingbutthegarage.com/
fredericksburg.html

Annual Historic Garden Week
Statewide event includes Alexandria,
Fairfax, Falmouth, Fredericksburg,
Leesburg, Warrenton
(804) 644-7776 or (804) 643-7141
vagardenweek.org

MAY

Spring Wine Festival & Sunset Tour
Mount Vernon
(703) 780-2000
mountvernon.org

census of 6,983 people, I'd guess there are many more trees than people. Yes, you could spend a lot of time exploring here and not duplicate a single day.

Year after year and now decade after decade, Patrick O'Connell and the **Inn at Little Washington** (Middle and Main Streets; 540-675-3800; theinn atlittlewashington.com) in **Washington** continue to garner praise. Just reading notes from the Inn—"The season's first wild morels and local asparagus have arrived"—or watching the "Dream Dinners" episode of *Avec Eric* on PBS and I'm ready to visit. Two tables are in the kitchen that features an enormous custom-made Vulcan range, allowing you to watch the action ringside. If you can't make it for dinner or a night or two in one of the 24 bedrooms and suites

JUNE

City of Fairfax Band Outdoor Concert Series
Veteran's Amphitheater at Fairfax City Hall
Thurs nights through Aug, Fairfax
(703) 757-0220
fairfaxband.org

JULY

World Championship Scottish Highland Games
Alexandria
(800) 388-9119 or (703) 912-1943
vascottishgames.org

AUGUST

Hot Air Balloon Festival
Bealeton
(540) 439-8661
flyingcircusairshow.com/balloon

SEPTEMBER

International Children's Festival
Wolf Trap Farm Park for the
Performing Arts
(703) 642-0862
wolftrap.org

OCTOBER

Art on the Avenue
Del Ray
(703) 683-3100
artontheavenue.org

Loudoun County Farm Tour
Leesburg
(703) 777-0426
loudounfarms.org

Waterford Fair American Crafts & Historic Homes Tour
Waterford
(540) 882-3018
waterfordfoundation.org/programs/
waterford-fair

DECEMBER

First Night
Alexandria
(703) 838-4200 or (800) 388-9119
funside.com

Colonial Market & Fair
Mount Vernon
(703) 780-2000
mountvernon.org/plan-your-visit/calendar/
events/colonial-market-fair

in the Inn (or the Parsonage, Carter House, Mayor's House, Gamekeepers Cottage, or Claiborne House), you can make pretend at home with Patrick's books *Patrick O'Connell's Refined American Cuisine* or *The Inn at Little Washington: A Magnificent Obsession*.

Stafford County

The **_Globe and Laurel Restaurant_** (3987 Jefferson Davis Hwy.; 703-221-5763; thebestgandl.com) was opened in old-town Quantico in 1968 by Richard

(Major, US Marine Corps, Ret.) and the late Gloria Spooner, but it burned, and the restaurant was reopened in Triangle in 1975. Now, due to the widening of US 1, the restaurant has moved again. Less than 2 miles from the Triangle location, in Stafford County, the new Globe is five times the size and has more fireplaces and all of the memorabilia.

Major Spooner was in the Marines for 29 years and 7 months and wanted a place with a pub atmosphere. You can read about some of the Major's battle experiences in his book, *The Spirit of Semper Fidelis: Reflections from the Bottom of an Old Canteen,* published in Nov 2004. The protagonist in the nearly 400-page book is named Private Chic Yancey, but you can figure out that this is a historical novel. Since then Spooner wrote *A Marine Anthology* and *The Dragon of Destiny and the Saga of Shanghai Pooley.* Music of swing bands or bagpipes fills the air as you dine. Of historic note are Spooner's Purple Heart medals and the hundreds, maybe thousands, of police department badges on the ceiling from police forces across the United States and from about 30 other countries. Also of interest is the collection of former military insignia, many of which aren't in the possession of military historians, for apparently no one thought to save them; many date from the Civil War. If you have military buttons or other memorabilia, check with the Major before you throw them away. Meat lovers should definitely try the prime rib. The restaurant is open Sun from 11:30 a.m. to 2:30 p.m., Mon from 9 a.m. to 10 p.m., and Tue through Sat 11:30 a.m. to 10 p.m.

Places to Stay in Northern Virginia

ALEXANDRIA

Kimpton Lorien Hotel and Spa
1600 King St.
(703) 894-3434
ihg.com/kimptonhotels/
hotels/us/en/lorien-hotel
-and-spa-alexandria-va/
wdclr/hoteldetail

Morrison House
116 S. Alfred St.
(703) 838-8000
morrisonhouse.com

Westin Alexandria
400 Courthouse Sq.
(703) 253-8600
marriott.com/hotels/
travel/wasxw-the-westin
-alexandria-old-town/

ARLINGTON

Westin Arlington Gateway
801 N. Glebe Rd.
(703) 717-6200
marriott.com/hotels/
travel/wasag-the-westin
-arlington-gateway

FREDERICKSBURG

Kenmore Inn
1200 Princess Anne St.
(540) 371-7622
kenmoreinn.com

Richard Johnston Inn
711 Caroline St.
(540) 899-7606
therichardjohnstoninn.com

LEESBURG

Lansdowne Resort & Spa
44050 Woodridge Pkwy.
(703) 729-8400
lansdowneresort.com

LINDEN

Blue Mountain Escape
1264 Freezeland Rd.
(703) 517-5700
bluemountainescape.net

MANASSAS

Bennett House Bed and Breakfast
9252 Bennett Dr.
(800) 354-7060

Places to Eat in Northern Virginia

ALEXANDRIA

Dairy Godmother
2310 Mount Vernon Ave.
(703) 683-7767
thedairygodmother.com

Rocklands Barbeque and Grilling
25 S. Quaker Ln.
(703) 778-9663
rocklands.com
also in Arlington and Washington, DC

The Light Horse
715 King St.
(703) 549-0533
thelighthorserestaurant
.com

ARLINGTON

Ambar
2901 Wilson Blvd.
(703) 875-9663
ambarrestaurant.com/
home-page-clarendon

Arlington Cinema and Drafthouse
2903 Columbia Pike
(703) 486-2345
acdh.arlingtondrafthouse
.com

Palette 22
The Village at Shirlington
4053 Campbell Ave.
(703) 746-9007
palette22.com

Jaleo
2250A Crystal Dr.
(703) 413-8181
jaleo.com

ASHBURN

Aggio
20462 Exchange St.
(703) 726-9800
ashburn.volt-aggio.com

Slapfish
44725 Thorndike St.
(703) 726-5254
slapfishrestaurant.com/
restaurant
also in Arlington

FAIRFAX

Coyote Grille and Cantina
10266 Main St.
(703) 591-0006
coyotegrille.com

Dolce Vita
10824 Fairfax Hwy.
(703) 385-1530
dolcevitafairfax.com

FREDERICKSBURG

2400 Diner
2400 Princess Anne St.
(540) 373-9049
facebook.com/2400diner

The Confident Rabbit
309 William St.
(540) 371-9999
bistrobethem.com

Tito's Diner
1695 Carl D. Silver Pkwy.
(540) 548-33406
titodiner.com

LEESBURG

Wine Kitchen
7 S. King St.
(703) 777-9463
thewinekitchen.com

MANASSAS

Carmello's
9108 Center St.
(703) 368-5522
carmellos.com

Okra's Louisiana Bistro
9110 Center St.
(703) 330-2729
okras.com

MIDDLEBURG

Market Salamander
200 W. Washington St.
(540) 687-8011
marketsalamander.com

RESTON

Clyde's of Reston
11905 Market St.
(703) 787-6601
clydes.com/reston

WASHINGTON

Inn at Little Washington
Middle and Main Streets
(540) 675-3800
theinnatlittlewashington
.com

Central Virginia

The central portion of Virginia is a huge mix of the cosmopolitan Richmond-Petersburg area and an almost 19th-century feeling of people still practicing rural folkways. This is the breadbasket of the state, the source of tobacco, cantaloupe, grains, forage, and tomatoes. You'll also see beef and dairy products. Here you'll travel through miles and miles of moderately rolling piedmont dotted with gracious plantations.

This is where you'll find Tiffany windows, museums, fine restaurants, good shopping, and what advertisers and marketing specialists call a great quality of life. This area is home to nationally renowned amusement theme parks and county fairs.

Traversing the central area can be done via several interstate highways, including I-95, I-85, both running north and south, and I-64, running east and west. There are several scenic routes, including US 29, 15, and 160.

Albemarle County

Charlottesville

Charlottesville, an independent city within Albemarle County, is the home of Thomas Jefferson's Monticello, the University of Virginia, and so much more.

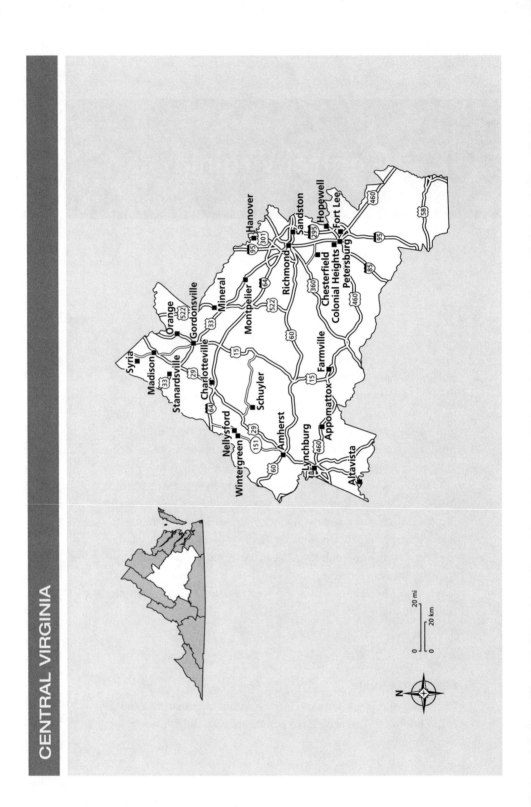

CENTRAL VIRGINIA

How Green Is My Ark?

Evan Almighty fans traveling through Crozet may notice a familiar look to the Old Trail Village development. It was used as a Washington, DC, suburb during the filming. Why Crozet? you may ask. The apparent reason is that Tom Shadyac, the director/producer, is an alumnus of the University of Virginia, and location director Tom Trigo lives in Crozet. Other buildings and locations around Charlottesville, Waynesboro, Staunton, and Albemarle County were used in the 2007 movie. Much to-do was made about the movie being perhaps the greenest movie ever made. Crew members were provided with bicycles to commute to the set; the lumber, windows, doors, flooring, etc., used in building the set were recycled, and the steel framing was sold and the money donated to Habitat for Humanity; and 2,050 trees were planted in the Rappahannock River Valley National Wildlife Refuge in Warsaw, Virginia, and the San Joaquin River National Wildlife Refuge near Modesto, California.

You can take a walking tour of **Historic Downtown Charlottesville** along the pedestrian mall with 30 restaurants, 120 shops, and flowering fountains, set in and around historic buildings. For your entertainment there are street performers, free concerts in an open-air amphitheater, an ice park, and other diversions. Art exhibitions are held the first Fri of the month.

I love historic theaters, particularly those built in the golden age of movie palaces, before the multiplex was invented. The **Paramount Theater** (215 E. Main St.; 434-979-1333; theparamount.net) in Charlottesville was constructed with a Georgian facade, an elegant lobby, chandeliers, and 18th-century-style scenes painted on silk panels. When constructed in 1931, it was one of the last of these fine theaters. It had remarkable sight lines and astonishing acoustics. It quickly became a landmark that lasted for the next four decades. By mid-1974 it had been shuttered and was threatened with demolition several times.

Fortunately, some community leaders bought the theater in 1992 and had it renovated and expanded, so the old 12-foot-deep stage is now 36 feet deep, and there's fly space above the stage for curtains, lighting, and scenery. There are also rehearsal rooms and scene shops. The orchestra pit in front of the stage has a hydraulic lift to raise the theater's mighty Wurlitzer theatre organ to stage level. It reopened on Dec 15, 2004, more than 30 years after it was closed. Now the Paramount is alive and well and doing what it's supposed to be doing—providing live entertainment, including Yo Yo Ma, Randy Rainbow, Chick Corea and Touchstone, *Swan Lake, The Prisoner of Second Avenue,* and a sing-along to the musical *Grease,* in the center of Charlottesville's Downtown Mall. In 2017 the Paramount was named "Outstanding Historic Theatre" by the League of Historic American Theatres, based on "excellence in community impact, quality of program and services, and quality of the restoration or reha-bilitation of its historic structure." Check the schedule for free theater tours.

The **Boar's Head Inn**'s (200 Ednam Dr.; 844-611-8066 or 434-296-2181; boarsheadinn.com) history started with an 1834 waterwheel gristmill that sur-vived the Civil War, ran for 60 years, and then, when John B. Rogan bought it in the early 1960s, was dismantled. Rogan had the pieces numbered and reconstructed on the Boar's Head Inn property. Fieldstones from the mill's original foundation were used in the inn's fireplace and in the arched stone entrance below the ordinary (a public house or tavern). The blue boar's head was a symbol of hospitality in Elizabe-than England and is well translated at the inn.

dmb

The **Dave Matthews Band** travels far and wide and has an extremely loyal following, but perhaps the most loyal are Charlottesville resi-dents. DMB was formed here and gave their first public performance on Earth Day of 1991.

Besides fresh mountain air, stunning scenery, proximity to the University of Virginia, gracious hospitality, spa services, sports and fitness facilities, and fine dining in the Old Mill Room, you can take a champagne hot-air balloon ride daily (weather permitting) between May and Dec with pilot Rick Behr at the controls. Ride over the foothills of the Blue Ridge, see deer running in and around the woods and farmlands, wathc people enjoying breakfast on their backyard patios. Even though you might catch them in their pajamas, they'll extend a friendly wave to you. When you're through with your hour-long ride, you'll be served Martinelli's Gold Medal apple cider and receive a color flight certificate, plus a disk of photos of your flight taken by the chase crew. Think of it as bed-and-breakfast-and-ballooning.

If you're feeling presidential (from your visits to the University of Virginia and Monticello) and you want to continue in this vein, then visit **Highland** (2050 James Monroe Pkwy.; 434-293-8000; highland.org), home of President James Monroe (our fifth president) and called Highland when it was owned by the Monroe family (Monroe lived here from 1799 to 1826). Do leave your UVA feelings in your car; Monroe attended the College of William and Mary. Oh, and leave any "stuffy" feelings in the car as well. Depending on the time of the year, you'll see people (and one hopes you will join them) flying kites, enjoying the Summer Festival of children's shows, listening to traditional music and opera in the boxwood gardens, and cutting their own Christmas trees.

Guided tours, lasting about 40 minutes, cover Monroe's life as he fought in the American Revolution, negotiated the Louisiana Purchase, pushed for the Missouri Compromise, and created the Monroe Doctrine. An augmented

UVA Library Collections

Included in the University of Virginia library collections are letters written to American novelist **John Dos Passos.** The gift was donated by Elizabeth Dos Passos, widow of the "lost generation" writer. Letters by poets e.e. cummings and Archibald MacLeish, critic Edmund Wilson, and Ernest Hemingway (which include gossip about mutual friends and tells about life in Key West) are also part of the collection. Manuscripts and typescripts of the author's novels, histories, works of journalism, poetry, and most of his short stories also are in the collection. Dos Passos was a writer-in-residence at the university and an admirer of the university's founder, Thomas Jefferson.

reality tour includes "conversations between individuals experiencing life at Highland in 1819" and other events. Highland is open daily 9 a.m. to 6 p.m. Apr through Oct and 11 a.m. to 5 p.m. Nov through Mar. Admission prices are $19 for adults, $13 for children ages 6–11 and local residents. There's a 10 percent discount for seniors, military, and AAA members. A self-guided tour is $13 for adult and youth.

Twelve miles west of Charlottesville, *Crozet Pizza* (5794 Three Notched Rd./Rte. 240; 434-823-2132; crozetpizza.net) is the reason people drive out of their way when they're visiting Charlottesville (although you can now find Crozet pizza at Buddhist Biker Bar in Charlottesville). It's an eatery and bar with red clapboard exterior, a wood stove in the middle of the restaurant, and lace curtains covering the country windows. A decade ago, the hours were more limited and the long lines formed early. While dining, take a look at the wall with business cards from around the world, or catch a look at family photos or the world map with pushpins indicating where patrons have been—all wearing the Crozet Pizza T-shirts. For lovers of nontraditional pizza, try such seasonal toppings as asparagus spears or snow peas, just two of the almost three dozen toppings available. The menu has been expanded and now includes appetizers, salads, sandwiches, burgers, and more. Open Mon through Sat 11 a.m. to midnight, Sun 11 a.m. to 10 p.m.

Amherst County

After a few years of residing in the 1891 jail, the *Amherst County Museum* (154 S. Main St., Amherst; 434-946-9068; amherstcountymuseum.org) moved into the Kearfott-Wood House, a Georgian Revival home built in 1907. You can explore the county's history from the early Woodland Indians to the Civil War

funfacts

The traffic circle in Amherst is the oldest traffic circle in the VDOT (Virginia Department of Transportation) system. The fountain and flowers were designed, installed, and maintained by the Village Garden Club.

and beyond. The *Amherst County Pathways* exhibit explores natural history, the bateaus, agriculture, and the Civil War. See Monacan projectile points, a copy of the original legislation creating Amherst County out of Albemarle County, and more. Check the website for monthly talks and field trips. The museum and the genealogy library are free, but donations are accepted. The museum is open Tues through Sat 10 a.m. to noon and 1 to 5 p.m. (closed from noon to 1 p.m.) and by appointment on Sat.

Appomattox County

Stop by the ***Appomattox Visitor Information Center*** (214 Main St.; 434-352-8999; virginia.org/listings/VisitorInformationCenters/AppomattoxVisitor InformationCenter) to see the original brick, wrought iron, and wood of the old railroad depot. The center has displays of local attractions, brochures, a theater, gift shop, and operates as a reservation center. You can pick up a self-guided walking tour brochure that highlights 50 stops, including buildings on the National Register of Historic Places, turn-of-the-(last)-century homes, and markers about the Civil War. The center is open daily from 9 a.m. to 5 p.m.

Once you've spent the day absorbing the past, stop by ***Baine's Books and Coffee*** (205 Main St.; 434-352-3711; bainesbooks.com), an independent, locally owned bookstore and coffee shop (with beans roasted by the Lexington Coffee Roasting Company). Once you've admired the cup holding your coffee, you can probably meet the staff member who made it or other cups, pitchers, bowls, etc. Then, listen to local and regional performers entertaining with folk, Americana, and bluegrass music on Fri and Sat evening from 7 to 10 p.m. Or, if you've always wanted to try your skills at an open mic night, stop by on Tues from 8 to 10 p.m. The store is open Mon through Wed 7 a.m. to 8 p.m., Thurs and Fri 7 a.m. to 9:30 p.m.; Sat 8:30 a.m. to 9:30 p.m.; and Sun 9 a.m. to 5 p.m.

Campbell County

In 1940 Herman Maril painted **The Growing Community** *mural* in the Altavista Post Office (700 Broad St.; 434-369-9955; wpamurals.com/AltaVist.htm). The oil on canvas painting was funded by the Section of Fine Arts under the Treasury Department, not the WPA (Works Progress Administration). It depicts the train station on the right and the Lane Furniture factory on the left. The Lane Furniture Company was opened in 1912 by John and Edward Lane when John Lane bought a box plant for $500. The company developed the first known moving-conveyor assembly system in the furniture industry during World War I and became known through advertising in such national publications as the *Saturday Evening Post* and the "girl graduate program," which gave miniature cedar chests to some 15 million female high-school graduates between 1930 and a decade or so ago.

Chesterfield County

The Ruritan Clubs of Chesterfield County established the ***Chesterfield County Museum & Historic 1892 Jail*** (6813 Mimms Loop; 804-768-7311; chesterfield history.com) in the early 1950s. In 2007 new exhibits were mounted that depict Virginia Indian culture, early settlement of the area, the Revolutionary and Civil Wars, and the first ironworks and coal mines in America. Visiting hours are 10 a.m. to 4 p.m. Tues through Fri; and Sat 10 a.m. to 2 p.m. Tours of the Old Jail start at the museum. No admission, but donations are accepted.

   Colonial Heights is the home of ***Violet Bank*** (the name Violet Bank seems to have come from the profusion of violets growing on the hillside), a spreading cucumber tree (planted in 1833, it's one of the largest in the world and rare east of the Blue Ridge Mountains), and Robert E. Lee's headquarters for the Siege of Petersburg for five months beginning June 8, 1864 (he had to leave when the falling leaves bared his position). The ***Violet Bank Museum,*** housed in Thomas Shore's home (303 Virginia Ave.; 804-520-9395; colonial heightsva.gov/499/Violet-Bank), is an excellent example of Federal design with American interior decorative arts. The museum boasts an autographed photograph of "Stonewall" Jackson and other items of interest to Civil War buffs. The Colonial Heights Federated Women's Club is responsible for the restoration of the ornamented ceilings and the 1815 reproduction furniture.

   The museum is open Tues through Sat 10 a.m. to 5 p.m. and Sun 1 to 6 p.m. A donation is requested.

Hanover County

The Hanover County seat in the town of Hanover Courthouse is where the historic ***Hanover Tavern*** (13181 Hanover Courthouse Rd.; 804-537-5050; hanovertavern.org) was given a license as an ordinary (tavern) in 1733. Patrick Henry, Virginia's first governor, and his wife, Sarah Shelton Henry, lived here, as did George Washington and Lord Cornwallis.

Hot Tomato

The *Hanover tomato,* hero of the annual *Tomato Festival* and title of the annual football bowl game between Patrick Henry and Lee-Davis, was bred to ripen early enough that people could have ripe, juicy, delicious tomatoes with their hamburgers when they celebrate July 4 with family cookouts. This was long before hothouses and "place-saver" objects that look like tomatoes but certainly don't taste like them. The festival has musicians, artisans, vendors, a Bow-Wow beach, and, of course, all things tomato (edible, wearable, and who knows what else). It usually takes place in the middle weekend of July at Pole Green Park (8996 Pole Green Park Ln.; hanover tomatofestival.com).

Time, the automobile, Prohibition, and any number of other factors led to the tavern's decline and disuse. It saw a rebirth in 1953 when an acting troupe opened Barksdale Theatre, combining dinner with a show (not at the same time), and then they moved on to other projects.

By 1990, the Hanover Tavern Foundation acquired the property and set about the massive task of restoration. A second phase was completed in 2005, and the tavern now has refinished interior flooring and painting, two dining rooms, and a restored theater that seats 156 people. A brick terrace has been laid, with an accessible ramp, and now serves as the new entrance. The space is used for art shows, lectures, and as an educational center promoting Virginia history. Meals are scratch-made under the direction of executive chef Mary Catherine Ortalani, with special menus for children. They're open for lunch and dinner, Sat and Sun brunch, and dinner and a show.

Hour-long guided tours are offered Wed through Fri at 2 p.m. ($4 for adults and $3 for children under 10). Self-guided audio tours of the tavern are available 11 a.m. to 4 p.m. for $5. They also offer haunted walking tours one Wed evening a month. Advance registration is required for groups of 10 or more on all tours.

Hopewell

Travel south on I-95 and branch off on Route 10 to *Hopewell* and *City Point Historic District,* where you can view the confluence of the Appomattox and James Rivers. This small, bustling town adjacent to Fort Lee had a population of 40,000 during World War I, with an additional 65,000 at the then Camp Lee. The DuPont Nemours plant was known for making guncotton for dynamite. At the end of the war, Hopewell's population returned to 1,369, about the same as after the Civil War. The national historic district has 85 buildings and three contributing sites at the tip of that confluence of the Appomattox and James Rivers. Notable buildings include St. John's Episcopal Church (1840), Civil War Catholic Chapel (1865), the Cocke House (ca. 1840, 1916), Miami Lodge (1912), Cook House (ca. 1858), St. John's Rectory (ca. 1848), and Christopher Proctor House (ca. 1800). The town of City Point was the Union headquarters of General Ulysses S. Grant during the siege of Petersburg (1864–1865).

If you've been tracing the trail of the **WPA murals** and sculptures through the two dozen post office buildings in Virginia, you've noticed a similarity in style and execution even though the paintings were created by many different artists. Now look at Edmund Archer's 1939 oil on canvas painting, *Captain Francis Eppes Making Friends with the Appomattox Indians,* representing a gesture of friendship, at the Hopewell Post Office (117 W. Poythress St.; 804-452-4350; wpamurals.com/hopewell.htm). Reportedly, Captain Eppes arrived on the ship *Hopewell,* which gave the city its name. Archer was born in Richmond, in 1904, and taught at the Corcoran School of Art in Washington, DC, before returning to Richmond in 1968. He was buried in Richmond's Hollywood Cemetery in 1986.

Hopewell's **Beacon Theatre** (401 N. Main St.; 804-446-3457; thebeacon theatreva.com) was built in 1928 as a silent movie and vaudeville theatre. Originally called the Broadway, the theatre transitioned into a movie theater during the 1950s to the 1970s. It was abandoned in 1981 and, as can be expected, fell into disrepair. In 2011, the Hopewell City Council approved a plan to refurbish the theater, in time for the city's centennial in 2016. Leon Russell played to a sold-out audience at the theater's reopening on January 13, 2014. It continues to play a major role in the cultural and recreational life of the area as a performance venue, conference center, and special event facility. BJ Thomas, Travis Tritt, the 5th Dimension, and the Oak Ridge Boys are among the recent headliners at the theater. Call for a tour.

Lynchburg

My childhood love of exploration is always heightened at a children's museum in **Lynchburg**. **Amazement Square** (27 9th St.; 434-845-1888; amazementsquare .org) delivers what its name promises. This is Central Virginia's first multidisciplinary, hands-on place where children can climb, slide, and discover on four floors of interactive exhibits, activities, and programs. Among the exhibits are explorations of Native Americans, *On the James, Once Upon a Building, Shipwreck Cove, Raceways, the Big Red Barn, Amazement Tower, On Stage, Beat Box,* and more and more and more. Do you suppose they have adult-only hours? The museum is open Tues through Fri 10 a.m. to 5 p.m.; Sun 1 to 5 p.m. Closed on Mon. Check with the museum for their Sponsored Admission Program.

Gravestones & More

Those with a curiosity about death should check out the *Old City Cemetery & Arboretum Center* (401 Taylor St., Lynchburg; 434-847-1465; gravegarden.org). This off-beat attraction has a cemetery records research center; a display of 19th-century mourning clothing, jewelry, and artifacts; and a gift shop. An adjacent caretaker's museum features a display on gravestone carving, a turn-of-the-20th-century hearse, and 19th-century cemetery-maintenance tools and equipment. The cemetery is open daily from dawn to dusk, unless ice and snow make the driveway impassable. A super-special time to visit is during the Antique Rose Festival that takes place in Apr and May.

The *Maier Museum of Art* (1 Quinlan St.; 434-947-8136; maiermuseum.org) at Randolph College has an outstanding collection of American art, primarily paintings, works on paper, and photographs from the 19th century to today, especially American Impressionism and early 20th-century Realism. It has changing exhibitions, rotating displays of the college's permanent collection, and educational programs. Nothing can beat the educational options at an institution of higher learning! This building was constructed in 1952 by the National Gallery of Art to protect the national art collection during wartime. Sarah and Pauline Maier gave a generous gift to the college in 1982 and gallery was named the Maier Museum of Art in honor of William J. Maier (1903–1981). You can still see art throughout the campus, particularly in the Lipscomb Library and the student center. The museum is open Tues through Sun from 1 to 5 p.m. during the academic year (Sept through Apr) and Wed through Sun 1 to 5 p.m. during the summer (May through Aug). There's no admission charge.

Madison County

With more than 200 wineries now in Virginia, a place has to be exceptional to be known as exceptional, and *Prince Michel Vineyards and Winery* (154 Winery Ln., Leon; 800-800-WINE or 540-546-3707; princemichel.com) definitely qualifies. It's set in the heart of Virginia wine country, just east of the Blue Ridge foothills, and is part of the *Monticello Wine Trail.* You can take a free self-guided tour of the winemaking facility, enjoy a picnic on the lawns, stroll through the vines, talk with the knowledgeable staff, and have a complimentary wine tasting of their award-winning wine in the "see-through" room atop the winery, or plan to continue the romantic getaway with a night in one of the one-bedroom suites. Prince Michel is open Mon through Thurs from 10 a.m. to 5 p.m.; Fri, Sat, and Sun from 10 a.m. to 5 p.m.

The folks at *Graves Mountain Lodge* (Rte. 670, 3626 Old Blue Ridge Tpke.; 540-923-4231; gravesmountain.com) in *Syria* have been welcoming guests for more than 135 years. They offer all the home-cooked food you can eat, natural beauty, and a wide range of outdoor activities, including hiking, fishing, swimming, and some "good old-fashioned porch sitting." Or you can observe the activities of their fruit and educational farm. There's just too much to mention. Accommodations range from dormitory to motel-style to an old farmhouse to cottages and cabins. When you see an event posted as "Let's Get Naked," they aren't talking about you; they're talking about spring shearing of sheep, goats, alpacas, and llamas. Should you breed fiber animals, professional shearers will be available to have a go at your future clothing and artistic works.

Nelson County

Just a few miles southeast of Charlottesville, over the James River a touch, is the town of *Schuyler* (pronounced SKY-ler), the fictional home of television's Walton family and the original home of Earl Hamner Jr., on whose work the television program was based. With such a memorable time of our lives spent watching the trials and tribulations of John-Boy and Mary Ellen and the other Waltons, people just assumed there really was a Waltons Mountain.

funfacts

Patrick Henry, of "Give me liberty or give me death" fame, played the violin, flute, and pianoforte.

Visitors came to Schuyler in droves, sometimes as many as 500 a day. There's little resemblance between the real and the fictional town, but visitors wanted to see "Ike's" general store, the Baptist church, the elementary school, and the Waltons' home.

Not able to do this, they'd stop by the old country store, owned by Rosie Snead, where they could buy a fact sheet detailing the history of the area, a postcard, or a color photograph of the Hamner home. Unfortunately, in 1989 the store burned down.

Waltons Mountain Museum (6484 Rockfish River Rd.; 434-831-2000; walton-mountain.org) opened in 1992 in the old school, which also serves as a community center. Each of four classrooms holds a re-creation of one of the program's sets.

funfacts

James Monroe's younger daughter, Maria Hester Monroe, became the first presidential daughter to have a White House wedding.

Each display set has an audio interview with Hamner, and he talks about growing up during the Depression; there are also video interviews with the actors.

In the school lobby there's a wall that's covered with newspaper articles of the press coverage of the museum's opening. On the other side local resident Barbara Marks assembled a photographic history of the area. Naturally, you can purchase Walton memorabilia in the museum store, including books by Hamner. Proceeds of the sales and admission fees support the community center, whose activities are held in the other classrooms. The **Walton Hamner House** (Earl Hamner Jr.'s homeplace) is under new ownership and is open for daily tours. Visit thewaltonhamnerhouse.com for more information.

funfacts

Hikers should know that 45 miles of the Appalachian Trail are in Nelson County, with multiple access points along the Blue Ridge Parkway.

The museum is open daily 10 a.m. to 3:30 p.m. from the first Sat in Mar through the first Sun in Dec. It's closed on Easter, Thanksgiving, and the last Sat in Sept, when the annual school reunion is celebrated. Admission is $10 for anyone 6 and older. Check the website or call for specific directions because, apparently, online map services and GPS tend to take you elsewhere.

Construction on a new bed-and-breakfast started in Feb 2019, with plans to open by late Oct. It will evoke the "Depression-era home where three generations of the fictitious family lived," according to Carole Johnson, the owner of the Walton Hamner House—*evoke* being the key word, with replicas of the furnishings. **John and Olivia's Bed and Breakfast Inn** (6483 Rockfish River Rd.; 434-831-2017; thewaltonhamnerhouse.com/john-olivias-bnb-inn) will have 5 bedrooms, 5 bathrooms, and a gift shop.

The new **Quarry Gardens at Schuyler** (1643 Salem Rd.; 434-466-3988; quarrygardensatschuyler.org) are naturalized gardens surrounding abandoned soapstone quarries (Schuyler was the soapstone capital of the world since 1890). There were 90 quarries in the area, and 6 of them are now rock-sided pools of water, about an acre in size each, and they're central to the Quarry Gardens. Exhibits in the Visitor Center illustrate the history of the soapstone industry and a small library of books about the industry. There are plant communities in 14 ecozones and 7 conservation areas, supporting plant communities that are unusual for Central Virginia woodlands. Come see the butterflies, flowers, and other "locals." Among the activities are mushroom forays by the Blue Ridge Mycological Society (they added 14 fungal species after all the rain in the fall of 2018). Visits are by appointment only. They're normally open Fri through Sun between Apr and Nov. There's no admission charge, but a $10 per person donation is suggested. This site is in a natural state for the most part, so read the precautions on their website before visiting.

Orange County

Horton Cellars Winery (6399 Spotswood Trail; 540-832-7440; hortonwine .com) in ***Gordonsville*** is where Dennis Horton has created a winery that's "functional during the winemaking season, someplace wine lovers would visit again and again because of its beauty and atmosphere, and ideal for storage." The 24.5 acres of Viognier grape acreage at Horton is one of the largest commitments to the grape in the country, a grape he chose because it has a thick skin and loose clusters to handle Virginia's temperatures and summer humidity. He also grows Marsanne, Mourvedre, Cabernet Franc, Syrah, and several other varieties, including Norton, the only native Virginia grape. Horton built underground cellars that fit the contour of the land and provide a constant temperature and humidity that's ideal for wine storage and an energy-efficient building.

Architect Angus McDonald created an Old English Tudor building that includes a spacious tasting room with an impressive fireplace. The Horton Cellars are open for tours and tastings. Tastings are $6 a person. You're invited to stop by daily from 10 a.m. to 5 p.m.

While you're in Gordonsville, stop by the ***Exchange Hotel Civil War Museum*** (400 S. Main St.; 540-832-2944; hgiexchange.com) to see an 1860 railroad hotel that served as a Civil War hospital for the sick and wounded. Some 23,000 men were treated in one year; 700 Confederate soldiers and 28 Union soldiers died on the grounds of the former hospital. In addition to medical artifacts and surgical tools, there are weapons, uniforms, and other personal items from Union and Confederate cavalrymen, artillerymen, and infantrymen. It's said to be one of America's most haunted places.

The 1860s train depot is undergoing renovation and is closed until the work is completed. The museum is open Mon through Sat 10 a.m. to 4 p.m. (except Fri and holidays); Sun 1 to 4 p.m. Admission is $10 for adults and $3 for children (8–12).

Just minutes away is ***Montpelier*** (11350 Constitution Hwy., Montpelier Station; 540-672-2728, ext. 140; montpelier.org), lifelong home of James Madison Jr., fourth president and "Father of the Constitution." Madison was a successful businessman, the primary author of the US Constitution, one of the authors of the Federalist Papers, a key player in negotiating the Bill of Rights, a member of the US Congress, and secretary of state under Thomas Jefferson.

Madison's home was considered a "commodious building," well worthy of entertaining the most important people of the country. The estate sat on 5,000 acres of rolling countryside, woodland, pastures, and cropland. The first portion of the existing building was constructed around 1760.

To pay debts incurred by Dolley Madison's son, Montpelier had to be sold, a transaction that could have led to disastrous results. The house changed hands six times until it was purchased in 1900 by William and Anna Rogers duPont. They enlarged the house to 55 rooms, reestablished the gardens, and added new outbuildings. When its last inhabitant, Marion duPont Scott (former wife of the late actor Randolph Scott), died, she left it to the National Trust for Historic Preservation.

The big news from Montpelier is that the mansion has been restored to the 1820s house that the Madisons called home. The project removed alterations made to the mansion, including the wings added by the duPont family in the early 1990s and reduced the home to 22 rooms. A Montpelier Education Center houses Madison furniture, furnishings, and exhibits.

Activities are scheduled throughout the year, including a wine festival (usually late May), celebration of Dolley Madison's birthday, a hot-air balloon festival, and the Orange County Fair. Montpelier is open daily 9 a.m. to 4 p.m. (Nov through Mar) and until 5 p.m. the rest of the year. Regular tour admission, which includes a 1-hour guided tour of the Madison home (given from 10 a.m. to 3 p.m.), access to the gardens and grounds, and any seasonal and themed tours on your day of visit is $22 for adults and $9 for children (6–14). Other tours are "The Mere Distinction of Colour," "Madison & The Constitution," and "Montpelier's Enslaved Community" (offered on Sat and Sun at 1 p.m. and included in the regular admission). Friends of Montpelier enjoy free admission, and National Trust members are $8. A gift shop features books, handicrafts, and decorative items.

Nearby, in the town of **Orange,** is the ***James Madison Museum*** (129 Caroline St.; 540-672-1776; jamesmadisonmuseum.org), housed in a 1928 Nash automobile dealership. The museum exhibits feature possessions of James and Dolley Madison, including a Campeachy chair (also lolling or hammock chair) made from a type of mahogany grown in Mexico. The Hall of Agriculture contains antique farming tools and implements from the area. It naturally focuses on Madison's interests in the Constitution, but it also features his involvement in agrarian reform, as illustrated in the 18th-century "cube" house contained in the agricultural display at the museum.

The museum is open Mon through Sat 10 a.m. to 4 p.m. and Sun 1 to 4 p.m. all year except Jan 1, Easter, Thanksgiving, and Dec 25. Admission is $5 for adults; $3 for seniors (60+) and AAA members; $1 for students.

For lodging and dining in an 18th-century plantation steeped in history, try the ***Willow Grove Inn*** (14079 Plantation Way; 540-672-7001; theinnatwillowgrove

.com), complete with period furnishings. Willow Grove began as a modest frame structure built by Joseph Clark in 1778. His son added a brick portion in 1820, and the exterior is an example of Jefferson's Classical Revival style, with a simpler Federal-style interior. Set on 37 acres of rolling hills and pastures, the plantation has been carefully preserved to look the way it would have naturally evolved. Hundreds of ancient trees, Victorian gardens, the original wide pine flooring, fireplace mantels, and wainscoting set the background for your long or short visit.

Dine in the elegant Dolley Madison dining room, enjoy the casual Clark's Tavern bar and pub, relax in the bright and sunny Jefferson Library, or contemplate nature from the antebellum veranda overlooking the Victorian gardens.

Petersburg

There are two **murals** in the **Petersburg Post Office** (29 Franklin St.; 804-732-2939; wpamurals.com/petersVA.htm). The first, *Riding to Hounds,* by Edwin S. Lewis, is a 1937 painting about fox hunting (he also did the mural in the Berryville Post Office), and supposedly his wife is portrayed as the central figure in this painting. The second, on the east wall, is a 1937 oil on canvas by William Calfee (who did the Tazewell and Phoebus murals as well); it's more pastoral and entitled *Agriculture Scenes in Virginia,* with tobacco on one side and peanuts on the other.

The **Old Blandford Church and Cemetery** (319 S. Crater Rd.; 804-733-2396; petersburgpreservationtaskforce.com/museums/blandford-church), also known as the Brick Church, is the highest spot in the Petersburg area. The church, built in 1735 with an inverse ship's hull ceiling design, is a Confederate memorial and one of the art treasures of the country. It's known for its 15 magnificent Louis Comfort Tiffany stained-glass windows, reportedly the only building in the country with every window an original Tiffany production. The original plan called for windows to represent each of the Confederate states, each depicting one of the Apostles, and smaller ones for the states whose sympathies had been divided. The windows took 8 years to complete, and each cost between $100 (for the smaller Maryland window) and $400, including shipping. The Cross of Jewels window was donated by Tiffany. If possible, you might want to see the church twice or even three times: the first when there isn't much sun, the second when there's a brilliant sun, and the third at sunset, to see the magnificent beauty of the Cross of Jewels. The windows seem to change from moment to moment, with a three-dimensional effect coming from the Tiffany talents. Three visits may seem a large demand on your time, but these windows are worth it.

The church was restored in 1901 through the efforts of the Ladies Memorial Association of Petersburg, whose remembrances of the war dead launched the Memorial Day tradition. Reportedly a Union general's wife saw "Miss Nora" Davidson and schoolchildren placing flowers on Confederate graves. The general persuaded Congress to declare a national holiday to honor the war dead.

The cemetery began before the church building was constructed, and the oldest known grave dates to 1702. Some of the finest examples of cast and wrought iron in the nation are found here. Many locals are buried here, along with 30,000 Confederate soldiers who were brought in from other areas. William Phillips, a British general, was secretly buried here—the only British general to have been buried in American soil for many, many years. But the Blandford cemetery is not just for Civil War casualties. Joseph Cotten—actor, Petersburg native, and narrator of the film at the Siege Museum—is interred here.

The church and cemetery are open Thurs through Sat 10 a.m. to 5 p.m.; Sun 1 to 5 p.m. Old Blandford Church Memorial Day services are held on June 9 each year.

Over in Old Towne Petersburg (which was referred to as Old Towne years ago) is the Petersburg tour's second most outstanding attraction, the **Siege Museum** (15 W. Bank St.; 804-835-9630; petersburg-va.org/tourism/siege.htm), which tells the tale of life in Petersburg during the 10 months the city was under attack, the longest siege of any city during the Civil War. The museum is in the former Bank of Petersburg, and it, like the other 800 buildings in the city, was under attack for 2 to 3 hours a day. Conditions were terrible, and the museum shows the war's effect on the economy, industry, and the people themselves. View the film first, shown every hour on the hour, and then wander through to learn how the women were the real heroes. Learn how ladies' hoop skirts hid food, supplies, and ammunition for the defenders. You'll see two bullets that met in midair and fused. Also on display is one of only two

A Quadrilateral Having No Two Sides Parallel

Recall your math to define what a trapezium is, or be satisfied to know that Charles O'Hara built his home in 1817 without parallel walls. Legend says his West Indian servant told him evil spirits could not reside in such a building. Or it could be O'Hara just had an unusually shaped lot on which to build. *The Trapezium House* (244 N. Market St. Petersburg; 804-733-2400). This is a private residence, so please be respectful of the owner's privacy.

revolving cannons ever built—the first exploded when it was fired, and the second was never shot. View the photographs, eyewitness descriptions, and artifacts. When I visited this museum for the first time, Sergei Troubetzkoy showed me the sites. After decades in Virginia tourism, including stints in Bedford and Lynchburg, Sergei has returned to promote Petersburg tourism. Nice symmetry and a good choice for Petersburg. The museum is open Thurs through Sat 10 a.m. to 4 p.m., and Sun 1 to 4 p.m., except Thanksgiving Day, Dec 24 and 25, and New Year's Day.

Think of Civil War battlefields, and you most likely think of the National Park Service. But just south of Petersburg, between I-95 and I-85, there's a privately owned attraction called *Pamplin Historical Park and the National Museum of the Civil War Soldier* (6125 Boydton Plank Rd.; 804-861-2408 or 877-PAMPLIN [726-7546]; pamplinpark.org). This is where the "beginning of the end" occurred, as Federal troops outnumbered a small brigade of North Carolinians. Within a week, Lee surrendered at Appomattox. In private hands since then, the area was ignored and overgrown.

A highly dramatic-looking museum and interpretive center with an unusual design replicates (interpretively) the shape of the Confederate defensive line. You can see exhibits of Civil War artifacts and relics and learn at the interactive stations. You can follow the breakthrough from Apr 2, 1865, via maps, a diorama, and a state-of-the-art fiber-optic battle map.

Outside, there are 1.1 miles of walking trails among the trees and original earthworks fortifications (some 12 feet high) built to protect Petersburg. Along the trail is a reconstructed soldiers' hut of the kind used by Confederates in the winter of 1864–1865. Park guides provide tours, and special programs explain the life, weapons, and uniforms of the era from spring to fall.

Tudor Hall, on an additional 68 acres, is an 1812 plantation owned by the Boisseau family until 1864, when the opposing armies turned their farm into a battle and camping ground. It was a descendant of this family, Dr. Robert B. Pamplin Jr. (a great-great-nephew), and the Pamplin Foundation that funded the purchase of the property as it was about to be sold for lumbering. The home has been restored and is open for exhibition. The park is open daily 9 a.m. to 5 p.m. The admission fee is $13 for adults; $12 for seniors (62+) and military; $8 for children (6–12).

The US Army Quartermaster Corps is the branch of the service that supplies food, clothing, and military equipment to our armed forces. The *US Army Quartermaster Museum* (1201 22nd St.; 804-734-4203; qmmuseum.lee.army .mil) at *Fort Lee* (formerly Camp Lee) shows life-size exhibits of colorful uniforms, weapons, and other examples of how quartermaster offices have looked over the years. You'll also see a drum used in President Kennedy's funeral cortege and the architect's original model for Arlington National Cemetery's Tomb of the Unknowns. The library and archives are available for research by appointment. There is no admission charge (donations accepted), but you must have a government-issued photo ID. The museum is open Mon through Fri from 10 a.m. to 5 p.m., and Sat from 11 a.m. to 5 p.m.

When Fort McClellan, Alabama, was closed, the Women's Army Corps Museum there was also closed. Fort Lee, where members of the WAC were trained from 1948 to 1954, was chosen as the new site for the museum because of its historical ties to the WAC. Today hundreds of Army women are trained at Fort Lee.

The *US Army Women's Museum* (2100 A Ave.; 804-734-4327; awm.lee .army.mil) depicts the day-to-day service and duties of women in the military from Revolutionary days through Desert Storm. There are 40 exhibits, thousands of artifacts and archival material, and more than 300 videos in the 13,325-square-foot museum. Apparently, the museum receives a lot of requests to identify the first to do this or that, or the oldest or youngest. Most likely, they don't have an answer, so don't bother asking. Ergo, the US Army Women's Museum "will not sanction any claim of 'firsts, etc.'" It is open Tues through Sat from 10 a.m. to 5 p.m. There is no admission charge, but you must present government-issued photo identification to the gate personnel.

Prince Edward County

Green Front Furniture (316 N. Main St.; 434-392-5943; greenfront.com), in *Farmville,* is known for its bare-bones 900,000 square feet of furnishings in 12 old tobacco and other warehouses, mostly located along Main Street, and then along South, Depot, 2nd, and, well, you get the idea. Check the website to determine what is in which building (e.g., upholstery is in buildings 5, 6, 8, 9, and 10). There are thousands of pieces of furniture. Green Front features traditional furniture, with owner Richard "Dickie" Cralle (son of the original owner) and his son Richard "Den" Cralle III carrying lines from more than 200 manufacturers, alphabetically from Althorp Living History to Zimmerman. There are case goods, authentic English antiques, unique accessories, and more. The Oriental rugs come from India, Afghanistan, Pakistan, Iran, China, and Nepal. Another store is located in Manassas, Virginia. Green Front is open Mon through Fri 10 a.m. to 5:30 p.m. (noon for building 7); Sat 9 a.m. to 6:15 p.m.

You can visit the area's history at the *Robert Russa Moton Museum and the Center for the Study of Civil Rights in Education* (900 Griffin Blvd.; 434-315-8775; motonmuseum.org). In 1951 this was the site of the first nonviolent student demonstration when Barbara Johns walked out of R. R. Moton

High School, an all-black segregated school to protest its disgraceful conditions. That became part of the 1954 *Brown v. Board of Education* case heard before the US Supreme Court. That case led to the mandate of equal education for all Americans, not just separate but equal. It's located in the Moton High School, which is one of more than 100 locations in the US Civil Rights Trail. Admission is free. The museum is open Mon through Sat from noon to 4 p.m.

Richmond

Richmond, Virginia's capital, is a good home base while exploring other parts of the state. You can see how central and significant the city was for transportation when you look at the railroad structure at 15th and Dock Streets. Three main railroads crossed here, the Seaboard Air Line, the Southern, and the Chesapeake and Ohio. Reportedly, this is the only three-level train crossing in the world.

Start your day with a hearty "buy-the-farm" breakfast at the *Dairy Bar* (formerly known as Curles Neck Dairy Bar), said to have the best milk shakes in town. A Richmond tradition since 1946, a cow mascot adorns the building (1602 Roseneath Rd.; 804-355-1937; dairybarrestaurant.com), invites you inside, and encourages young diners to color the mascot and have their art displayed on the walls. The diner is open Mon through Sat 7 a.m. to 3 p.m.; Sun 9 a.m. to 2 p.m.

A lot of the Civil War was fought in Virginia, and a look at a map shows what a strategic part it played. Richmond, the capital of the Confederacy, was under frequent attack from 1861 to 1865. The *Richmond National Battlefield Park* (470 Tredegar St.; 804-226-1981) commemorates 11 sites involved in three battles that came within miles of the city. These include skirmishes at Gaines' Mill, Malvern Hill, and Cold Harbor. Stop by the park visitor center on E. Broad Street; park rangers will provide maps so that you can tour the battlefield.

Within Gaines Mill, Cold Harbor, Malvern Hill, Fort Harrison, and Drewry's Bluff, there are interpretive walking trails, with ranger-guided tours, scheduled talks, living history programs, and summer season youth programs (also at other times by request). Cold Harbor (5515 Anderson-Wright Dr.) and Fort Harrison (8621 Battlefield Park Rd.) have tour roads, and their visitor centers have exhibits about the battles. In May, June, July, and Sept, there are activities that coincide with the anniversary of one of the park's major battles.

Within the Chimborazo Visitor Center are a scale model of the Chimborazo hospital (the Confederacy's largest) and Civil War artifacts. A 22-minute motion picture depicts the battles that took place near the city. Some research facilities are available.

New-and-Improved Virginia Museum of Fine Arts

In May 2010, the newly expanded *Virginia Museum of Fine Arts* (200 North Blvd.; 804-340-1405; vmfa.museum) reopened to the public with more special exhibition space, public areas, an amazing-looking atrium, and a sculpture garden—a mere $150 million project. Within 10 months, the VMFA brought in an exhibit of 176 works by Pablo Picasso for a 3-month visit. It was the only museum on the East Coast and only one of three in the United States to host the exhibit. Today you can participate in a number of age-related activities, see the permanent and temporary exhibits, and enjoy a variety of tours. They include free daily walk-in tours (subject to docent availability), multidisciplinary student group and guided tours, adult tours, and audio tours with mobile apps. General admission is free; the cost for special exhibitions and programs varies. Open daily from 10 a.m. to 5 p.m. (Thurs and Fri until 9 p.m.)

The ***American Civil War Center at Historic Tredegar*** is the first museum in the nation to tell the Civil War story from the perspectives of Union, Confederate, and African-American men, women, and children whose lives were forever changed by this powerful event. This 10,000-square-foot center incorporates artifacts, media, and interactive features so you'll be engaged and enlightened. The tour starts with the causes for the war, moves into the war years, and then finishes with the legacies it left.

Scouts (including Brownies, Daisies, Cubs, Junior Girls, etc.) can earn a patch, specially designed for them, by completing a scavenger hunt booklet covering the campus. There are two workbooks, one for kindergarten through 5th and one for 5th through 12th (parents and teachers are encouraged to enjoy the fun and learning process, too). The program fee is $5, including the workbook, patch, and admission. Opportunities to satisfy several other requirements for merit badges, belt loops, pins, or patches are offered, covering such themes as heritage, culture, archaeology, and nature.

The Tredegar Visitor Center is open daily from 9 a.m. to 5 p.m.; winter hours for Cold Harbor Visitor Center and Chimborazo Medical Museum are Wed through Sun from 9 a.m. to 4:30 p.m.

seacreatures

Embedded in the black limestone squares of the checkerboard-patterned floors around the rotunda and halls of the capitol in Richmond, you can see snails (including a giant marine snail shell from the Ordovician period), nautiloid, shell, sea lily, coral, and algae fossils.

For pure architectural and historical enjoyment of a structured nature, visit **Richmond's Fan District** (fandistrict.org), bordered by Monroe Park, the Boulevard, and Monument Avenue on the north and Cary Street on the south. The Fan, a mile-square, tree-lined district of streets, radiates, or fans out, and a map of the district slightly resembles the fashionable accessory Southern ladies are so noted for. The town houses carry Victorian, Greek Revival, Italianate, Tudor, and Georgian touches. They're joined by party walls or separated by narrow walkways. With about 2,000 town houses, the Fan is said to be the largest intact Victorian neighborhood in the United States. A suburb of this bustling town back in the 1890s, the Fan District is now incorporated into the city of Richmond. For walking and driving tour maps, you can contact the Fan District Association, 208 Strawberry St., Richmond 23220.

A visit and tour of the 1790 **Capitol** (1000 Bank St.; 804-698-1788; virginia capitol.gov) is a special treat, particularly the hidden dome, which Thomas Jefferson designed, in the Italian-architecture–inspired building. Beneath that dome is the only statue of George Washington that was modeled from life. Sculptor Jean Antoine Houdon visited Washington at Mount Vernon to mold his head in a gooey plaster mix and measured his body as accurately as a tailor would. Such details as the vein in his thumb and the stitching in the cloak facing are included. This Washington does not look like the Washington of the ubiquitous Gilbert Stuart painting, and most likely it's a much more accurate interpretation of his appearance.

The Capitol has undergone a $74 million renovation that includes an underground visitor center on the south side (Bank Street, near 10th Street) of the building. The Capitol is open Mon through Sat 9 a.m. to 5 p.m.; Sun 1 to 5 p.m. Guided 1-hour and self-guided tour options are available.

The large equestrian statue of George Washington in the northwest corner of the square was constructed to be his final resting place, before his body was buried at Mount Vernon. If you're interested and can find an agreeable guard, you can climb up the inside of the statue.

Of course, there is the option of doing nothing, or almost nothing, and a great place to do that is at the **Lewis Ginter Botanical Garden.** Ginter made his first fortune in dry goods, his second in the stock market, his third in tobacco (he sold the rights to his cigarette-paper rolling invention to Duke, figuring it would never fly), and his fourth fortune in real estate development. The obvious—and correct—implication here is that he lost his fortunes in between earning them. It was through the real estate fortune that he most directly affected Richmond. Among other things he built the Jefferson Hotel, Ginter Park (Richmond's first suburb), and a number of buildings that are part of Virginia Commonwealth University.

It's a Grave Matter

Richmond's *Hollywood Cemetery* (412 S. Cherry St.; 804-648-8501; hollywood cemetery.org) was designed by John Notman, who pioneered romantically land-scaped cemeteries. A Gothic Revival chapel marks the entrance, and outstanding examples of Victorian monuments and ornamental ironwork can be found almost everywhere. A 90-foot pyramid honors the 18,000 Confederate soldiers buried on the property. US presidents James Monroe and John Tyler and Confederate president Jefferson Davis are also buried here. Walking tours are offered regularly from Apr through Nov; call (804) 649-0711, ext. 301, for more information. You can also take a virtual tour, a Segway tour, a Gem electric car tour, a self-guided tour from your car, and a trolley tour. Oh, and the name Hollywood is for the large holly trees that grace the ground, not that city out in California, Florida, or southern Maryland. Open daily 8 a.m. to 5 p.m. (6 p.m. during daylight saving time).

This world-class botanical garden contains the 3.5-acre *Henry M. Flagler Perennial Garden* (1800 Lakeside Ave.; 804-262-9887; lewisginter.org), one of the largest on the East Coast. The Ginter garden people aren't aware of any connection between Flagler and Ginter; although surely Ginter would have known of Flagler, they aren't sure if Flagler knew of Ginter. Nevertheless, the Flagler people donated this garden. It is the largest single display, with some 12,000 plants and with 4,000 species planted within bordered walkways and meandering streams. New is a program called "A Million Blooms." It started with orchids that created what is thought to be the largest collection of orchids on public display in the mid-Atlantic area. The garden changes just about daily and is appealing even into the deepest of winter because there is something blooming all the time or because of the interesting foliage. Check the website to see what's blooming the day of your visit.

The 23,000-square-foot E. Claiborne Robins Visitor Center is a classic, Georgian-style building and features an exhibit hall, garden shop, meeting and banquet room, and cafe.

Spring highlights include tulip week, beginning about Apr 16 or a week before Virginia's Garden Week. The Ginter garden sponsors a plant sale in the last full week of Apr and a Mother's Day concert in early May, complete with food.

The garden is open daily 9 a.m. to 10 p.m. (check for details about the other attractions within the garden), with Tues and Thurs evening hours until 9 p.m. from June through Aug. Admission is $13 for adults; $11 for seniors (55+); and $8 for children (3–12).

If you love nature, the *Robbins Nature and Visitor Center at Maymont* (2201 Shields Lake Dr. [visitor center]; 804-358-7166; maymont.org) is for you.

This 100-acre park was the country home of Richmond financier James H. Dooley and his wife. They had no heirs, so they willed the land to the city in 1926. The 33-room Victorian mansion has been restored to its glory days, and there are formal Italian and Japanese gardens, an arboretum, a children's farm, and a petting zoo. All attractions are open to the public and free, although there is a $4 suggested donation.

Within the center is a state-of-the-art complex that houses 13 aquaria that follow the life and ecosystems of the James River, including shallow pools, open water, backwaters, a turtle pool, estuaries, and channel runs. Along with lots of fish, there are snapping turtles (in the turtle pool, of course) and even two otters, the center's mascots, in an indoor-outdoor tank.

Children 8 and up can explore the natural world with microscopes and other lab equipment. A discovery room is available for younger children, and there's an area that explores nightlife—not of discos and bars, but of such nocturnal animals as owls, meadow voles, and white-footed mice. There's also a gift shop with science-related items and a cafe for a brief bite to eat.

The visitor center, the grounds, gardens, farm pastures, and wildlife are open daily 10 a.m. to 5 p.m. The nature center is open Tues through Sun 10 a.m. to 5 p.m. The Maymont Mansion is open Tues through Sun noon to 5 p.m. Carriage rides are offered on Sun from noon to 4 p.m. (Apr through Oct). Tram rides run a loop Tues through Sun noon to 5 p.m. Fees are charged or a donation is requested, depending on what you do.

The *Science Museum of Virginia* (2500 W. Broad St.; 804-864-1400 or 804-25-STARS [257-9277]; smv.org) features, among many things, a tilted hemispherical projection dome, 23 meters in diameter and almost 5 stories tall. The dome's 6-channel audio system has 34 three-way speaker systems and 6 subwoofers driven by 54 BGW amplifiers capable of a combined output power of more than 13,000 watts.

This is definitely a hands-on museum, and you're invited to discover and explore the scientific world in language and displays that reach all levels. Other attractions at the museum are the computer works sections, where you can pick up the basics or go one-on-one against the superbrains. After you've played mind games, head for the visual perception area and play games with your eyesight using mirrors and other optical illusions. Five crystal-shaped structures fill the rotunda floor, and these crystals house a complete display on the formation of crystals and their importance.

The science museum is located in the historic former Broad Street Railroad Station. Originally opened in 1919, the building was designed by John Russell Pope. The exhibits are open daily 9:30 a.m. to 5 p.m. Admission prices to the exhibits are $15 for adults; $13.50 for seniors (60+), youths (6–12), and active military; and $10 for children (3–5). An exhibit/Dome ticket is $19 for adults; $17.50 for seniors, youths, and active military; $14 for children. Exhibit admission is always free for members. Children 2 and younger and museum members are admitted free.

The 1895 *Jefferson Hotel* (101 W. Franklin St.; 804-649-4750; jefferson hotel.com), a massive, white-brick hotel blending Louis XVI and Colonial Renaissance styles, was once the finest hostelry in the South. It burned in 1901 and again in 1944. Live alligators lived in the two reflecting pools in the Palm Court lobby from the early 1900s until 1948, with "Old Poppy" being one of particular note. Several of the bellhops during that period told stories about finding the alligators crawling on the upholstered chairs in the lobby and chasing them back into their pools.

The alligators are now enshrined in bronze, permanently situated at the foot of the Thomas Jefferson statue; however, when the Ringling Brothers, Barnum and Bailey Circus came to town a few years ago, they brought a real alligator to the Jefferson for some publicity photographs. You never know what you'll find here. Just be sure when you put your feet up on a footstool that it doesn't walk away.

The grand staircase, which legend says was the model for the staircase in *Gone with the Wind,* is back. Film buffs might recognize the hotel from the film *My Dinner with André,* which was shot at this location. History seems to invade your pores at the Jefferson Hotel, and the new Lemaire restaurant will take you back to living off the land with their farm-to-table cuisine.

The *Virginia Holocaust Museum* (2000 E. Cary St.; 804-257-5400; va holocaust.org), is a tribute to Richmond Holocaust survivors and a unique hands-on children's museum specifically geared for students in the 8th through 10th grades. The first five exhibit rooms cover Kristallnacht (the Night of Broken Glass), life in the Jewish ghetto, and other significant elements from the history of the Holocaust. A time line features the story of Jay Ipson (the museum's first executive director) and his parents, who moved to Richmond in 1947. During the Holocaust the family lived in Lithuania in a 9-by-12-by-4-foot area hidden under a potato field. There is no admission fee to the museum. It is open Mon through Fri 9 a.m. to 5 p.m.; Sat and Sun 11 a.m. to 5 p.m. It is closed on Jan 1, the first day of Rosh Hashanah, Yom Kippur, Thanksgiving, and Dec 25.

Once you've finished some sightseeing, stop by *Buz & Ned's Real Barbecue* (1119 North Blvd., 804-355-6055; and 8205 W. Broad St., 804-346-4227; buzandneds.com) for a serving of slow-roasted pork barbecue that comes from a 150-year-old recipe. Look for the billboard with the big red arrow pointing to the restaurant on North Boulevard. Buz and Ned's is open Sun through Thurs 11 a.m. to 9 p.m.; Fri and Sat 11 a.m. to 10 p.m.

Sussex County

Virginia's first commercial peanut crop was grown in Sussex County in 1844. The climate is ideal, and because of their large kernels, the peanuts are hailed as the "Cadillac" of peanuts. Today peanuts represent a multimillion-dollar

ANNUAL EVENTS IN CENTRAL VIRGINIA

JANUARY

Charlottesville Restaurant Week
Charlottesville
(434) 817-2749, ext. 51
c-villerestaurantweek.com

MARCH

Annual Virginia Festival of the Book
Various venues
Charlottesville
(434) 924-7548
vabook.org

APRIL

Richmond Restaurant Week
Richmond
richmondrestaurantweek.com

Historic Garden Week
Statewide event includes Ashland,
Charles City, Petersburg, Richmond
(804) 644-7776, ext. 22
vagardenweek.org

MAY

Dominion Riverrock
Richmond
(804) 649-1861
dominionriverrock.com

JUNE

**Summer Solstice Wine Festival at
James River Cellars**
Glen Allen
(804) 550-7516
jamesrivercellars.com

JULY

Hanover Tomato Festival
Mechanicsville
(804) 365-4695
hanovertomatofestival.com

AUGUST

Powhatan County Fair
Powhatan
(804) 598-9808
powhatanfair.org

SEPTEMBER

State Fair of Virginia
Doswell
(804) 994-2800
statefairva.org
through October

**Taste of the Mountains Main Street
Festival**
Madison
(540) 948-4455
madisonva.com/event/26th-annual
-taste-of-the-mountains-main-street
-madison/

OCTOBER

Blues Festival at Mountain Vineyards
Lovingston
(434) 299-5080
mountaincovevineyards.com

Richmond Restaurant Week
Richmond
richmondrestaurantweek.com

OTHER ATTRACTIONS IN CENTRAL VIRGINIA

Freedom of Speech Wall
Charlottesville
(434) 295-4784

Grand Kugel
Richmond
(804) 864-1400
smv.org

Henrico
Markel Building, Doswell
henrico.us/locations/markel-building

Kings Dominion
Doswell
(804) 876-5000
kingsdominion.com

Leander McCormick Observatory
Charlottesville
(434) 924-7494
astronomy.as.virginia
.edu/public-outreach/
observatory-public-night-program

Lewis Ginter Botanical Gardens
Richmond
(804) 262-9887
lewisginter.org

Monticello
Charlottesville
(434) 984-9800
monticello.org

Montpelier
Montpelier Station
(504) 672-2728, ext. 100
montpelier.org

The Plunge
Wintergreen Resort, Wintergreen
(855) 699-1858
wintergreenresort.com/tubing

Richmond Braves
Richmond
(804) 241-0833
richmondbraves.org

Richmond Performing Arts Alliance
(RPAA; formerly Richmond CenterStage
Foundation)
Richmond
(804) 592-3330
https://rpaalliance.com/

Scotchtown, Home of Patrick Henry
Beaverdam
(804) 227-3500
preservationvirginia.org/historic-sites/
patrick-henrys-scotchtown/

Valentine Richmond History Center
Richmond
(804) 649-0711
battlefields.org/visit/heritage-sites/
valentine-richmond-history-center

Virginia Discovery Museum
Charlottesville
(434) 977-1025
vadm.org

industry in the state, so it's not surprising that you'll find "peanut this" and "peanut that" all along US 460 and throughout the Southside. The peanut, filled with protein, is the basis for several recipe booklets, which include recipes for crunchy chicken bits, cookies, glazed peanut bread, peanut-stuffed squash, peanut party biscuits, wine-cheese logs, cream of peanut soup, peanut broccoli salad, peanut spinach balls, Oriental crepes, peachy peanut spread, and, of course, peanut butter pie. Write to Production Promotion, Division of Markets, Virginia Department of Agriculture and Consumer Services, 102 Governor St., Richmond 23219, for a copy. For more information call (804) 225-3663 or visit vdacs.virginia.gov/vagrown/peanuts.shtml.

The **Virginia Diner** (322 W. Main St., Wakefield; 888-823-4637; vadiner .com), noted for its treatment of peanuts, is an old 125-seat diner that is singularly unimpressive in appearance, but don't let that deceive you. It started life in 1929 as a refurbished 1860 train car and has grown ever since. The car has been replicated, including the quaint atmosphere that makes diners so endearing. Buckets of free peanuts for munching greet you at the door. Virginia Fancy and Virginia Jumbo peanuts are first boiled in water, then roasted in special vegetable oil, causing the peanuts to blister and giving them extra crunch. Remember to visit the diner's gift shop for all those ham and peanut needs. The diner is open daily, except Dec 25, from 6 a.m. to 9 p.m. in summer, and until 8 p.m. in winter.

A younger entry into the peanut world (they started in 1984), **Plantation Peanuts** (509 N. County Dr., Wakefield; 800-233-8788; plantationpeanuts.com) has a select variety of nuts (peanuts, pecans, almonds, and cashews) chosen for their classic style and flavor. Each batch is slightly cooked and hand salted (ask them how they salt peanuts in the shell), and it's all done in the back room, except for the candied or sugared nuts, which are prepared elsewhere.

Places to Stay in Central Virginia

CHARLOTTESVILLE

The Clifton
1296 Clifton Inn Dr.
(434) 971-1800
the-clifton.com

English Inn of Charlottesville
2000 Morton Dr.
(434) 971-9900
englishinncharlottesville
.com

Foxfield Inn
2280 Garth Rd.
(434) 923-8892
foxfield-inn.com

Inn at Monticello
1188 Scottsville Rd.
(434) 979-3593
innatmonticello.com

GORDONSVILLE

Shenandoah Crossing Resort
174 Horseshoe Circle
(540) 832-9400
bluegreenvacations
.com/resorts/virginia/
shenandoah-crossing

LYNCHBURG

Carriage House Inn Bed & Breakfast
404 Cabell St.
(434) 846-1388
thecarriagehouseinnbandb
.com

Craddock Terry Hotel
1312 Commerce St.
(434) 455-1500
craddockterryhotel.com

MADISON

Ebenezer House Bed and Breakfast
122 Seville Rd.
(877) 514-2510
theebenezerhousebb.com

MINERAL

Littlepage Inn
15701 Monrovia Rd.
(540) 854-9861 or
(800) 248-1803
innsite.com/inns/A101663
.html

NELLYSFORD

Mark Addy
56 Rodes Farm Dr.
(434) 361-1101
mark-addy.com

ORANGE

Holladay House
155 W. Main St.
(540) 672-4893
holladayhousebandb.com

Inn on Poplar Hill
278 Caroline St.
(540) 672-6840
innonpoplarhill.com

Mayhurst Inn
12460 Mayhurst Ln.
(540) 672-6840
mayhurstinn.com

RICHMOND

Berkeley Hotel
1200 E. Cary St.
(804) 780-1300
berkeleyhotel.com

Jefferson Hotel
101 W. Franklin St.
(804) 649-4750
jeffersonhotel.com

Linden Row Inn
100 E. Franklin St.
(804) 783-7000
lindenrowinn.com

STANARDSVILLE

Lafayette Inn
146 E. Main St.
(434) 985-6345
thelafayette.com

WINTERGREEN

Wintergreen Resort
Route 664
(434) 325-2200
wintergreenresort.com

Places to Eat in Central Virginia

CHARLOTTESVILLE

Albemarle Baking Company
418 W. Main St.
(434) 293-6456
albemarlebakingco.com

Alley Light
108 2nd St. SW
(434) 296-5003
alleylight.com

Cavalier Diner
1403 Emmet St. N
(434) 977-1619
facebook.com/
CavalierDiner

Citizen Burger Bar
212 E. Main St.
(434) 979-9944
citizenburgerbarcville.com

Hamiltons' at First & Main
101 W. Main St.
(434) 295-6649
hamiltonsrestaurant.com

Public Fish and Oyster
513 W. Main St.
(434) 995-5542
publicfo.com

Maya Restaurant
633 W. Main St.
(434) 979-6292
maya-restaurant.com

Sultan Kebab
333 2nd St. SE, Ste. 100
(434) 981-0090
sultankebabcville.com

Michie Tavern
683 Thomas Jefferson
Pkwy.
(434) 977-1234
michietavern.com

LYNCHBURG

Market at Main
904 Main St.
(434) 847-9040
marketatmain.com

PETERSBURG

Brickhouse Run
409 Cockade Alley
(804) 862-1815
brickhouserun.com

Freda Mae's
3849 S. Crater Rd.
(804) 733-9396
facebook.com/fredamaes

RICHMOND

Cobblestone Bar & Grill
Berkeley Hotel
1200 E. Cary St.
(804) 225-1300

Galaxy Diner
3109 W. Cary St.
(804) 213-0510

Millie's
2603 E. Main St.
(804) 643-5512
milliesdiner.com

Proper Pie Co.
2505 E. Broad St.
(804) 343-7437
facebook.com/ProperPieCo

River City Diner
803 E. Parham Rd.
(804) 266-1500
rivercitydiner.com
also Southside

Strawberry Street Cafe
421 N. Strawberry St.
(804) 353-6860
strawberrystreetcafe.com

SANDSTON

Ma and Pa's Diner
5600 Williamsburg Rd.
(804) 226-0329

Southern Virginia

Brunswick County

Film buffs will be interested to know that **Brunswick** has been home to a few movie scenes. Jeff Nichols's movie *Loving*, with Ruth Negga, Joel Edgerton, and Will Dalton, told the story of a couple arrested for an interracial marriage in 1960s Virginia and was shot entirely in Virginia; the Lawrenceville/Brunswick airport was used for the drag strip scenes with 1950s vintage cars. Lake Phoenix (formerly Lake Rawlings), in North Brunswick, was used for several films, including *The Replacements* with Keanu Reeves (the sunken sailboat scene) and Colin Farrell's Jamestown story, *The New World*. See if you can spot them all.

According to local historians, Lawrenceville is the original home of beef stew. The story goes that one day in 1828 Dr. Creed Haskins went hunting with some friends. While they were out, the camp cook, Jimmy Matthews, shot squirrels and started making a thick stew with butter, onions, stale bread, and seasonings, thus creating **Brunswick stew.** Because game animals are used, the stew cooks for a long time, much longer than a soup would. Now, you may hear—in other parts of the country and elsewhere—that Brunswick, Georgia, is the home,

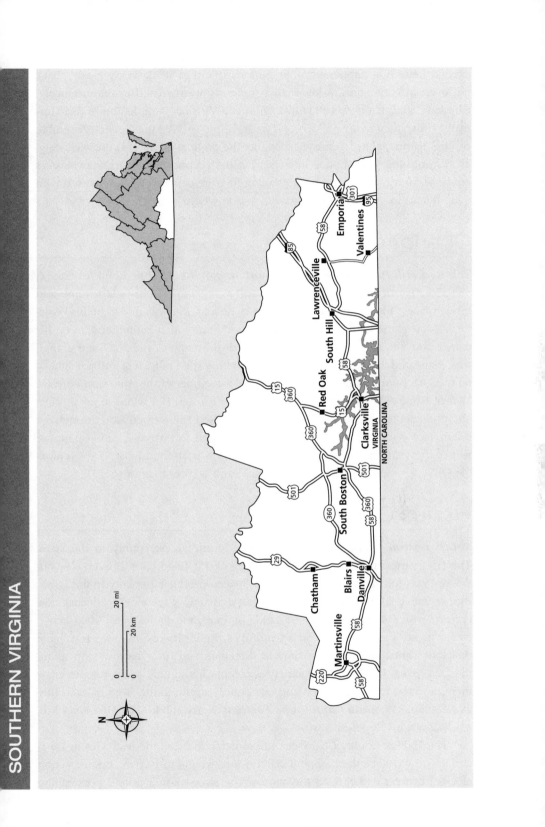

except they say it happened on St. Simons Island in 1898, so obviously, that's not even in contention. Additionally, some say it originated in Braunschweig, Germany, and that it was a favorite of Queen Victoria. Sure, let the British/Germany conspiracy people take credit for it. Nope. In 1988 the General Assembly of Virginia proclaimed Brunswick County the original home of Brunswick stew, an "astonishing gastronomic miracle!" On the second Sat of Oct, stewmasters convene for a battle of the best, cooking in large caldrons that are stirred with oars. It's up to you and the judges to decide whose is best.

Charlotte County

The ***Red Hill Patrick Henry National Memorial*** (1250 Red Mill Rd./Rte. 2; 434-376-2044 or 800-514-7463; redhill.org) was Patrick Henry's last home and burial place. One of seven different homes he had, this was said to be his favorite as "one of the garden spots of the world." Start with a 15-minute film on his career and life at Red Hill. It's the home of the nation's oldest Osage orange tree, estimated to be 350 to 400 years old, with a span of 85 feet and a height of 60 feet. It's both a National Champion and a member of the American Forestry Hall of Fame. The museum shop is the place for Red Hill wines, books, prints and documents, apparel, and children's items. Red Hill is open Mon through Sat 9 a.m. to 5 p.m. and Sun 1 to 5 p.m. Apr through Oct 31; and until 4 p.m. the rest of the year and by appointment. Admission is $8 for adults; $7 for seniors (65+); $6 for military, AAA, and NPS pass; and $4 for students (6–17).

Halifax County

South Boston, in Halifax County, is the fourth-largest county in the state. The land varies from level to gently rolling and is filled with tobacco (Halifax County was for many years the largest tobacco-producing county in the country), commercial forests (the state's largest agricultural revenue producer), and large tracts of seemingly endless land. At one time there were 4,000 active farms, most of them small, and a handful of them produce the sweetest, most delicious cantaloupes, grown only in Wickham soil on a narrow strip along the Dan River. The Turbeville variety is patented, and only seven people grow them, and the fruit is honored and celebrated on the fourth Wed of each July at the annual ***Virginia Cantaloupe Festival*** (Berry Hill Resort, 3105 River Rd.; 434-572-3085; valopefest.com).

The Halifax County Chamber of Commerce initiated the festivities in 1981, and it's grown since then. The official fun runs from 4 to 10 p.m., but the action clocks in much earlier with the start of the slow-roasted pulled pork taking many hours. It's much like a "big old homecoming," says the chamber of commerce's Nancy Pool. All you have to bring is your appetite, your lawn chair, and the cost of admission, which for 2018 was $35 each, advance purchase only (no door sales).

The cantaloupe is so delicious by itself that it seems logical it would make other foods taste even better, so a cantaloupe cutup recipe contest was held in 1985. The contest brought in recipes for melon with chicken, melon franks (slit a hot dog and stuff with a slice of melon, wrap with bacon, and secure with a toothpick before roasting on the grill), cantaloupe pancakes, melon with Chablis or piña colada mix, and cantaloupe preserves.

With so much history here (the county seat dates back to 1777 and two military campaigns—the Retreat to the Dan in the Revolutionary War and the Battle of Staunton River in the Civil War—culminated or occurred in Halifax County), it's natural to have a historical museum. In 1982 the Tuesday Women's Club established the ***South Boston–Halifax County Museum of Fine Arts and History*** (1540 Wilborn Ave.; 434-572-9200; sbhcmuseum.org), which houses the permanent collections and loans of items relating to Halifax, including Civil War artifacts, glassware, Indian artifacts, military uniforms, and memorabilia from Halifax County families. A research center is open during museum hours so you can go through newspapers, archives, yearbooks, and other sources for your genealogy work. The museum is open Wed through Sat 10 a.m. to 4 p.m. There's no admission charge, but donations are accepted.

Stars & Stripes Forever

Annin & Company (3011 Philpott Rd., South Boston 24592; 434-575-7913; annin .com), with plants in South Boston and Cobbs Creek In Mathews County, is the oldest and largest flag manufacturer in the United States, and they've been busy making flags since 1847. The company is responsible for the design of the black-and-white POW-MIA flag created by (the late) Newt Heisley, a military man who flew transport planes in the South Pacific during World War II. The company has also designed flags for new United Nations member nations and the Flag of Honor and Flag of Heroes that honor the victims of the Sept 11, 2001 attacks. The Flag of Honor includes the names of everyone who died on the planes and in the buildings, the names creating red and blue strips. The Flag of Heroes includes the names of the emergency services personnel from the FDNY, PAPD, NYPD, and court officers creating the red strips across the flag. Proceeds from the flags are donated to the Voices of 911, the National 911 Museum at Ground Zero, the Flag of Honor Fund, and the Wounded Warrior Project. Unfortunately, they do not offer tours, but you can contact them with your flag questions or special requests.

For great family entertainment in **South Hill**, stop by during the South Hill Chamber of Commerce Beef Festival, Relay for Life, Jazz by the Lake, wine tasting extravaganza, live theater, cooking school, or hydroplane challenge. However, the activity that seems to draw the most attention here is the 3-day July **Pontoon Boat Parade** that kicks off the annual **Virginia Lake Festival,** also known as Lakefest (105 2nd St.; 434-374-2436; clarksvilleva.com/recre ation/on-the-lake). Decorated like parade floats, the boats look like anything from pirate ships to trains.

The **South Hill Model Railroad Museum** is located, appropriately enough, in the restored Historic South Hill Train Depot. It represents more than 200 miles of fun tracks in Virginia known as the Wiggle, Bump and Agony. The focal point of the museum is the Atlantic & Danville Model railroad, a scale model of the trains and towns, circa 1950, running from Lawrenceville to Clarksville, Virginia. The museum is intimate and not overwhelming and fun for the three-year-old (Thomas is there), the history buff, and the train enthusiast. The depot is also home to the **South Hill Chamber of Commerce** (201 S. Mecklenburg Ave; 434-447-4547; southhillva.org/visitor-information/museums -attractions) and the **Virginia S. Evans Doll Museum**. Open 9 a.m. to 4 p.m. No admission charge.

Henry County

Martinsville is the home of the **Piedmont Arts Association** (215 Starling Ave.; 276-632-3221; piedmontarts.org), a Museum Partner of the Virginia Museum of Fine Arts. Exhibits might include paintings and graphics or three-dimensional works and installations in one or more of the five galleries. They also offer

Fossils in Focus

Virginia boasts one of the top-five fossil sites in the world, a proliferation of dinosaur tracks, and modern animals found nowhere else on Earth. Many exhibits at the **Virginia Museum of Natural History** (21 Starling Ave.; 276-634-4141; vmnh.net) in Martinsville are the result of original research conducted by seven scientists on staff. Exhibits have included *Rock Hall of Fame, Age of Mammals, Age of Reptiles,* and *Dan River People.* After years of being located in the old Joseph Martin elementary school, the museum moved to new digs and 89,000 square feet of space in 2006, and it's growing again. The museum is open Mon through Sat from 9 a.m. to 5 p.m. It is closed on Sun, Thanksgiving Day, Dec 25, and Jan 1. Admission is $7 for adults, $5 for seniors (60+) and children (3–18). AAA and AARP discounts are available.

Hot Time in the Old Town Today

On a cheerful Dec 12, 1936, at 3:45 in the afternoon, as shoppers were going about their holiday errands in uptown Martinsville, an employee at the newly opened fireworks manufacturing company on the Courthouse Square demonstrated a new cap pistol that set off a massive series of fireworks explosions as firecrackers, pinwheels, skyrockets, and other items (about two truckloads' worth) ignited. The building suffered extensive damage, and a few coffins stored upstairs were charred. However, the clerk, in escaping out a back window, hurt his ankle and was the only injury of the day.

classes, performing arts, and the opportunity to see (and purchase) one-of-a-kind craft items in the gift shop. Pottery, jewelry, carved wooden objects, dried flower wreaths, and more come from craftsmen from the region and across the country, with price ranges to fit every budget. The R. P. Gravely–A.J. Lester Art Garden is free is open to the public from dawn to dusk. The Piedmont Arts Association is free and open to the public Tues through Fri 10 a.m. to 5 p.m.; Sat 10 a.m. to 3 p.m. Summer hours are extended.

The **Circus mural** (191 Fayette St.; 276-632-3221; visitmartinsville.com/venues/details/id/72066/circus-mural-in-uptown-martinsville), on the wall of New College Institute in uptown Martinsville, was commissioned and produced as part of the Piedmont Arts' Public Art Exhibit. John Stiles, graphic designer and artist, used a contemporary style in creating, basing it on a picture owned by Dr. Mervyn and Virginia King. It shows a parade of elephants and other performers in front of the courthouse, advertising the arrival of the circus in Martinsville, around 1920.

Mecklenburg County

Buggs Island Lake (105 2nd St.; 434-374-2436; clarksvilleva.com/recreation/on-the-lake/#Buggs), covering 50,000 acres and straddling the North Carolina–Virginia border, was constructed by the US Army Corps of Engineers between 1946 and 1953 as one of a series of dams along the Roanoke River. It is the largest lake in Virginia. It's really the John H. Kerr Dam and Reservoir (named after a North Carolina congressman who supported its construction), and 169-acre Buggs Island is downstream of the dam.

Besides 800 miles of shoreline, with the expected water fun of fishing (striped bass or rockfish, crappie, and largemouth black bass—said to be the "best bass fishing in the state"—and hybrid muskie, bream, sunfish, carp, and

Don't Return to Sender

Valentines is a small community of rural Southside Virginia, with an internationally recognized name. Normally it's smaller than your typical sleepy country town, but beginning in mid-Jan every year, there's a loving buzz in the air, particularly at the post office. The story goes that William H. Valentine established the Valentines post office (23 Manning Dr.; 434-577-2456) in 1887. In 1951, when Willie Wright became the postmaster of the office in the corner of Wright's General Store, he started stamping envelopes "With Love," and the tradition has grown since then. Business really started booming in 1955 when the "LOVE" stamp was unveiled here. Shortly after the New Year, bags of mail came in containing some 35,000 to 40,000 letters, all waiting for the postmark with a red heart and several dogwood flowers on the envelope before being sent to that special person.

gar), boating, and swimming, there are 5 campgrounds on the Virginia side. On land, you can enjoy picnicking, hunting, horseback riding, and hiking.

Pittsylvania County

The largest county (in area) in the state is Pittsylvania County, where 18th-century houses still stand and more than 100 water-powered gristmills created a merger between the agrarian and industrial worlds. That was down to four a few years ago, then three that are still operational, with five still standing but idle. If you're fascinated with the role these gristmills played as post offices, churches, schools, country stores, polling places, and the local rec centers, read Herman Melton's book *Pittsylvania's Nineteenth-Century Grist Mills*. It also provides genealogical data for 300 families. Genealogy can take on a new dimension in this county, for the courthouse records date from 1747, and the library has in-depth Virginia records and research tools.

Chatham has won several "Keep Virginia Beautiful" awards and has earned a reputation as the prettiest little town in the Southside. A beautiful view seems to make a beautiful wine, at least that's part of the attraction for the **Tomahawk Mill Vineyard and Winery** (9221 Anderson Mill Rd.; 434-432-2037; tomahawkmill.com). A Confederate soldier built the water-powered grist-mill in 1888, and it operated for about 100 years before the first grapes were planted. They also make mead, apple wine, and blends that include a country blush and a Vidal Blanc. They're open for tastings (and picnicking or looking at the restored millpond and dam). They're open Mar 15 through Dec 15, Tues through Sat 11 a.m. to 5 p.m.; Sun 1 to 5 p.m.

Danville

Danville (danville.com) is the place where, on September 27, 1903, a south-bound Southern Railroad express mail train left the tracks on a trestle and plunged into the ravine below, killing nine people. This incident was the inspiration for the song "The Wreck of the Old '97" and is recorded on a historical marker on Highway 58 between Locust Lane and N. Main Street. A 46-by-74-foot canvas mural was created by Wes Hardin on the side of the Atrium Furniture building at the Gateway to downtown. A second mural, at 121–125 N. Union St., features the downtown historic area and was created in 2006. Funds were provided by six local residents who paid $500 each to have his or her likeness included in the mural.

The *American Armoured Foundation Tank Museum* (3401 US 29; 434-836-5323; aaftankmuseum.com) takes you to the beginning of military history. Stop here to see reenacters, military model shows, a military bicycle exhibit, and more. Founded in 1981 and opened in May 2003, the museum has a mission to educate, collect, restore, preserve, and display as varied a collection of military tank and cavalry artifacts as is possible. There are 112 tanks and artillery pieces, the most extensive collection in the world. Some items date from 1509. You'll also find 150 machine guns, mortars, flamethrowers, recoilless rifles, rocket launchers, tank and artillery optical instruments, small arms, uniforms, and more. Stop by to see an exhibit dedicated to Elvis Presley during his military years. With more than 300 items pertaining to women in the military, the museum needs only money to present an exhibit devoted to women in the military.

Among the other facilities (research library, gift and hobby shop, classroom, etc.), the museum is home to the largest and only under-a-roof radio-controlled-tank battlefield in the world. At this time it's set up to represent a World War II–era town in France. Some exhibits are interactive, including a tank turret trainer with a machine gun attached and a gunsight that shoots out tennis balls using compressed air. The collection includes the largest and only (would have to be largest, then, wouldn't it?) indoor radio controlled tank battlefield in the world!

birthplaceof ladyastor

Viscountess Nancy Astor, born in Danville on May 19, 1879, was the first woman to sit in British Parliament. Her sister Irene inspired the famous "Gibson Girl" artwork done by her husband, artist Charles Dana Gibson. Their birthplace at 117 Broad St. has a historical marker located at the corner of Broad and Main Streets, Danville.

ANNUAL EVENTS IN SOUTHERN VIRGINIA

2nd Thursday Science Talks
Martinsville, monthly
(276) 634-4141
vmnh.net/events/details/
id/541/2nd-thursday-science-talks

Fast Friday
Martinsville Speedway
Martinsville, monthly
(276) 956-7200
martinsvillespeedway.com/News-and
-Media/Events.aspx

Museum Sleepovers
Virginia Museum of Natural History
Martinsville, monthly
(276) 634-4141
virginia.org/listings/Events/
MuseumSleepovers

FEBRUARY
Nail the Rail 9 Miler
Martinsville
(276) 632-1772
milesinmartinsville.com

MARCH
The Sledge Trail Run
Anglers Park
Danville
(434) 799-5150
playdanvilleva.com/226/
The-Sledge-Trail-Run

APRIL
Clarksville Lake Country Wine Festival
Clarksville
(434) 374-2436
clarksvilleva.com/festivals-celebrations/
clarksville-va-wine-festival

Historic Garden Week
Statewide event includes Danville
(804) 644-7776
vagardenweek.org

JUNE
Annual Rosemont Wine & Art Festival
La Crosse
(434) 636-9463
rosemontofvirginia.com/event/artfestival

JULY
Virginia Lake Festival (Lakefest)
Clarksville
(434) 374-2436
clarksvilleva.com/festivals-celebrations/
virginia-lake-festival

Virginia Cantaloupe Festival
South Boston
(434) 572-3085
valopefest.com

AUGUST
Smith River Fest
Axton
(276) 634-4640
visitmartinsville.com/smith-river-fest

SEPTEMBER
South Boston Harvest Festival
South Boston
(434) 575-4208
soboharvestfest.com

Virginia Peanut Festival
Emporia
(434) 348-4219
thevirginiapeanutfestival.com

OCTOBER
Harvest Days Festival
Clarksville
(434) 374-2436
clarksvilleva.com/festivals-celebrations/
harvest-days-festival/

The museum is open Fri and Sat from 10 a.m. to 4 p.m. (Apr through Dec); Sat from 10 a.m. to 4 p.m. the rest of the year. Admission is $12 for adults and $10 for children (5–12) and adults over 60.

The ***Danville Science Center*** (677 Craghead St.; 434-791-5160; dsc.smv .org) occupies an 1899 Southern Railway passenger train station and lets you experience science with hands-on exhibits where you can discover how things work. You can make sparks fly while discovering electricity. To understand orbits, you can launch balls. You can also see an astronaut's view of Danville.

If you visit the ***Butterfly Station*** at the Science Center, you will learn that more than 160 species of butterflies inhabit Virginia. You can also learn that most adult butterflies live from 20 to 40 days, they have footpads that act as taste buds, and butterflies and moths fold their wings differently. You can also learn how to make your own butterfly garden and learn which caterpillar-host plants attract which butterfly species. A guided tour of the butterfly garden is available for $1 a person. The butterfly season is Apr through Oct.

The Science Center is open Tues through Sat 9:30 a.m. to 5 p.m.; Sun 11:30 a.m. to 5 p.m. Admission costs $7 for adults and $6 for seniors (60+), active military, and children (4–12). There's an extra fee to see the Digital Dome show or a combined ticket for both.

OTHER ATTRACTIONS IN SOUTHERN VIRGINIA

Clarksville Regional Museum
Clarksville
(434) 374-4434

Danville Museum of Fine Arts & History
Danville
(434) 793-5644
danvillemuseum.org

Halifax County War Memorial
Halifax
(434) 476-3300
oldhalifax.com/warmem

JTI Fountain
Danville
(434) 791-0210

L. E. Coleman African-American Museum
Halifax
(434) 222-6757
oldhalifax.com/county/ColemanMuseum/default.htm

South Boston Speedway
South Boston
(434) 572-4947
southbostonspeedway.com

Southern Virginia Wild Blueway
South Boston
(434) 572-2543
sovawildblueway.com/

Southern Virginia Botanical Gardens
Halifax
(434) 575-5370 or (434) 476-5370
svbgeec.wixsite.com/svbg

As you travel through Danville, take some time to drive or walk along ***Millionaire's Row*** (434-709-8398; danvillehistory.org/millionaires-row.html), 8 blocks of one of the finest collections of Victorian and Edwardian architecture in the South. Look for such details as gables, gingerbread scrollwork, columns, porticos, cupolas, and minarets. You'll also find five architecturally different churches (Romanesque, Gothic Revival, Tudor Gothic, Neoclassical Revival, and High Victorian Gothic) along the row, which helps explain why Danville is frequently called the "City of Churches."

Pick up a *Victorian Walking Tour* brochure at the visitor center. The homes are closed to the public most of the year but are open the second Sun in Dec for the Danville Historical Society's annual Holiday Walking Tour.

Along your tour you'll see the 1857 Italian villa–style Sutherlin house, now the ***Danville Museum of Fine Arts and History*** (975 Main St.; 434-793-5644; danvillemuseum.org), also known as the "Last Capitol of the Confederacy." Confederate president Jefferson Davis resided in this home during the final week of the Civil War, and it was here that Davis and his Confederate government received word that Lee had surrendered at nearby Appomattox. Exhibits depicting the history of the area and revolving art exhibits are featured.

The museum is open Tues through Sat, 10 a.m. to 5 p.m., Sun 2 to 5 p.m., and Mon by chance or appointment. Admission is $10 for adults, $8 for seniors (62+), $4 for students, and free to members.

Places to Stay in Southern Virginia

BLAIRS

The Finch's Nest Bed and Breakfast
9109 Spring Garden Rd.
(434) 250-6716
finchsnest.com

CLARKSVILLE

Cooper's Landing Inn & Travelers Tavern
801 Virginia Ave.
(434) 374-2866
cooperslandinginn.net

Magnuson Hotel on the Lake Clarksville
105 2nd St.
(434) 374-5023
conradusa.com/magnuson/index.html

LAWRENCEVILLE

Brunswick Mineral Springs Bed & Breakfast
14910 Western Mill Rd.
(434) 848-4010
brunswickmineralsprings.com

MARTINSVILLE

The Church Street Guesthouse
409 E. Church St.
(276) 638-6068
martinsvilleguesthouses.com/index.html

RED OAK

CornerStone Farm
525 Barnes Rd.
(434) 735-0527 or
(866) 977-3276
cornerstonefarm.net

Old Crowe Farm Bed & Breakfast
815 Little Retreat Rd.
(434) 735-0139
oldcrowefarm.com

SOUTH BOSTON

Greenwood Inn
909 Pace Dr.
(434) 447-5001

Places to Eat in Southern Virginia

CLARKSVILLE

Traveler's Tavern
801 Virginia Ave.
cooperslandinginn.net

DANVILLE

The 616 Farm to Table
616 N. Main St.
(434) 797-3463
dine616.com

EMPORIA

Logan's Diner
414 S. Main St.
(434) 634-5512

MARTINSVILLE

Wild Magnolia
730 E. Church St.
(276) 666-6666

SOUTH BOSTON

Bistro 1888
221 Main St.
(434) 572-1888
bistro1888.com

SOUTH HILL

The Hungry Farmer
122 N. Mecklenburg Ave.
(434) 447-3145

Shenandoah Valley

Some things you should know about the Shenandoah River and valley:

The **Shenandoah River** runs "uphill" from south to north (the mouth empties into the Potomac River, on the north). Yes, there are a few other rivers like that in the world, but not many. The valley was the main thoroughfare for settlers moving south from Pennsylvania. More major battles of the Civil War were fought in Virginia than any other state, and this lush, fruitful valley was a grand prize that changed hands dozens of times.

The two-lane **Skyline Drive** runs 105 miles through the 194,000-acre **Shenandoah National Park** (nps.gov/shen/planyourvisit/fees.htm), with 75 overlooks and parking areas that lead to trails, waterfalls, and nature areas. There are more than 500 miles of trails in the park (most of them are pet-friendly), and 30 percent of them are designated wilderness. The **Appalachian Trail** runs 101 miles through the park. President Franklin D. Roosevelt, in dedicating the park in 1936, said visitors would find an experience "good for their bodies and good for their souls." Seventy-five years later, this is even truer. There are four entrances to the park, at Front Royal (near

Routes 66 and 340), Thornton Gap (at Route 211), Swift Run Gap (at Route 33), and Rockfish Gap (at Routes 64 and 250), which is also the entrance to the Blue Ridge Parkway.

Basic admission to Skyline Drive is $30 per car for one vehicle and passengers for seven days, motorcycles are $25 for one motorcycle and one passenger for seven consecutive days, or $15 per person (16+ when entering by other than a private vehicle). An annual pass is $55. There are LOTS of other passes and exceptions and rules and regulations.

The park is always open; however, portions of Skyline Drive are closed during inclement weather and at night during the deer hunting season. You should check these details before you start hiking.

At its southern end the parkway meets with the northern end of the 469-mile Blue Ridge Parkway as it winds along mountain crests toward the North Carolina border. Virginia state parks had their beginning in 1936, starting with 6 parks and growing to today's 34.

I call our Virginia mountains friendly because they invite the hiker, the stroller, the skier, the river rafter, the daydreamer, and the explorer into their sanctuary, their tranquility. Perhaps most important to casual visitors, the scenery is breathtakingly beautiful, with each curve and bend in the road more extraordinary than the previous one.

The **South River** (578 South River Rd.; 540-463-3777; lexingtonvirginia .com/outdoors/activities/attractions/south-river) is one of only two urban trout fisheries in the state. The spring-fed waters keep the temperatures just right for trophy-sized trout and smallmouth bass. The serene freestone stream is designated as "stocked trout water" by the Virginia Department of Game and Inland Fisheries and is stocked five times between Oct 1 and May 15. All of these fish are of "catchable" size and many are much larger. You may catch 6 fish per day larger than 7 inches, although as many of the stocked fish aren't caught after each stocking, you may find a true trophy.

Augusta County

The **Natural Chimneys** (94 Natural Chimneys Ln.; 540-350-2510 in season or 540-245-5727; co.augusta.va.us/government/parks-recreation/parks-facilities/ natural-chimneys) regional park area in **Mount Solon** is the home of seven towering limestone structures (the area was a seabed many years ago), impressive scenery indeed. Does your mind see 120-foot chimneys or massive castle turrets? Admission to the Chimneys is free. A seasonal 145-site campground has water and electric hookups and a primitive/tent section.

Steeles Tavern

About halfway between Lexington on the south and Staunton on the north is the community of **Steeles Tavern**. The **Sugar Tree Inn** (145 Lodge Trail, Hwy. 56; 800-377-2197 or 540-377-2197; sugartreeinn.com) sits about 5 minutes off the Blue Ridge Parkway, 1/2 mile high and surrounded by its own hardwood forest. It was built and designed as an inn (not a readapted old barn) by local people using hand-hewn chestnut, oak, and poplar timbers taken from original buildings throughout Rockbridge County. Logs as much as 200 years old were mortised and pegged together without nails, just as in pioneer days.

Its rooms (each with its own wood-burning fireplace) in four buildings and the main lodge are spacious, "with human-size private baths and generous chairs in which to rock or relax." Some rooms have a whirlpool bath, ceiling fan, and air-conditioning. A full breakfast is provided in a glass-walled dining room, and dinner is available Thurs through Sat if you just can't bring yourself to leave these woods. Sugar Tree Inn is open Feb through Dec.

Clarke County

Clarke County and **Berryville** are still mostly bucolic, although things have changed around here. Gone are the mortuary museum and a general store where your payment was put in a trolley that rode a pulley to the second floor office, and your change was placed in the trolley to be returned to you. (Think a tiny Mister Rogers ski lift.)

The **Old Clarke County Courthouse** was designed and built by David Meade soon after Clarke County—named for George Rogers Clark (without the "e")—was formed from Frederick County in 1836. The **Clarke County Historical Association** (32 E. Main St.; 540-955-2600; clarkehistory.org) maintains the museum and archives that are located in the Coiner House. The exhibits tell the unique story of the county and the region. Families have donated papers, photographs, and memorabilia, and they encourage you to donate items so they can be shared with historians. If you wish, they'll scan your originals and return them to you, along with a CD of the scans. The museum is open Tues through Fri 11 a.m. to 4 p.m. and by appointment.

The bread and fruitcake (2 pounds, 4 ounces each) from the cloistered **Trappist Abbey of the Holy Cross Monastery** (901 Cool Spring Ln.; 540-955-4383; monasteryfruitcake.org) is legendary. Locally, Safeway and Giant grocery stores carry the baked goods, free of preservatives and made from unbleached and stone-ground flours, spring water, and unsulfured molasses. Or you can order a cake for $37.95. They also sell creamed honeys and truffles.

The monastery is on the site of the historic ***Wormley Estate,*** a well-preserved, 200-year-old stone building.

What isn't as well known is that you can stay at the Abbey. Accommodations are available for 16 men and women, with no scheduled activities other than meals, and three of them are included each day. Each room has a private bathroom and a large window that opens onto the scenic beauty of the Blue Ridge Mountains. This is a great, quiet retreat, scheduled from Fri afternoon through Sun afternoon and Mon afternoon through Fri morning. If you're going off the beaten path to escape or find something, this is the place to do it. Oh, and there is a gift shop, open from 9 a.m. to noon and then from 1:30 to 5 p.m., where you can buy the aforementioned goodies.

At the University of Virginia's ***Blandy Experimental Farm and the Orland E. White Arboretum*** (which is the State Arboretum of Virginia) in ***Boyce,*** you can enjoy a bucolic experience as you travel through 172 acres of maintained landscapes and gardens featuring more than 1,000 varieties and species of plants representing 100 generations and 50 families. View the most extensive boxwood collection in North America. Feel free to drive the circular route or take a leisurely walk through a shady dogwood lane. Picnicking is allowed.

Among the types of activities planned by the staff here might be a bus trip to the Maymont Flower and Garden Show, an exhibit of wildflower pictures by Richmond photographer Hal Horwitz, a popup planetarium, a talk about why some song sparrows are wimps, and an apprentice gardener workshop. Some of these events have an admission fee; some are free. The arboretum (400 Blandy Farm Ln.; 540-837-1758; virginia.edu/blandy) is open to the public daily from dawn to dusk. There is no charge for admission.

The ***Burwell-Morgan Mill*** (Rte. 624, 15 Tannery Ln.; 540-837-1799; burwell morganmill.org) is an operating overshot waterwheel with wooden gears. It's made of stone and dates from 1782 (built by former Hessian soldiers who were captured at the Battle of Saratoga in 1777); clapboard was added in 1876. Lieutenant Colonel Nathaniel Burwell and Brigadier General Daniel Morgan started the operation, and during the Civil War flour and feed from the mill were sold to both armies. It was an unusual mill in that the abundant water supply and huge 20-foot-diameter wheel achieved 45 horsepower, compared to an average of only 20 horsepower at other mills. The mill remained in operation until 1953. The Clarke County Historical Association acquired it in 1964 and spent years doing extensive restoration work. The mill is open Fri through Sun, noon to 5 p.m., with grindings every Sat, May through Nov.

It's not exactly in the same league as a historic mill, but if you like prehistoric stuff, ***Dinosaur Land*** (3848 Stonewall Jackson Hwy.; 540-869-2222;

dinosaurland.com) in **White Post** could be the place to visit. Built in the mid-1960s, 50 nasty-looking fiberglass critters, from allosaurus to yaleasaurus, roam (statue-wise) the woods waiting to inform you and have their pictures taken with you and your youngsters. For your convenience, there's also a little store with souvenirs.

Dinosaur Land is open daily Mar 1 to Memorial Day 9:30 a.m. to 5:30 p.m.; Memorial Day to Labor Day 9:30 a.m. to 6 p.m.; Labor Day through Dec 31 9:30 a.m. to 6 p.m. It is closed on Thurs from Oct through Dec, and all month in Jan and Feb. The admission price is $8 for folks ages 11 and older and $6 for children (2–10).

Frederick County

The Inn at Vaucluse Spring (231 Vaucluse Spring Ln.; 540-869-0200; vaucluse spring.com) in **Stephens City** is run by Derrick and Tiffany Niide and their two children, all native Hawaiians. Tiffany was a practicing physician who specialized in teaching mindfulness and wellness programs. Derrick has a background in teaching and hospitality. After an extensive search, they found this property and decided it was the perfect place for their Aloha spirit. They have 6 guesthouses (including 3 private cabins, an 1850s log house, and an elegantly restored Manor House built in the 1790s) on 44 serene acres. Each room has a jet tub, fireplace, and fabulous views. Seating areas (indoor and outdoor) abound, and a pool is open seasonally. The Vaucluse spring generates about 1.5 million gallons of crystal-clear water daily. Come, watch birds and other wildlife, hike, bike or just relax. Do not expect a TV in your room; you're here to unwind. Tiffany offers mindfulness classes and retreats

The Battle of Kernstown, 5.3 miles north of Stephens City, is the only battle in which Stonewall Jackson was defeated (8,000 Federals against Jackson's 3,500 Confederates). Ironically, two years later, in June 1864, the Second Battle of Kernstown was the last Confederate victory in the Shenandoah Valley. Follow the walking trails through the 388-acre Civil War battlefield park for insights into the events of these battles, stop by the battlefield visitor center, and see the 1854 Pritchard-Grim Farm house. Private tours are available by appointment. Special events are scheduled throughout the year. Open Sat from 10 a.m. to 4 p.m. and Sun 11 a.m. to 4 p.m. from the second weekend in May through Oct. No admission charge; donations gladly accepted. For more information contact the Kernstown Battlefield Association, 610 Battle Park Dr., Winchester 22602, or visit kernstownbattle.org.

Page County

A network of caverns runs beneath the town of **Luray,** and they're hiding many treasures. The world's largest musical instrument is the Great Stalacpipe Organ in the Cathedral Room of **Luray Caverns** (101 Cave Hill Rd.; 540-743-6551; luraycaverns.com). Reportedly the largest bell at the Luray Singing Tower weighs 7,640 pounds. The caverns open daily at 9 a.m., with tours starting about every 20 minutes. The fee is $28 for adults, $15 for children (6–12), $25 for seniors, and it includes admission to the caverns, the Car and Carriage Museum, Luray Valley Museum, and the Toy Town Junction.

If you're a fly-fishing enthusiast, check out **Shenandoah Valley Fly Fishing** (571-606-0307; shenandoahvalleyflyfishing.com). Take an all-day class and learn entomology, knots, fly choice, and more in one-on-one classes. They provide the necessary gear; you bring your raincoat, polarized sunglasses, sunscreen, etc. You must have a Virginia fishing license and trout stamp.

Rockbridge County

If your idea of a bed-and-breakfast includes an early Victorian setting, antique furnishings, wraparound verandas on the first and second floors, a fireplace to relax in front of as you listen to classical music, and a wide trout stream defining the property line, then you might want to stop at the **The Hummingbird Inn Bed and Breakfast** (30 Wood Ln.; 540-997-9065 or 800-397-3214; hummingbirdinn.com) in **Goshen.** Sandra and Jeff are the current innkeepers of this comfy place with 5 guest rooms, and they serve seasonal, farm-fresh local fare at the two-course country breakfast. They'll also pack a picnic/brown-bag lunch for your travels.

Gertie's Country Store and Deli (563 Tye River Tpke.; 540-377-9313) in **Vesuvius** is an authentic, down-home experience just off the Blue Ridge Parkway and along the TransAmerican Bike Route. Enjoy good food (try the fried bologna sandwich), find a bargain among the vintage and antique furniture, and scan the walls covered in signatures for a few famous names. That's the "guestbook," so be sure to add your signature. Gertrude Virginia "Gertie" McPherson, the store's namesake and matriarch, died on March 18, 2017, but her tradition continues.

Captain Joseph Kennedy constructed what is now called **Wade's Mill** (55 Kennedy-Wade's Mill [4 miles west of I-81 at the Raphine exit]; 540-348-1400; wadesmill.com) sometime around 1750, and his family owned it for more than a century. James F. Wade, hence the name, purchased it in 1882, and his family operated it for the next four generations. The 4-story mill is powered by a 21-foot waterwheel from a nearby stream (known originally as Captain Joseph Kennedy's Mill Creek) and is one of the few remaining mills still producing a wide variety of flours on millstones. On your free self-guided tour, you can see all the gears and pulleys used to grind the wheat. It's listed on the National Register of Historic Places. Check for such events as Mike Lund (formerly of Staunton's Zynodoa Restaurant and the incomparable Inn at Little Washington) teaching how to prepare three special spring meals.

Check their website for some mouthwatering recipes that will have you ordering from the catalog immediately, if you don't decide you really want to stop by in person. Admission and parking are free, and dogs are welcome to stretch their legs and have a swim in the creek. Wade's Mill is open Wed through Sun from 10 a.m. to 5 p.m., from Mar 31 through Dec 23. It's closed on Sun from June through Aug, and on July 4 and Thanksgiving Day.

One of the more spectacular sights on the eastern side of the Continental Divide is *Natural Bridge State Park* (6477 S. Lee Hwy.; 540-291-1326; dcr.virginia.gov/state-parks/natural-bridge), the newest Virginia state park. It's more than 100 million years old, 215 feet high, and 90 feet wide. It was surveyed by George Washington in 1750 (you can see his initials carved on the wall of the bridge) and once owned by Thomas Jefferson (he bought it and 157 acres of land from King George III of England for 20 shillings in 1774). The nightly illumination of Natural Bridge is a tradition that started on May 22, 1927, when President Calvin Coolidge pressed the start button for the first time. Henry Parsons explored the caverns in 1889–1891, and when modernization took place, some tools, a ladder, a lantern, and rope were found where they had been left almost 100 years before. The park has 6 miles of hiking trails, including the accessible Cedar Creek Trail that leads from the bridge to the Monacan Indian Village and Lace Falls with its 30-foot cascade. Living history programs explore how previous generations lived. Admission is $8 for adults (13+) and $6 for children (6–12). Open daily from 8 a.m. to 5 p.m.

Fly over Larry Krietemeyer's *Halcyon Days Cidery Company* (4135 S. Lee Hwy.; 540-291-1338; halcyondayscider.com) and you'll notice the 2,500 dwarf apple trees are in the shape of the Chartres labyrinth in France. The tree limbs are trained to create the labyrinth's walls, providing about 2 miles of pathways to stroll so you can "lose yourself to find yourself." The processing plant is located in a renovated dairy barn.

Rockingham County

For a wonderful repurposing story, look to the *Hardesty-Higgins House* (212 S. Main St.; 540-432-8935; visitharrisonburgva.com), or as they say in *Harrisonburg,* it's "Where History and Hospitality Meet." Today it holds the visitor services offices, the *Rocktown Gift Shoppe,* the *Valley Turnpike Museum* (Route 11, or Main Street), the *Harrisonburg-Rockingham Civil War Orientation Center,* and the executive offices for the *Harrisonburg Downtown Renaissance and Harrisonburg Tourism.*

It started life when Dr. Henry Higgins began construction in 1848 and was completed in 1853 by Isaac Hardesty (the city's first mayor). Over the years, it has served as an inn and a showroom for handcrafted-furniture makers, and finally landed in the city's hands in 2001. You can stroll around or "Do Downtown" with a self-guided tour, shopping, something cultural, or dining. It's open daily 9 a.m. to 5 p.m.

One dining option is the *L & S Diner* (255 N. Liberty St.; 540-801-0110) that was opened in 1947, and where they say its pan-fried chicken is the most popular item on the menu. A winning competitor is the Garbage Omelet (need you ask?) with three eggs, cheese, a variety of meats, onions, green peppers, tomatoes, and potatoes. Seems natural, as this is one of Virginia's big poultry centers. If you'd like to stop and try some, the diner is open Mon through Sat from 5:30 a.m. to 1 p.m. Look for the railway car.

Quilting is a favorite pastime, whether for the wonderful historical patterns created over the years, the heirloom quality, or the physical and mental warmth they create, and you can explore all these facets at the *Virginia Quilt Museum* (301 S. Main St.; 540-433-3818; vaquiltmuseum.org). Here, at the largest quilt museum in the state, you'll discover the roles and significance of quilts in American society and be amazed and delighted at the ingenuity, the

Gobble Gobble

Two turkey statues, one at each end of Route 11, welcome you to *Rockingham County,* the top turkey producer in Virginia, signifying the county's status as Turkey Capital. Carl Roseberg was the sculptor and Norwood Bosserman the designer of the bronze sculpture and limestone base. The statues are about 3 feet tall and set on a 5-foot base, and they were dedicated in 1955. Gerald Harris, then a sixth grader, originated the idea, and three of them were made, with the third located at the Elkton High School. Unfortunately, it was stolen by vandals and, apparently, flew the coop permanently.

creativity, and just the beauty of all the quilts on display. You can take lessons, perhaps learn about that beloved quilt that's been handed down in your family for generations, or stop in the gift shop. The museum is open Tues through Sat 10 a.m. to 4 p.m., closed mid-Dec through mid-Feb. Admission is $7 for adults, $5 for students (5–18); the first Fri of the month (Apr through Oct) is free. Group tours are available; please call to reserve a day and time. Closed during exhibit installation periods.

Known as Harrisonburg's "most unusual store," shoppers will find just about everything at this historic **Glen's Fair Price Store** (227 N. Main St.; 540-434-8272; glensfairprice.net) that was opened in 1941. This includes cameras, collectibles, toys, nearly 2,000 costumes (for rent or purchase), nostalgic candy, and slightly disgusting pranks. Whether you're looking for a monkey that doubles as a slingshot, the drinking/dunking bird you had as a child, or a deer business-card holder, if brother and sister co-owners, Gary and Melinda (children of Glen) don't have what you want, they'll find it for you—if it can be found. Open Mon through Fri 11 a.m. to 6 p.m. and Sat 11 a.m. to 5 p.m.

Every interesting town has its independent book store, and **Downtown Books** (49 W. Water St.; 540-433-1155) is that store. They have a "free book" table daily, used books, videos, comic books, CDs, cards, and postcards. Owner Bob Schurtz admits that the organization is "random," so, come, browse, and be surprised at what you find. Open Mon through Fri from 9 a.m. to 6 p.m. and Sat from 9 a.m. to 5 p.m.

The **Daniel Harrison House** (335 Main St.; 540-879-2280; fortharrison va.org) is known also as **Fort Harrison.** The front part of this sturdy stone structure was built about 1748, with the rest of the house constructed in the 1850s. When the nonprofit organization formed by the Harrisonburg-Rockingham Historical Society purchased the property in 1978, the members immediately began restoration, including dismantling and rebuilding the east and west stone walls. Since then, they've painted the interior and exterior, redone the floors, and reconstructed a 19th-century summer kitchen. Some original cedar shingles were found in the attic and replicated. A 1962 electric map that's 13 by 20 feet has been revised with new electronics and bells and whistles (figuratively, anyway). The map, recalling the campaign of 1862, explains how General Jackson delayed the Union forces on their way to Richmond. The house is open Fri and Sat 1 to 4 p.m. from mid-May through Oct, and by appointment.

About 25 miles west of Harrisonburg on US 33, on the Virginia/West Virginia line, is **High Knob Fire Tower** (401 Oakwood Dr.; 540-432-0187; virginia .org/Listings/HistoricSites/HighKnobFireTower) at an elevation of 4,107 feet.

World War I veterans started construction in 1939, and it was completed the following year by men in the Civilian Conservation Corps (CCC). It stopped being used as a fire tower many years ago and was designated a National Historical Lookout in 1994. What's unusual about it is that it was built of rocks while other towers were made of wood or metal. You are allowed to climb the tower and just try to absorb the spectacular views. That's easier said than done, for some people anyway. Park along US 33 (limited availability) and hike about 40 minutes to the tower. You will be going through private property, so please stay on the trail. There was another High Knob Observation Tower farther south in Wise County, a 2-story wooden structure that was destroyed by a Halloween arsonist in 2007. So, if you read a website that says it doesn't exist, make sure you're reading about the right tower.

Among the accommodations available along Skyline Drive, **Skyland** (Skyline Drive mile markers 41.7 and 42.5, Shenandoah National Park; 877-847-1919; goshenandoah.com/lodging/skyland) has the distinction of being located at the Drive's highest elevation: 3,680 feet. Lodgings range from small, rustic cabins to comfortable rooms to newly renovated rooms, some with a fireplace. Pet-friendly (cats and dogs only) rooms are available for an additional $25 fee. Be prepared to slightly disconnect. There's no phone in your room, and cell service depends on your carrier. A gift shop, Mountain Taproom, Pollock dining room, family-friendly nightly entertainment, a constant stream of activities (astronomy, culinary, apple harvest time, etc.), and guided horseback rides (departing from Skyland Stables) are among the attractions, beyond the natural beauty, of course. Open mid-Apr through mid-Nov.

Lexington

The **Virginia Horse Center** (487 Maury River Rd.; 540-464-2950; horsecenter .org) in **Lexington,** said to be the largest facility of its type in the east, is fascinating regardless of how much you know (or don't know) about horses. Every weekend, from spring through fall, there are horse sales, 4-H horse-judging competitions, Grand Prix jumping, dressage exhibitions, breed shows, and much more. There's a covered grandstand with seating from which to watch the events in the main rings, or you can stand around the rail and talk to contestants, participants, or others related in a peripheral or major way. Even when the horses and riders are being led through some basic riding events, you can feel the excitement charging through the audience. A 4,000-seat coliseum allows year-round operation and houses an exhibit area, concession concourse, offices, and meeting rooms.

It may seem strange to see a **Sam Houston Wayside** (73 Sam Houston Way; 540-463-3777; lexingtonvirginia.com) park in Virginia, but he was born in a cabin just north of downtown Lexington on March 2, 1793. As commander-in-chief of the Texas army, he won the battle of San Jacinto, which secured Texas independence, on Apr 21, 1836. He was president of Texas (1836–1838, 1841–1844), US senator (1846–1859), and governor (1860–1861). He died in July 1863. A 38,000-pound piece of Texas pink granite marks the spot at the Sam Houston Wayside. It's open daily, from dawn to dusk. Pets are welcome, and the site is wheelchair accessible.

That delicious aroma you smell comes from the **Cocoa Mill Chocolate Company** (123 W. Nelson St.; 800-421-6220; cocoamill.com), started in 1993. They handcraft their chocolates with premium chocolate, natural flavors, fresh cream and butter, and authentic liqueurs. Chocolates are prepared in small batches because they believe freshness contributes as much to flavor as quality ingredients. Each piece is hand-dipped, hand-decorated, and hand-packed so that careful attention is paid to every detail. During some times of the year—not around Valentine's Day—you can view the operation and then buy your favorites after watching them being made. The store is open Mon through Sat from 10 a.m. to 5 p.m. There's also a store in Staunton.

On display at the **George Marshall Museum** are the Nobel Peace Prize bestowed on Marshall and the Oscar won by General Frank McCarthy, an aide to Marshall, as producer of the movie *Patton*. Also in the museum are exhibits tracing Marshall's life and an electric map tracing the significant events of World War II. The Soldier of Peace Gallery illustrates Marshall's contributions in the post–WWII years, as secretary of state, secretary of defense, and as the head of the American Red Cross. The museum is open Tues through Sat 11 a.m. to 4 p.m. and closed on Thanksgiving Day, Dec 24 and 25, and Jan 1. Admission is $5 for adults, $3 for seniors, $2 for students, free for children 12 and under, active military personnel, and veterans. The museum is located on Virginia Military Institute grounds: 1340 VMI Parade, Lexington 24450. Call (540) 463-7103 or visit marshallfoundation.org for more information.

About 4 miles east of the visitor center, out US 60 E at the **Ben Salem Lock and Wayside Park** (1615 E. Midland Trail; 540-463-3777; virginia.org/Listings/OutdoorsAndSports/BenSalemLockandWayside) are the remains of the James River and Kanawha Canal. Conceived by George Washington as part of the "Great Central American Waterway from the Rockies to the Atlantic Ocean," this was the earliest canal system in the Western Hemisphere. The wayside is a delightful place for a picnic, swimming, fishing, or a quiet afternoon spent watching the waters frolic over the river rocks.

Located just outside Lexington, **Hull's Drive-In Theatre** (2367 N. Lee Hwy; 540-463-2621; hullsdrivein.com) has been part of the community since 1950 and operated initially by the late Sebert Hull and his wife, Effie. In 1999

The Cyrus McCormick Museum

Cyrus McCormick, the inventor of the mechanized reaper, was born in Steele's Tavern. Visit his farm to discover his achievements through a museum, restored blacksmith shop, and gristmill. Spend a few minutes enjoying a picnic. The 634-acre farm, now known as the *Shenandoah Valley Agricultural Research and Extension Center,* is part of Virginia Tech University. The *Cyrus McCormick Museum* (128 McCormick's Farm Circle; 540-377-2255; lexingtonvirginia.com/directory/attractions/cyrus-mccormick-farm) and grounds are open daily from 8 a.m. to 5 p.m., weather permitting.

the drive-in was rescued from closure by a group of community members who formed Hull's Angels and became America's first nonprofit drive-in theater. The mission of Hull's Angels is to sustain the historic Hull's Drive-In Theatre and to serve the community by providing quality, affordable, family entertainment in a safe, clean, and welcoming environment. Run by a group of dedicated volunteers and a few paid staff, Hull's operates not to make a profit but to offer the public a place to gather and enjoy a classic American experience. Weekend nights Mar through Oct, you can catch a double feature movie for just $7 for adults and $3 for children (5–11). Children under 4 are free.

Staunton

Staunton is a year-round destination featuring a historic downtown, and a hip culinary, arts, and music scene. The calendar seems to have a different festival every month, so there's almost always something happening in this vibrant town. Because Staunton (pronounced STAN-tehn or STANT-en) was unscathed during the Civil War, there are plenty of 18th- and 19th-century buildings, many of which have been beautifully restored and preserved. There are six National Historic Districts—Gospel Hill, Stuart Addition, Newtown, Beverly, the Villages at Staunton, and the Wharf District (no, there's no waterfront wharf there; just a reminder that similar warehouses would be associated with a wharf as with the local train station).

Pick up the *Self-Guided Tour of Staunton's Historic Districts* brochure from the visitor center (35 S. New St.; 540-332-3971 or 800-342-7982; visitstaunton .com) and at many downtown merchants.

One of the many highlights in the area is the *Andre Viette Gardens* (994 Long Meadow Rd.; 800-575-5538; viette.com) with one of the largest collections of perennial flowers in the eastern United States, as in "more than 3,000 varieties of rare and unusual perennials, trees, shrubs, and evergreens for the sun and shade." Check his website and you can find where Andre will be lecturing or doing a radio or online broadcast, talking about this and that and the monthly flower, etc. The gardens are open even when the Garden Center is closed. The center is open late Apr through Oct Mon through Sat 9:30 a.m. to 4:30 p.m. and Sun noon to 4:30 p.m.

When you want that perfect Virginia souvenir, visit the ***Virginia Made Shop*** (54 Rowe Rd.; 540-886-7180; vamade.com), which features a wide collection of Virginia products, including peanuts (of course), Wade's Mill pancake mix, Millcroft Farms products, wines, crafts, colonial gifts and accessories, and souvenirs. They do a particularly good Christmas-craft business. Many of the crafts appear more modern than old-timey, but you're likely to find cornhusk dolls, cornhusk flowers, grapevine and pinecone wreaths, and cotton rugs, the best-selling item in the shop. Everything promotes Virginia, and almost everything is made in Virginia except some souvenirs made elsewhere in the United States (they couldn't find Virginia manufacturers for some of these items). Nothing is foreign-made, and about half the artists are from the Staunton area. The shop is open Mon through Sat 10 a.m. to 6 p.m. and Sun until 5 p.m. This shop has been open since early 1984, when then Virginia governor Church Robb started a campaign to buy Virginia products and Terry and Ginger LeMaurier opened this shop.

It's time to brush up your Shakespeare, your Ben Jonson, and your Tom Stoppard at the ***Blackfriar Playhouse at the American Shakespeare Center*** (10 S. Market St.; 877-682-4236; americanshakespearecenter.com) in Staunton. Hoping to duplicate, or go several levels higher than, the annual Shakespeare Festival in Ashland, Oregon, Ralph Cohen has directed the fundraising ($4 million worth) and construction of the world's only indoor replica of the Bard's favorite theater (the Globe was an outdoor theater; the Blackfriar an indoor facility). It's oak, and has wooden benches for about 300 (you can rent a cushion and backrest), and the houselights don't go down when the acting starts so you have a much more intimate relationship with the cast, who can see who the audience is and how they're reacting. And it's jaw-droppingly beautiful. Their American Shakespeare Center on Tour travels the country to visit performing arts centers, universities, and select high schools. The company presents plays and workshops in one-day or week-long interactive residences.

The Blackfriar Playhouse production days and times vary according to the season, so check their website for sales and packages.

On display in the ***Staunton firehouse*** (500 N. Augusta St.; 540-332-3886; ci.staunton.va.us/departments/staunton-fire-rescue/tours) is ***Jumbo,*** a 1911 Robinson fire engine lovingly restored by Billy Thompson's White Post

ANNUAL EVENTS IN THE SHENANDOAH VALLEY

JANUARY

Polar Bear Horse Show
Virginia Horse Center
Lexington
(540) 464-2950
vahorsecenter.org

2019 Wine and Chocolate Pairing Party
Bluestone Vineyard
Bridgewater
(540) 828-0099
bluestonevineyard.com

Martin Luther King Jr. Weekend
Wintergreen Resort
Wintergreen
(434) 325-2200
wintergreenresort.com

FEBRUARY

Historic Staunton Foundation Annual Winter Wine Festival
Stonewall Jackson Hotel
Staunton
(540) 885-7676
historicstaunton.org/hsf-events/
winter-wine-festival

MARCH

Shamrock 5K Trail Run
Hillendale Park
Harrisonburg
(540) 433-2474
harrisonburgva.gov/shamrock-trail-run

APRIL

Virginia Hot Glass Festival
Staunton
(540) 885-0678
sunspots.com

Shenandoah Apple Blossom Festival and Parade
Winchester
(540) 662-3863
thebloom.com

Wildflower Weekend in Shenandoah National Park
Shenandoah National Park
(540) 999-3500
nps.gov/shen

Historic Garden Week
Statewide event includes Harrisonburg, Lexington, Staunton
(804) 644-7776
vagardenweek.org

MAY

New Market Day Parade & Ceremony
Virginia Military Institute
Lexington
(540) 464-7207
vmi.edu

Restorations (Billy died in 2011, but his son and grandson continue the restoration company). The first motorized fire truck of its kind to be used in Virginia, it's also the only surviving fire truck of its kind. Stop by during the day and the firefighters on duty (if they aren't on a call) will show you into the room with the truck and other fire service items, some from the Civil War era; or if you come at night, you can look through the windows. By the way, the station is one of the oldest in the state. Because it cost $143,000 to restore the fire truck, they'll gladly accept donations.

JULY

Summer Jam at Massanutten
Massanutten Ski Area
McGaheysville
(540) 437-3368
massresort.com/play/live-events/
summer-jam/

Happy Birthday America
Gypsy Hill Park
Staunton
(540) 424-4445
happybirthdayamerica.org

AUGUST

Harrisonburg's Annual International Festival
Downtown Harrisonburg
(540) 434-0059 ext. 5
harrisonburg-international-festival.org

SEPTEMBER

Annual Buena Vista Labor Day Festival
Glen Maury Park
(540) 261-7321
bvcity.org/glen-maury-park

OCTOBER

Mountain Day Festival
Buena Vista
(540) 261-1514
celebratebuenavista.wordpress.com/
celebrate-buena-vista-org

Fall Festival at Massanutten
Massanutten Ski Area
McGaheysville
(540) 437-3368
massresort.com/play/live-events/fall-festival

Haunted Harrisonburg Tours
Harrisonburg
(540) 315-4685
facebook.com/HarrisonburgGhostTours

NOVEMBER

Shenandoah Uncorked Wine Festival
American Celebration at Shenandoah
Caverns
Quicksburg
(540) 477-3115
shenandoahcaverns.com/
shenandoahuncorked.html

DECEMBER

Annual Lexington Christmas Parade
Lexington
(540) 319-4181
mainstreetlexington.org

New Year's Eve Glow Run 5K
Harrisonburg
(757) 478-0495
vamomentum.com/nye-glow-run-5k.html

It's said that the *Frontier Culture Museum* (1290 Richmond Rd.; 540-332-7850; frontiermuseum.org) is the only one of its kind in the world. The outdoor museum with 11 permanent exhibits started with four working 19th-century farmsteads. Two of the log cabins were brought to the site from European nations—Northern Ireland and Germany—and the English farm was reconstructed (it couldn't be removed because of English preservation law). It is said that although the countless stones that made up the Irish farmhouse were numbered in place, somehow they multiplied like so many wire hangers, and quite a few were left over after it was reassembled here in the United States.

The fourth farmstead was donated by Phyllis Riddlebarger of Botetourt County, Virginia, and reflects the melding of European influences. Her late husband's grandparents bought the farm in 1884. You can see the adaptations in the German V-notched log barn construction, and the A-frame roofed smokehouse has English derivations. The center is amassing and preserving archival and genealogical collections and artifacts. Historical research, academic outreach, intern programs, and the preparation of appropriate materials and publications play a vital role in the museum programs. West Africans were brought to the American colonies by the hundreds of thousands in the 1600s and 1700s, and now there is a West African Farm exhibit depicting the lives of the Igbo people. Their most notable and enduring contributions to American culture are found in foodways, music, folklore, and religious worship. There's also a 1700s Irish forge, an Early American schoolhouse, and a 1850s American farm.

Guided tours (advance registration) and self-guided tours are available. The museum is open daily 9 a.m. to 5 p.m. mid-Mar through Nov, and 10 a.m. until 4 p.m. the rest of the year. Admission is $12 for adults, $11.50 for seniors, $11 for students (13 through college), and $7 for children (6–12).

Wright's Dairy Rite (346 Greenville Ave.; 540-886-0435; dairy-rite.com) is not the last curb-service (where you order from the speaker on a "Servus-fone" at your parking place) hamburger joint in the state—a few Sonic Burgers offer the same service—but it's probably the most historic. Forester and Alka Wright opened this eatery in 1952 and insisted that only the highest-quality and freshest ingredients be used in the kitchen. The Wrights created a tradition in Staunton that has existed for more than 65 years. To this day Wright's is still family-owned (by son-in-law James E. Cash and Shirley Wright Mckee). While everything's tasty, the onion rings are worth the drive from wherever you are. This is where the Statler Brothers used to hang out and perhaps where they began composing one or more of their songs. Although the '50s have remained here, Wright's now offers free wireless internet service.

Anyone seriously interested in "beyond organic" farming has probably heard of **Joel Salatin** and his **Polyface Farm** ("the farm of many faces") in **Swoope,** just outside of Staunton, where he uses holistic methods of animal husbandry to raise his livestock. He produces salad bar beef, pigaerator pork, pastured poultry, forage-based rabbits, and forestry products. His farming techniques are environmentally responsible, sustainable, and ecologically advantageous. Salatin is the author of numerous articles and books, including *Everything I Want to Do Is Illegal, The Raw Milk Revolution, Folks, This Ain't*

Normal, Holy Cows and Hog Heaven, and *Sheer Ecstasy of Being a Lunatic Farmer.* He also spends a fair amount of time lecturing to college students and instructors, and environmental groups, and he attended at least two TEDx-MidAtlantic conferences.

You are welcome to take a free self-guided tour of the farm (43 Pure Meadows Ln.; 540-885-3590; polyfacefarms.com) Mar 1 through Dec 14, Mon through Sat 9 a.m. to 4 p.m. Two-hour escorted tours may be arranged. Fees vary. If you want to purchase some Polyface products, you can visit the farm Mon through Fri 9 a.m. to noon, and on Sat until 4 p.m. or by appointment on weekday afternoons. From mid-Dec through the end of Feb, the farm store is open only on Sat. Additionally, buying clubs in Virginia and Maryland carry his products, and you can find a list of local stores that do, too, on the Polyface website.

Waynesboro

The historic ***Wayne Theatre/Ross Performing Arts Center*** (521 W. Main St.; 540-943-999; waynetheatre.org) in ***Waynesboro*** opened as a vaudeville house in 1926. As with many theaters, it was closed (in 1999) and was restored and reopened on March 1, 2016. This is a restoration "by the community, for the community, and ultimately is being given back to the community." They are the first theater experience for many students, and, as of 2018, more than 14,000 students have been here for an Arts Education Program. Among the performers who have provided live entertainment is "Carole King: The Soundtrack of a Generation," Bumper Jacksons, Koresh Dance Company, and LIVE @ the WAYNE with Rhythm Road and the Boogie Kings house band. An exhibit gallery is open to the public Tues through Fri 10 a.m. to 2 p.m. and to ticket holders an hour before and during all performances.

Craft food meets craft beer at ***Hops Kitchen*** (1010 E. Main St.; 440-487-9037; hops-kitchen.com; basiccitybeer.com), where they infuse Basic City beer (they're located in the brewery) into most of the items they prepare. The beer, made with artesian spring water and housed in an old brass foundry, is combined with foods from Southeast Asia, Central America, southern Florida, New Mexico, Colorado, Ohio, and, of course, Virginia. Those are the places where head chef Mike has lived and worked. In addition to the brewery, he networks with Sunrise Farms and Purple Cow. Open Sun noon to 8 p.m., Tues through Thurs 3 to 9 p.m.; Fri from 3 to 10 p.m.; Sat noon to 10 p.m. Hops Kitchen has a food truck open Mon through Thurs from 11 a.m. to 2 p.m. for lunch at 2101 W. Main St. They're also located in Richmond at 212 W. 6th St.

Shenandoah County

America's oldest motor inn is located in **Middletown**. The **Wayside Inn** (7783 Main St.; 540-869-1797; alongthewayside.com) has been in operation since 1797, when it was known as Wilkerson's Tavern. It has always been a marvelous place to dine (Larrick's Tavern and 7 dining room options, each with colonial-attired waitstaff) and to stay (with 22 unique rooms and suites). The furnishings make the place an antiques-lover's paradise. Some rooms are said to be haunted and some are pet-friendly. Whether you enjoy a meal in the Lord Fairfax Room or the Old Servant Kitchen (both favorites), a walk through the inn, or an extended stay, you'll always receive gracious Southern hospitality. The tavern and restaurants are closed on Mon. They have karaoke on Wed night and live music on Fri and Sat nights (beginning at 7 p.m.) and some Thurs nights.

Yes, that's a basket filled with apples painted atop the water tower along I-81 as you head toward **Mount Jackson.** Hmm, maybe it should be filled with apple cider instead. Alas, I've not been able to determine what type of apples they are.

For information about the friendly town of Mount Jackson, the Historical District that's listed on the National Register of Historic Places, the Shenandoah Lanes duckpin bowling alley (ca. 1947), the Union Church that was used as a hospital, and the Our Soldiers Cemetery, call (540) 477-2252 or visit mountjackson.com.

Right outside of Mount Jackson and New Market is the **Meems Bottom Covered Bridge,** crossing the north fork of the Shenandoah River, and you can drive through it! It was built in 1893 of materials hewn and quarried nearby and was nearly destroyed by fire in 1976. It was reopened in 1979 and then closed again due to structural problems. It has since reopened. The Mount Jackson community says the bridge is 191 feet long; the Virginia Department of Transportation says it's 204 feet. In any case it's the longest covered bridge in the state and the only one still open for vehicular use. This single-span Theodore Burr truss, built under the supervision of F. S. Wisler, succeeded at least two other bridges. Records show that one was burned in 1862 as Stonewall Jackson went up the valley ahead of General John C. Fremont prior to the battles of Harrisonburg. Another was washed away during a flood in 1870. ("Up the valley" here is southward, since the river flows northward to join the Potomac at Harpers Ferry.)

The bridge, and the adjacent picnic ground on Wisler Road, is easily reached by taking exit 269 from the south or exit 273 from the north off I-81 to Highway 11 and turning west on Route 720. Call (540) 459-2332 or visit virginia dot.org/info/faq-covbridge1.asp for more information.

West of Mount Jackson is **Orkney Springs,** where the summertime **Shenandoah Valley Music Festival** (221 Shrine Mont Circle; 540-459-3396; musicfest.org), one of the outstanding events of its type, is held every summer. Their explanation is "We didn't invent summertime—just the finest way to enjoy it!" First opened in 1962, the festival offers programs that vary from the great masterworks for orchestra to light classical music, lilting pops, vocal music, and big-band sounds. You could not ask for a more beautiful setting in which to hear beautiful music (and it's mountain informal to boot). Concerts are presented rain or shine. Food is available to purchase, or you're invited to bring your own picnic to eat on the lawn before the concert.

It's amazing what a little fame will do, or more important, what a great reputation will do to garner that fame. So goes the story with the **Route 11 Potato Chip Factory** (11 Edwards Way; 540-477-9664; rt11.com). It's been covered in the *Washington Post, New York Times, Winchester Star, Bon Appétit, Gourmet,* and *Southern Living. Today, Good Morning America,* and *The Early Show* have had segments about the yummy products, and perhaps most important, it's been featured on the *Food Finds* show on the Food Network.

Virginia's Country Classic

Winchester's most famous daughter, Virginia "Ginny" Patterson Hensley Dick (Sept 8, 1932–Mar 5, 1963), was buried at the Shenandoah Memorial Park following her plane-crash death in Tennessee. You may know her better as award-winning country singer **Patsy Cline.** A bell tower has been erected here in her memory. Enter the north gate and take the first right to the bench on the left.

Other places of Cline history include her Winchester home, where she married Charlie Dick on Sept 15, 1957; Gaunt's drugstore (1 Valley Ave.), the currently vacant soda fountain and drugstore where she was a waitress in 1950–1951; G & M Music (38 W. Boscawen St.), where she recorded; WINC Radio 520 (N. Pleasant Valley Road), where Patsy often performed; and Handley High School on Valley Avenue, where she attended high school. An exhibit on Patsy's early years is on view at the Winchester–Frederick County Visitors Center (1400 S. Pleasant Valley Rd.). It's open daily, free of charge.

Her home (608 Kent St.; 540-662-5555; celebratingpatsycline.org) has been restored and is open for tours Apr through Oct, Mon through Sat 10 a.m. through 4 p.m.; Sun 1 to 4 p.m. Admission is $8 for adults, $7 for seniors (65+), free for active military with ID. In addition to Patsy Cline Boulevard in Winchester, the 7-mile stretch of US 522 running south out of Winchester is known as the Patsy Cline Memorial Highway. It was dedicated in Nov 1986. For a brochure highlighting Cline landmarks and historic sites, contact Celebrating Patsy Cline, Inc., PO Box 3900, Winchester 22604.

grayandblue

The remains of 2,576 Confederate and 4,500 Union soldiers killed in nearby Civil War battles were laid to rest at the **Mount Hebron Cemetery** (305 E. Boscawen St.; 540-662-4868; mthebroncemetery .org).

They note that they use sea salt (real salt) from an ancient Utah seabed (think Salt Lake) on their lightly salted chips and their sweet potato chips. Some of the many steps they've taken toward a green earth are shipping all potato peelings and chip rejects to a herd of cattle down Route 11, and the used chip oil is sold to a company that roasts their horse feed in it. They also recycle the steam from the cookers to help heat the kitchen, and the list continues.

With increased demand for their chips, they had to either expand or move, so they relocated from Middletown to Mount Jackson in 2008. You're invited to watch them make the chips (the entire process except for the peeling), but you should call if you specifically want to view the frying. There are plenty of samples (you are required to taste some if you're going to watch the frying) and a shop full of goodies to buy. They are open Mon through Sat 9 a.m. to 5 p.m.

Shenandoah Caverns (261 Caverns Rd.; 540-477-3115; shenandoahcaverns .com), part of a "family" of attractions, has a large (really large) elf statue welcoming you to one of the many caverns available for touring in this part of the state. The hour-long guided tour descends a staircase into the 56-degree cavern system (bring a light jacket and comfortable shoes), or you can take the elevator—the only cavern system in Virginia that has one. The caverns open daily at 9 a.m., with the last tour time varying by season. Admission, which includes the caverns, American Celebration on Parade, and the Yellow Barn (the latter

Can You Canoe?

Front Royal, northern gateway to Skyline Drive and Shenandoah National Park, has been officially granted the title *"Canoe Capital"* by the state because of the more than 40,000 people who annually explore the north and south forks of the Shenandoah River. If you want to join them, call the *Front Royal Canoe Company* at (800) 270-8808 (8567 Stonewall Jackson Hwy.; frontroyalcanoe.com). Closed during the winter.

Another canoe, tube, kayak, and raft rental place is *Shenandoah River Outfitters, Inc.* (6502 S. Page Valley Rd., Luray; 540-743-4159; shenandoahriver.com). They also have river cabins and a tent campground. Open spring through fall.

OTHER ATTRACTIONS IN THE SHENANDOAH VALLEY

Boxerwood Nature Center & Woodland Garden
Lexington
(540) 463-2697
boxerwood.org

Camera Heritage Museum
Staunton
(540) 886-8535
cameraheritagemuseum.com

Coyner Springs
Waynesboro
(540) 942-6735
waynesboro.va.us/218/
Coyner-Springs-Park

Edith J. Carrier Arboretum
at James Madison University
Harrisonburg
(540) 568-3194
jmu.edu/arboretum

Luray Zoo—A Rescue Zoo
Luray
(540) 743-4113
lurayzoo.com

Old Town Winchester Splash Pad
(seasonal)
Winchester
oldtownwinchesterva.com/business
-directory/attractions-museums/
old-town-winchester-splash-pad

Shenandoah Valley Art Center
Waynesboro
(540) 949-7662
svacart.com

Shenandoah Valley Folk Art and Heritage Center
Dayton
(540) 879-2616
heritagecenter.com

Skyline Caverns
Front Royal
(540) 635-4545 or (800) 296-4545
skylinecaverns.com

Staunton/Augusta Arts Center
Staunton
(540) 885-2028
saartcenter.org

Strasburg Museum
Strasburg
(540) 465-3175

Virginia Beer Museum
Front Royal
(540) 313-1441
facebook.com/VABeerMuseum

two are open seasonally), is $25 for adults, $22 for seniors (62+), and $13 for children (6–12). AAA and military discounts are available.

Another attraction at Shenandoah Caverns is the *American Celebration on Parade* (397 Caverns Rd.; 540-477-4300). Here you can see, pose by, and even climb on some of the most extensive and glorious parade floats that have graced such events as the Presidential Inaugural, Mardi Gras, Rose, Miss America Pageant, and Thanksgiving parades. You are guaranteed to be amazed at their beauty, complexity, and size. They come from the shop of Hargrove,

Inc., a Maryland company that started in the 1940s. The company has been decorating the National Christmas Tree in Washington, DC, since the Pageant of Peace was established in 1954, and some of the lights and decorations from the trees are included in the holiday exhibit. The 40,000-square-foot facility has changing exhibits, and the Shenandoah Jubilee singers perform about a dozen concerts a year at the facility.

A night at the *Hotel Strasburg* (213 Holliday St.; 540-465-9191 or 800-348-8327; hotelstrasburg.com) in *Strasburg* is like stepping back in time to the 1890s. The hotel combines Victorian history and charm to make a special place for lodging and dining. Tastefully decorated with many antique pieces of period furniture and an impressive collection of art, the inn's dining rooms and quaintly renovated sleeping rooms invite you to wander through them. Do arrive early so that you can peek into the rooms to view the varied quilts and furniture pieces. There are no elevators and no dedicated staff to take your luggage to your room; that means a steep set of stairs to navigate, so pack light.

Not as old as the Wayside Inn, the *Wyndham George Washington Grand Hotel* (103 E. Piccadilly St.; 540-678-4700; wyndhamhotels.com/wyndham-grand) has nonetheless been around for more than a century. This *Winchester* establishment has old-time charm and luxurious amenities that make you feel like you're staying at the country home of wealthy and genial friends. The stately Georgian Revival building has an indoor pool (looks like a Roman bathhouse), fine dining at George's Food & Spirits, and your favorite beverages at the Half Note Lounge, where there's live entertainment on weekends. A spa relieves your sightseeing tensions or lets you energize for the day, and your stay in one of the 90 rooms and suites are comfy enough to entice you to extend your stay.

So much has changed at the *Shenandoah Valley Discovery Museum* (19 W. Cork St.; 540-722-2020; discoverymuseum.net) since the last edition of this book. It's as if someone waved a magic wand and said abracadabra! First, it moved into a new facility, and then they created entirely new and different exhibits. The three levels offer permanent and temporary exhibits, including the Pollinator Plaza, Air, Apple Packing Shed (this is apple country), Health Works, Roller Coaster Alley, Moccasin Trail, and the Musical Garden. They're geared for interactive adult/child enjoyment. Open Tues through Sat from 9 a.m. to 5 p.m. and Sun from 1 to 5 p.m. Admission is $9 for ages 2 and up, except it's free on the first Fri of each month from 5 to 7:30 p.m. The museum store is almost as much fun as the museum, with items starting at 75 cents. Look for science kits, art kits, wooden puzzles, and more. The third floor is the place for special outdoor programs.

Places to Stay in the Shenandoah Valley

BERRYVILLE
Waypoint House Bed and Breakfast
211 S. Church St.
(540) 955-8218
waypointhouse.com

HARRISONBURG
Hotel Madison
710 S. Main St.
(540) 564-0200
hotelmadison.com

LEXINGTON
Shenandoah Manor Bed and Breakfast
325 Union Run
(612) 221-1140
shenandoahmanorbandb
.com

NATURAL BRIDGE
The Inn at Forest Oaks
20 Houston Tavern Ln.
(540) 291-1005
theinnatforestoaks.com

STAUNTON
Stonewall Jackson Hotel & Conference Center
24 S. Market St.
(540) 885-4848
stonewalljacksonhotel.com

WAYNESBORO
Iris Inn
191 Chinquapin Dr.
(540) 943-1991
irisinn.com

WHITE POST
L'Auberge Provençale
13630 Lord Fairfax Hwy.
(540) 837-1375 or
(800) 638-1702
laubergeprovencale.com

WINCHESTER
Old Waterstreet Inn
217 W. Boscawen St.
(540) 665-6777
oldwaterstreetinn.com

Places to Eat in the Shenandoah Valley

BERRYVILLE
The Berryville Grille
9 E. Main St.
(540) 955-4317
theberryvillegrille.com

BUENA VISTA
Kenney's
1518 Magnolia Ave.
(540) 261-2592

FRONT ROYAL
Blue Wing Frog
219 Chester St.
(540) 622-6175
bluewingfrog.com

HARRISONBURG
Food.Bar.Food
126 W. Bruce St., Ste. 101
(540) 433-3663
foodbarfood.com

LEXINGTON
Carson's Food and Drink
362 E. Main St.
(859) 309-3039
carsonsfoodanddrink.com

LURAY
Moonshadows Restaurant
132 E. Main St.
(540) 743-1911
moonshadowsonmain.com

MCGAHEYSVILLE
Thunderbird
42-A Island Ford Rd.
(540) 289-5094
thethunderbirdcafe.com

NATURAL BRIDGE
Pink Cadillac Diner
4347 S. Lee Hwy.
(540) 291-2378
pcdinerva.com

STAUNTON
Depot Grill
42 Middlebrook Ave.
(540) 885-7332
depotgrille.com/staunton

Kathy's Restaurant
705 Greenville Ave.
(540) 885-4331
kathys-restaurant.com

Zynodoa
115 E. Beverly St.
(540) 885-7775
zynodoa.com

WAYNESBORO

Farmhaus Coffee Co.
908 W. Main St.
(540) 941-1550
farmhauscoffee.com

WINCHESTER

Bonnie Blue
334 W. Boscawen St.
(540) 686-7490

Virginia Mountains

Bath County

This is Bath County, where the population boasts that there are no traffic lights in the county, no billboards (there are advertising signs on the roads, but no "billboards"), and, because the weather is cool enough, no mosquitoes. I must admit that, in traveling through this area, I have never met a mosquito in Bath County. What Bath has to offer is lots of pretty scenery, some of the oldest rock formations known to geology, and a few pleasant ways to spend some time.

Bath County may be best known for ***The Omni Homestead*** (7696 Sam Snead Hwy.; 540-839-1766 or 800-838-1766; theomnihomestead.com) at ***Hot Springs***, one of those venerable resorts dating back for what seems forever. Actually, they celebrated their 250th birthday in 2016, three years after it joined the Omni Hotels & Resorts family (July 1, 2013). It's set on 2,300 acres, offers 2 golf courses, an expansive spa, 4 tennis courts, natural hot springs, swimming pools, falconry, trap, skeet, sporting clays, zip line, skiing, ice skating, horseback riding, carriage rides, stream fishing, children's activities, and countless other amenities. If you haven't visited in a while, they

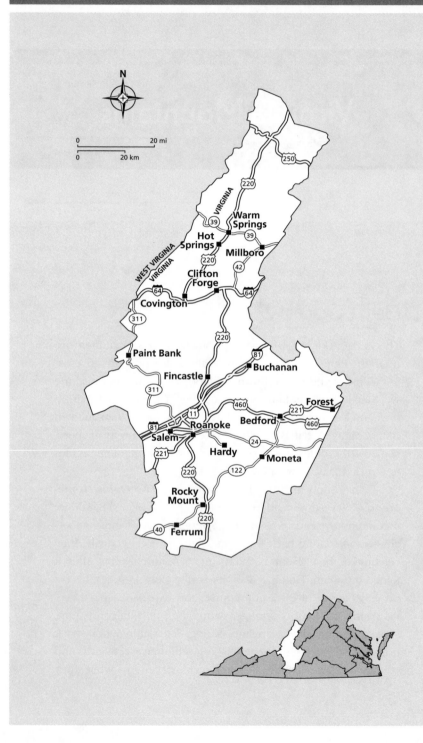

added water slides and a lazy river in 2012, and they now have hayrides and make s'mores at the fire pit on the lawn. They have a grand Easter egg hunt on the lawn with about 10,000 eggs. They also now have a chef's garden and a bee apiary (added in 2017).

Playing golf in this area can be devastating to your ego. The courses are tough, but some people say it's the magnificent view (which tends to add a few strokes to your average score) that's so distracting to your concentration.

Although not inexpensive (no one would expect it to be), you can sometimes book packages—such as golfing, spa, or skiing—that will reduce the overall price. As can be expected, fall foliage is a busy time, and you can have trouble getting a shadow in this place without prior reservations.

Garth Newel (Welsh for "new house") **Music Center** (403 Garth Newel Ln.; 540-839-5018 or 877-558-1689; garthnewel.org) in Hot Springs is Virginia's only center for studying and performing chamber music. Between Warm Springs and Hot Springs, on 114 acres, with the Allegheny Mountains as a background, you can hear concerts featuring string quartets or a piano trio or sometimes as many as an octet.

Check their website for a concert schedule, cuisine activities, and lodging options. Several spring and fall holiday music weekends are scheduled, and guests can stay for the entire weekend or may obtain lodging elsewhere in the vicinity. Reservations are sometimes made up to a year in advance, particularly for Thanksgiving weekend, but they definitely should be made at least two months ahead.

Movie buffs might find the hills familiar looking because Jodie Foster and Richard Gere filmed *Sommersby,* a movie about the struggles of a couple following the Civil War, in these beautiful Allegheny Mountains.

On one of my exploratory trips, I took off from Hot Springs toward West Virginia on Route 39, a designated scenic byway, and just marveled at this pristine area. A tape of Vivaldi's *The Four Seasons* (what else?) was cranked up fairly high to serenade the woodland creatures through the car's open windows, whether or not they wanted to be entertained. There was no one else on the road for miles. In fact, other than the road, there was barely a sign that a human had happened by this way.

Suddenly, as though from a scene from the movie *Close Encounters of the Third Kind,* I turned a corner, and stretched out below me were the workings and company town of Virginia Power's **Bath County Pumped Storage Project.** As I recall, there were about 3,000 people working on this facility. There was on-site housing for 1,000. This meant that another 2,000 were commuting daily, some from as far as 90 miles away. I must have just missed rush hour.

It was my introduction to the pump storage concept. Virginia Power (now Dominion Power) took two streams, the Big Back Creek and the Little Back Creek, and dammed both, creating huge reservoirs. During the day, water is released from the upper storage area to the lower storage area via 1,000-foot-high pipes that are nearly 29 feet in diameter. The upper reservoir is 1,262 feet higher than the lower one. Water gushes through the turbines, generating electricity in the world's most powerful pumped storage generating station. When evening and weekends come, the turbines and the procedure are reversed, and the water is sent back up to the original reservoir area.

Why? you might ask. For several reasons. One, the procedure works as both a flood- and drought-prevention program. The water's recycled, so there's no fear of a dry season, and the downstream farmers and residents are assured of a constant supply of water and power. The only water loss is from evaporation. Second, it's a relatively inexpensive means of power generation. Approximately 1 kilowatt is lost (in the return water process) for every 4 generated. This station provides power to 750,000 homes in Virginia.

You can visit the pump station, but you can't use the two lakes because they can fluctuate in level up to 60 feet in a short time. There is, however, a 325-acre recreational lake, a 30-site RV campground, a group/family picnic shelter, a sandy beach with swimming area and bathhouse, a hiking trail, and other recreational facilities. The campground doesn't have individual electric hookups (I've always thought that strange), but there is a comfort station with hot-water showers, flush toilets, and a dumping station.

A stocked trout stream, also occupied by smallmouth bass, is available, and the ponds have largemouth bass (18 inches is about the record), red-eared sunfish, bluegill, and channel catfish enjoying the habitat. There's a charge of $2 per vehicle for day-use activities.

Millboro

Fort Lewis Lodge (603 Old Plantation Way; 540-925-2314; fortlewislodge .com) is a country escape set on a historic 3,365-acre estate in ***Millboro.*** They offer guests an array of outdoor activities including miles of hiking trails through the mountains, bikes and helmets for rides, acres of land to be explored, a wood-fired sauna, outdoor fireplace, star gazing deck, and 3 miles of private river access for canoeing, kayaking, swimming, fishing, or simply relaxing by our swimming hole. Family-owned and operated for over 30 years, Fort Lewis is also a working farm, where fresh produce is grown on property, chickens and pigs are raised, maple syrup is made, and the pastureland is used for a grass fed cattle herd. Mornings and evenings are highlighted by seasonally inspired cuisine served in the historic Lewis Gristmill, followed by a fire in the timber-framed pavilion. The 21 accommodations include 3 "in the round" silo bedrooms, 4 hand-hewn log cabins with stone fireplaces, the main lodge, and 2 private homes. All reservations include a farm-fresh dinner and breakfast. They are a seasonal business and open only from Apr through Oct.

Some of the cabins and campgrounds that surround the oval-shaped Douthat Lake at **Douthat State Park** (14239 Douthat State Park Rd.; 540-862-8100; dcr.virginia.gov/state_parks/dou.shtml) in **Millboro**—as well as the roads, trails, dams, and picnic areas—were built by the Civilian Conservation Corps between 1932 and 1942.

Although (or because) it's off the beaten path, more than 180,000 people visit here annually. The 4,493-acre park has some incredible scenery, 24 trails that cover 43 miles of wooded hiking trails (easy to strenuous), waterfalls, boating, camping, environmental center, sandy beach, swimming, interpretive programs, playgrounds, amphitheater, 4 miles of stream fishing, 50-acre lake (stocked with trout), and a visitor center. Open 6 a.m. to 10 p.m. Fishing is a major activity, with trout stocked twice a week from Apr through Sept. Check at the camp store for fishing permits. Overnight reservations can be made online or by calling (800) 933-PARK.

The **Lakeview Restaurant** (14239 Douthat State Park Rd.; 540-862-8111) in Douthat State Park is one of only three in the state park system, and the view competes with the food. It's been renovated and now has a glass-enclosed porch overlooking the lake, and central heat and air. Generally, the restaurant is open weekends from Easter through Memorial Day and Labor Day through Oct for breakfast, lunch, and dinner; then Wed through Fri for lunch and dinner and weekends for brunch, lunch, and dinner from Memorial Day through Labor Day. Call or check the above website for operating hours. From the screened-in porch, you can see the lake, canoes, paddleboats, and rowboats.

Bedford County

The **Peaks of Otter** (milepost 86, 85554 Blue Ridge Pkwy.; 540-586-1081; peaksofotter.com) overlook the town of **Bedford** (in Bedford County), "The World's Best Little Town" (population about 6,100). Before entering the town you can hike up the 3,875-foot-high Sharp Top, said by Bedford residents to be Virginia's most famous mountain. A stone from the top of Sharp Top was Virginia's contribution to the Washington Monument in 1852. Stop here for astronomy, hiking, live entertainment, birding, spending the night, or enjoy a specialty drink or craft beer at the Peaks Bar & Lounge. The lodge is open weekends only for the winter.

In the middle of the **Bedford City Historical District** is the **Bedford City/County Museum** (201 E. Main St.; 540-586-4520; bedfordvamuseum .org), housed in the 1895 Masonic building on Main Street since 1979. It features two floors of displays, including old photographs, surgical instruments, a 100-year-old wedding dress worn by Miss Anspaugh (daughter of Colonel David Anspaugh), and a Benjamin Franklin printing press used at the *Bedford Bulletin*. The only other press like it is at the Smithsonian Institution in Washington, DC.

The museum's library of historical and genealogical materials is well used by those trying to find their family histories. Special lectures and films are shown in the evening. The library also has a file on the legendary Beale's treasure. There are some who say a treasure (worth about $65 million as of 2010) was buried in a cave near Montvale by a party of adventurers who returned from a trip to the West laden with gold and other valuables "long years prior to the War Between the States." Others say the treasure's been recovered, whereas still others say there wasn't any treasure in the first place. Where was Snopes debunking urban legends when we needed them? The directions to the treasure were left in a sealed box in a Lynchburg bank. When the box was opened, there were three intricate codes describing the treasure and its location. Reportedly, two of the codes have been deciphered, but so far no one seems to have broken the third code. You can come to your own conclusion after looking at the file and checking the maps.

Admission to the museum is free, but a $3 donation is suggested. It's open Mon through Sat 10 a.m. to 5 p.m.

The **National D-Day Memorial** (106 Main St.; 800-351-DDAY [3329] or 540-586-3329; dday.org) was dedicated on June 6, 2001, the anniversary of the battle. It's celebrating the 75th anniversary of D-Day in 2019. Thirty-five Bedford residents went ashore at Normandy, and 21 of them died on the spot or soon after. It's said Bedford, which had a population of about 3,500 at the time, suffered the highest per capita loss of any city in the United States. The sprawling monument sits atop 81 acres at the highest point in Bedford, with a sweeping 360-degree view of the Blue Ridge Mountains and surrounding countryside. It consists of two reflecting pools and an archway with a statue of a soldier titled *The Final Tribute* in the archway. Life-size statues, replicating soldiers approaching the beach, face a story wall that explains the unfolding battle. An education center has exhibits and works on an oral history project and is available for conferences and seminars. The memorial has been overwhelmingly more popular than even its staunchest supporters had imagined. Instead of 150,000 people a year, more than 200,000 had visited in the first months it was open. A gift shop has a variety of D-Day-related items.

If you want to see the invasion pool with water (it's drained during cold weather), schedule your visit from mid-Mar through Dec (call 540-587-3619 to make sure the pool is operating). Other than on days of inclement weather, the memorial is open daily from 10 a.m. to 5 p.m., although it's closed on Mon from Dec through Feb and closed on Jan 1, Thanksgiving Day, and Dec 25. Admission is $10 for adults and $6 for students, $8 for veterans. A combination ticket with Thomas Jefferson Poplar Forest is available.

Most people think of Monticello when they think of Thomas Jefferson, but there's another place he called home—the place he went to when he wanted to get away from the crowds of people who filled his Charlottesville home after his presidency. That place is ***Poplar Forest*** (1542 Bateman Bridge Rd.; 434-525-1806; poplarforest.org), a home he started constructing in 1806 while still in office. It's an octagonal plantation home, set on 4,800 acres, in Bedford County.

You're invited to stroll, hike, or amble along the trails connecting native woodlands, agricultural fields, streams, and historic sites. Events, from historical theater to craft beer and wine tastings, musical performances to academic lectures, are scheduled regularly. Save time to stop by the museum shop where the range of books and other items match Jefferson's range of interest. Guided 40-minute tours, covering such topics as the design and construction of the retreat, his landscaping design, the restoration, and the plantation community, are offered daily Mar 15 through Dec 15 from 10 a.m. to 4 p.m. except Thanksgiving Day. Admission, including a guided house tour and self-guided grounds tour, is $16 for adults, $14 for active military and seniors (60+), $19 for a combo ticket for Poplar Forest and the National D-Day Memorial, and reduced rates for children, students, and AAA members.

Covington

Stop for a moment or more by the ***Humpback Covered Bridge*** (Midland Trail; 540-962-2178; virginiadot.org/info/faq-covbridge5.asp) in ***Humpback Bridge State Wayside Park,*** a graceful, arched span erected in 1835 just west of ***Covington,*** making it the oldest of Virginia's remaining covered bridges. It is said to be the only existing bridge of this type in the country and perhaps in the world, although apparently three of them were originally built within a mile of one another. The bridge received its name because of a rise of 4 feet from the ends to the center. It has no center support. Reportedly, 18-year-old Thomas Kincaid (no, not the "light" painting guy), using an axe as his principal tool, cut the hand-hewn timbers and made the locust pins that join the timbers. No nails were used.

The structure was part of the 200-mile-long James River/Kanawha Turnpike and, when completed, linked the head of bateau navigation on the James

River from Covington with the Ohio River at the Kentucky line. Apparently it was saved from destruction by an unwritten agreement between the Confederate and Union soldiers during the Civil War.

The 100-foot, single-span walled structure over Dunlop Creek carried traffic for nearly 100 years before being abandoned in 1929 and, for nearly a quarter of a century, stood derelict near its then-modern successor. Since 1954 it has been maintained as a part of a 5-acre highway wayside 3 miles west of Covington on US 60. At the wayside are several picnic tables, barbecue grills, and 2 portable toilets. You can wade through the creek for a better, or at least a different, view of the bridge. Several Civil War cannonballs have been found in the creek and along its banks, as both Union and Confederate troops moved across the bridge with cannons. Graffiti artists have used the walls and roof of the bridge as their canvas, but none of the words seems too objectionable, being mostly love notes from the young at heart and the young in mind.

Unlike most other covered bridges in the state, which take a detailed map to find, this one is easy to locate: There are signs off I-64 at exit 3 (the Callaghan Interchange) directing you to the Humpback. You can also get there by traveling west out of Covington for about 3 miles.

Falling Springs (540-962-2178) is a leaping cascade of about 200 feet noted by Thomas Jefferson in his book *Notes on Virginia,* written in 1781. The Westvaco Corporation, which owns the land on which the falls and the wayside are located, completed extensive renovations to the overlook in 1997, so you can more safely stop and enjoy the view. Take your camera and maybe look for some afternoon sun or early-morning mist. It's beautiful. Not far away are two natural areas where you might want to stay awhile.

Thomas M. Gathright Sr., a landowner, farmer, and avid sportsman, and Benjamin C. Moomaw Jr., executive director of the Covington–Alleghany County Chamber of Commerce, championed the cause for the construction of a water-control project on the Jackson River to protect Covington and other downriver communities from flooding. In their honor are **Lake Moomaw and Gathright Wildlife Management Area** (Morris Hill Road; 540-962-2214; virginia.org/Listings/OutdoorsAndSports/LakeMoomawandGathrightDam). The 12-mile-long lake, with its 43.5 miles of shoreline, was created by a dam that is 1,310 feet long and rises 257 feet above the Jackson River bed. The dam's appearance is misleading, particularly if you've seen such monumental projects as Hoover Dam. It's a clay and rock structure that you can drive over, and it looks like just another piece of shoreline. Many people ask, "Where's the dam?" It isn't until you go into the visitor center and see the display and then go outside to the overlook that you realize the water at the dam is 150 feet deep (the lake has an average depth of 80 feet). The visitor center, open daily from 8:30 a.m. to 3:30 p.m., has some interesting information.

The 2,530-acre stocked lake created by the Gathright Dam has year-round boating, boat ramps, lighted docks, water sports, sandy beaches, and fishing with its related activities of camping, picnicking, hiking, and hunting (in season). There are some wheelchair-accessible fishing decks. The area is abundant with wildlife, including bald eagle, white-tail deer, and turkey. You must possess a valid fishing license and a free permit from the Gathright Visitor Center.

Camping in the Gathright Dam and Lake Moomaw area is available in several USDA Forest Service camping areas on a first-come, first-served basis. Furnished cabins are available, and reservations can be made by calling (800) 933-PARK. Obviously, there are some peak times when the whoosh of a dog's wagging tail couldn't squeeze into the campgrounds, particularly during fall foliage time. The Morris Hill camping area (with 55 campsites and a dump site, potable water, and restrooms), about a 45-minute drive from recreational facilities at Lake Moomaw, doesn't always fill up when the leaves are changing.

For additional information write to the James River Ranger District, 810-A S. Monroe Ave., Covington 24426; (877) 444-6177, (540) 962-1138, or (540) 839-2521. The dam and lake are about 10 miles north of Covington. Take US 220 to Route 687, to Route 641, to Route 666, which will bring you to the facilities.

Craig County

In a Craig County valley is the town of **Paint Bank,** nestled between Peter's Mountain and Pott's Mountain, on the banks of Pott's Creek, not too far from Covington and Roanoke. It consists of **The Paint Bank General Store and Gift Shop** (said to have "the most ambitious worms in the county") with the **Swinging Bridge Restaurant** inside, post office, volunteer fire department, mill (with hopes for restoration), hotel, fish hatchery, and the creek. The General Store opens every morning at 8 a.m. with a variable closing time from 3:30 to 9 p.m., depending on the day of the week and month of the year.

In 1907 a train depot was constructed to serve the Norfolk and Western Railway that had just been extended to Paint Bank. The depot has been refurbished and is now available as lodging for hunters, hikers, birders, and others who want to get really off the beaten path. The **Depot Lodge Bed and Breakfast** (thedepotlodge.com) has 5 rooms, each with private bath and a cast-iron freestanding gas stove. Stephen Cutler, a New Yorker, owns the Depot Lodge (540-897-6000 or 800-970-DEPOT) and the General Store (540-897-5000) and sounds really excited about all the improvements to the area.

Rolling, Action!

Should you see the Robert Duvall, Stephen Lang, Jeff Daniels, and Mira Sorvino film *Gods and Generals,* you may recognize the VMI campus because part of the film was shot there in the fall of 2001. Ronald F. Maxwell chose the locale for the 1860s historical movie to shoot two scenes in the life of Confederate general Thomas J. "Stonewall" Jackson (Lang), who taught at VMI for 10 years prior to the war. The first scene is when Jackson is leading the VMI cadets to war in 1861, and the second is when his body was returned 2 years later. *Gods and Generals* is a prequel to Maxwell's 1993 movie *Gettysburg* and is based on the 1996 novel by Jeff Shaara. Duvall portrays Robert E. Lee.

Audie Murphy, the most decorated United States soldier of World War II, died in an airplane crash on May 28, 1971, on Brush Mountain. (Reportedly, there are four Brush Mountains and nine Brushy Mountains in Virginia.) You can visit the **Audie Murphy Monument** placed on the crash site by Post 5311 of the Veterans of Foreign Wars.

The monument's plaque reads:

AUDIE LEON MURPHY

JUNE 20, 1924–MAY 28, 1971

BORN IN KINGSTON, TEXAS. DIED NEAR THIS SITE IN AN AIRPLANE CRASH. AMERICA'S MOST DECORATED VETERAN OF WORLD WAR II. HE SERVED IN THE EUROPEAN THEATRE, 15TH INFANTRY REGIMENT, 3RD INFANTRY DIVISION, AND EARNED 24 DECORATIONS INCLUDING THE MEDAL OF HONOR, LEGION OF MERIT, DISTINGUISHED SERVICE CROSS, AND THREE PURPLE HEARTS.

Franklin County

For information and exhibits about the traditional life and culture of the Blue Ridge and its inhabitants, stop by the Ferrum College's **Blue Ridge Institute and Museum** (20 Museum Dr.; 540-365-4614; blueridgeinstitute.org). The institute's programming has an international reputation. Offered are gallery exhibits and a living-history farm/museum of the day-to-day lifestyle of the German Americans who settled here in 1800.

Look for costumed interpreters cooking meals in an open hearth, baking bread in an outdoor oven, blacksmithing, and doing other house and farm chores. There are educational workshops, audio and video productions, and an annual folk festival. Historical breeds of sheep, chicken, horses, pigs, and cattle are in the farm buildings, and heirloom vegetables are grown in the gardens around the home and farm buildings. If you'd like, you can inquire about participating in visitor programs in which you wear the costumes and take part in the farm activities and village crafts.

The one-day fall celebration at the institute's *Folklife Festival* (fourth Sat in Oct, 10 a.m. to 5 p.m.) shows old customs and competitions, with performers on three stages playing blues, gospel, and string band music. Dozens of artisans show their skills and sell crafts, and antique and contemporary quilts are displayed in the Mountain Comforts Quilt Show. You can also view restored automobiles and farm machines, and you might want to catch the horse pull and coon dog competitions. When you're ready for a bite to eat, try some of the dozens of regional specialties, but don't look for hot dogs or hamburgers.

The museum is open for walk-in visitors Mon through Sat 10 a.m. to 4 p.m. all year, and Sun 1 to 5 p.m. mid-May through mid-Aug. There is no admission charge.

Within the town *Rocky Mount* is the *Depot Welcome Center* (1255 Franklin St., Ste. 112; 540-483-3030; visitfranklincountyva.org), housed in a late 19th-century Norfolk Southern freight station. Local history is explored at the history museum, and music is enjoyed at jam sessions as this is the eastern gateway to the Crooked Road: Virginia's Heritage Music Trail. Glassblowing demonstrations are available at the granary, and other artists occupy the Artisan Center on the Crooked Road.

Hardy

Visit the *Booker T. Washington National Monument* (12130 Booker T. Washington Hwy.; 540-721-2094; nps.gov/bowa/index.htm) in *Hardy,* which memorializes the slave childhood of the man who would educate himself and go on to found Tuskegee Institute in Alabama in 1881. He was an important and controversial leader following the end of the Civil War, and you can see how the tobacco farm looked and worked when Washington was young. A 12-minute introductory video is shown in the welcome center, and you can participate in the interactive exhibit *Born Here, Freed Here.* Visitors are invited to step back in time and experience firsthand the life and landscape of people who lived in an era when slavery was part of the fabric of American life. The cabin, one of several reconstructed buildings on the site, is a replica of the slave cabin that Washington lived in as a child.

Within the grounds are living-history demonstrations during the summer and occasionally some costumed interpretation programs. There is a living-history farm, trails, and a picnic area. The Plantation Trail is a 0.25-mile walking trail through the historic area of the park. Jack-O-Lantern Branch Heritage Trail is a 1.5-mile walk through woods and fields. The visitor center facilities are wheelchair accessible, and the historic area is partially accessible.

Groups of 10 or more can reserve a 30-minute walking tour by contacting the ranger. Open daily 9 a.m. to 5 p.m. (it may be closed during inclement weather), with no admission charge. It is closed on Thanksgiving Day, Dec 25, and Jan 1.

Roanoke

Roanoke (at one time, possibly Rawrenock or Roenoak, an Indian word meaning "white shell beads" or "money") is the largest Virginia city west of Richmond. A huge neon star atop *Mill Mountain,* reportedly the country's largest manufactured star, was erected by the chamber of commerce in 1949. You can see this star from 60 miles away (at least from the air—quite a sight when you're flying into town on a foggy night and 17,500 watts of neon light beam through the mist). It is 88.5 feet high (1,045 feet above sea level) and weighs 10,000 pounds. There are 2,000 feet of neon tubing, and several color combinations are possible. There are two good times to visit the star: first, in the daytime for an overview of Roanoke; second, at dusk, when the star is lit and crackling with electricity. It is illuminated every night until midnight, and it's almost as though Roanoke is saying, "Come on by, we'll leave the star on for you." Webcams have been installed in a lot of interesting places so you can watch eaglets learn to fledge or crabs crawl out of the water, and now there's one to see you wave. Yes, a webcam has been installed on the star. When you're on the overlook, the camera is overlooking you at roanokeva.gov/1687/StarCam. Smile!

Mill Mountain is within the city limits, and it's said to be the only mountain in Virginia, and perhaps east of Phoenix, that's located inside a city. Oh, although statistics just don't seem to be available for an accurate account, it's been said that the best and perhaps the most popular place to propose in Roanoke is at the *Mill Mountain Star* (210 Reserve Ave.; 540-853-1133; (roanoke va.gov/gallery.aspx?PID=218).

The *Art Museum of Western Virginia,* which was the Roanoke Museum of Fine Arts, which was Roanoke Fine Arts Center, which started as the Roanoke chapter of the American Association of University Women, has been active since 1947, accomplishing so many miracles made purely from hard work and willing them so. They have presented shows covering Thomas Eakins, Andy Warhol, Edward Steichen, and from Howard Finster's Mountain Lake folk art workshop. Its home has moved from pillar to post. In 2000, the city granted money and property, and an architectural search was started. Randall Stout Architects, Inc., was selected in 2002, and Georganne C. Bingham was named new executive director in 2003.

It took until September 10, 2005, before ground was broken for the 81,000-square-foot design (16,000 square feet of gallery space) and construction started in May 2006. Two years later, the ***Taubman Museum of Art*** (110 Salem Ave. SE; 540-342-5760; taubmanmuseum.org) opened, honoring US Ambassador to Romania Nicholas F. Taubman and Mrs. Eugenia L. Taubman for their generous gift toward the project. The soaring wings seem to fly off into the mountains, or that's how I see the building. What's your opinion?

Admission is $7 for adults, $6 for seniors (65+), $3.75 for children (5–13). Members are free. The museum is open Tues through Sat 10 a.m. to 5 p.m. (extended to 8 p.m. on Thurs with free admission beginning at 5 p.m.) and Sun noon to 5 p.m.

Among the interesting shops in the downtown area is the ***Historic Roanoke City Market*** (213 Market St.; 540-342-2028; downtownroanoke.org/explore/farmers-market), which is the oldest in continual use in Virginia. A number of local artisans also present and sell their creations here. The produce travels an average of 25 miles, so you know it's fresh! From May through Sept, there's free, family-friendly activities every Sat. The market is open daily from 8 a.m. to 5 p.m., however, many vendors take off Sun, Mon, and Tues so they can plant, pick, or otherwise prepare items for sale, Also, during the growing season, the farmers tend to show up around 7 a.m. and depart by 3 p.m.

Then venture to the ***Center in the Square*** (1 Market Sq. SE; 540-342-5700; centerinthesquare.org) and plan to spend some time here. Within this renovated 1914 warehouse building are 10 dynamic arts and cultural organizations, including the Mill Mountain Theatre (millmountain.org), Roanoke Pinball Museum (roanokepinball.org), O. Winston Link Museum (linkmuseum.org), Roanoke Symphony (rso.com), Science Museum of Western Virginia with the Hidden Butterfly Garden (1 Market Sq. SE; 540-342-5710; smwv.org), Harrison Museum of African American Culture (harrisonmuseum.com), Opera Roanoke (operaroanoke.org), History Museum of Western Virginia (vahistorymuseum.org), Roanoke Ballet Theatre (roanokeballet.org), and Kids Square. More than 400,000 people visit this unique complex annually, about half of whom are schoolchildren. Each component of this facility has its own operating hours, so check the site for what you want to see and do. The Atrium Aquariums and Green Rooftop (floors 6 and 7) are open without charge. The building hours are Mon 10 a.m. to 5 p.m., Tues through Sat 10 a.m. to 5 p.m., and Sun 1 to 6 p.m.

As usual, my favorite is the Science Museum (my high school science teacher, Mrs. Mitchell, would never believe that—surprise!). Whether it's an exhibit called *The Ins and Outs of Anatomy* or summer camp, I want to be there. The museum and butterfly garden are open Tues through Sat from 10 a.m. to 5 p.m., also Mon from June through Aug. Admission starts at $15 for adults; $13.50 for senior (60+), military, youth (6–17) and students; $7.50 for children (3–5).

When it's time to rest your weary bones, consider the *Hotel Roanoke and Conference Center* (110 Shenandoah Ave.; 540-985-5900; hotelroanoke.com), now a Curio Collection hotel by Hilton. Built for $45,000 in 1882 on a 10-acre knoll overlooking the city, it was constructed in the Tudor style, with hand-rubbed English walnut, carved oak, cherry, and ash woods, gaslight chandeliers, and floors polished to shine like glass. Much of the original Honduras mahogany remains, although part of the hotel burned in 1898. Through its history it has celebrated many firsts. It was the first hotel in Roanoke to have bathrooms with a porcelain or zinc tub, and the first sewer line in town ran from the hotel.

Telephones with multiple plugs (so you could move the telephone around the room) were installed in 1931. It also featured closets with lights that turned on automatically when the door was opened, electric fans, full-length mirrors, and running ice water. In 1937 it became one of the first hotels in the world to be air-conditioned. In 1940 Fred Brown, the hotel's chef, created peanut soup, an item that is still on the menu.

Extensive renovations and additions have been done in the past years, and in the entranceway you can see personalized bricks purchased by local citizens

OTHER ATTRACTIONS IN THE VIRGINIA MOUNTAINS

C&O Railway Heritage Center
(seasonal)
Clifton Forge
(540) 862-8653
cohs.org/heritage

Botetourt County Historical Museum
Fincastle
bothistsoc.wordpress.com

Buchanan Swinging Bridge
Buchanan
(540) 254-1212
townofbuchanan.com/attractions/
buchanan-swinging-bridge

Falling Creek Park
Bedford
(540) 586-7682
bedfordtrails.wordpress.com/about

Grandin Theatre
Roanoke
(540) 345-6177
grandintheatre.com

Mill Mountain Zoo
Roanoke
(540) 343-3241
mmzoo.org

Salem Red Sox (seasonal)
Salem
(540) 389-3333
milb.com/salem

Woodpecker Ridge Nature Center
Troutville
(540) 992-2743
dgif.virginia.gov/vbwt/sites/
woodpecker-ridge-nature-center

in a fund-raising effort to help the restorations. Residents of the Roanoke Valley (and others) took furnishings, utensils, accessories, and other memorabilia (either via auction or "otherwise") from the hotel when it was closed in 1989. As the hotel celebrated its 125th anniversary in 2007, the management started hunting for these items, encouraging former visitors to search attics and basements for artifacts illustrating the hotel's historical, social, and economic ties to the Roanoke Valley. Items could be given or loaned for the 125 days of celebration. If you missed the notice or the celebration, you can still contact the hotel if you have items you want to return. The Regency Room, under the leadership of executive chef Stephen DeMarco and chef de cuisine Collin Lloyd is Virginia Blue Ridge's only AAA Four Diamond restaurant. Look for French-inspired Southern cuisine, including crab cakes, peanut soup, and spoon bread. The Pine Room Pub, formerly a World War II officer's club, has craft beers and light snacks.

The *Virginia Museum of Transportation* (303 Norfolk Ave. SW; 540-342-5670; vmt.org), the official transportation museum of Virginia, holds the South's largest collection of steam locomotives, cars, boats, airplanes, and missiles. The exhibits may explain the railroad's part of the circus in America, a composite of rural stations from the last century, and a Norfolk Southern SD-40 Locomotive Cab #1594 that you can climb aboard. There's a gift shop on the premises with railroad memorabilia including hats, goggles, belt buckles, handkerchiefs, patches, pins, recordings, photographs, books, puzzles, train sets, whistles, mugs, decals, and postcards. As much of the collection is outdoors, they suggest (I concur) that you wear comfortable walking shoes and clothing.

The museum is open Mon through Sat 10 a.m. to 5 p.m.; Sun 1 to 5 p.m. It is closed on Easter Sunday, Thanksgiving, Dec 24–26 and 31, and Jan 1 and 2. Admission is $8 for adults, $7 for seniors (60+), and $6 for children (3–11).

What About Bob?

If you're stopping by *Smith Mountain Lake* for fishing, you may realize that this is where the movie *What About Bob?* was shot (with Bill Murray and Richard Dreyfuss). The story goes that the location scout loved the lake but needed a small town next to it. There was no small town next to Smith Mountain Lake, but Virginia Film Commission people took care of that by showing the film crew a nearby town and suggesting that people could drive by on power lawn movers with sail masts attached and bobbing around in the background. The production company bought the idea. So when you next watch the movie, check the shot of Bill Murray with the sail masts "floating" behind him while he's in town.

ANNUAL EVENTS IN THE VIRGINIA MOUNTAINS

JANUARY

Roanoke Regional Writers Conference
Hollins University
Roanoke
(540) 362-6451
hollins.edu

FEBRUARY

Clifton Forge Blues Festival
Clifton Forge
(540) 862-5655
historicmasonictheatre.com

MARCH

Highland Maple Festival
Highland
(540) 468-2551
highlandcounty.org/events/maple-festival

Fierce Films Festival
Roanoke
(540) 343-3241
mmzoo.org/experiences/events

Town of Buchanan Cherry Blossoms
Buchanan
(540) 254-1212
townofbuchanan.com

Inspired Piece Makers Quilt Show
Roanoke
(540) 853-2241
theberglundcenter.com

APRIL

Blue Ridge Marathon
Roanoke
(540) 343-1550
blueridgemarathon.com

Historic Garden Week
Statewide event includes Roanoke
(804) 644-7776
vagardenweek.org

JUNE

Annual Southwest Virginia Antique Farm Days
Rocky Mount
(540) 420-4172
svapf.org

JULY

Reggae by the River
James River
Buchanan
townofbuchanan.com/event/
reggae-by-the-river/

AUGUST

Warren Street Festival
Rocky Mount
(540) 483-8254
facebook.com/warrenstreetsociety

SEPTEMBER

Long Strange Night on the Mountain
Peaks of Otter Winery
Bedford
(540) 586-3707
peaksofotterwinery.com

Olde Liberty Fiber Festival
Bedford
(540) 313-1687
olfibrefaire.com

OCTOBER

Mountain Magic in Fall Bluegrass, Antiques and Crafts Festival
Buchanan
(540) 254-1212
townofbuchanan.com/mountainmagic

NOVEMBER

Buchanan Tree Lighting Ceremony
Buchanan
(540) 254-1212
townofbuchanan.com

Years ago, when I-95 was under construction in Connecticut, someone decided to gather the architecturally interesting aspects of the homes being destroyed for the right-of-way. That included windows, doorways, claw-footed bathtubs, and other items. It started a new enterprise that now includes Roanoke's **Black Dog Salvage,** a business that owners Mike Whiteside and Robert Culp say let's you do the "treasure hunting without the digging." You may have seen them in the TV series *Salvage Dawgs* on HGTV and other cable networks. They save interesting items to preserve history and prevent items from going into a landfill. Ted Ayers, Tay Whiteside, Grayson Goldsmith, Koiner Kulp Thomas, Susan Hudson, and Jeff Ellis make up the bulk of the rest of the genius crew. The aforementioned empire includes the salvage items from buildings around the Roanoke area and beyond (sometimes way beyond). What can't be reused in its original purpose, they repurpose—for example, a door becomes a desk or tabletop. They also have their own line of furniture paints and carry works by local and regional artists and artisans, garden statuary, Black Dog Custom Designs, and other antiques. And, you can shop online if you can't make it to Roanoke. Or, if you have items that can be salvaged, let them know. As if that weren't enough, they've been restoring the Old Stone House next to the main store, and it's available as lodging for up to 6 guests and for private receptions.

The showroom is open Mon through Sat 9 a.m. to 5 p.m., Sun 11 a.m. to 4 p.m. The salvage warehouse is at 629 Ashlawn St. SW, Roanoke 24015. The retail showroom is at 902 13th St. SW, Roanoke 24016. Call (540) 343-6200 or visit blackdogsalvage.com for more information.

Places to Stay in the Virginia Mountains

BEDFORD

Peaks of Otter Lodge
85554 Blue Ridge Pkwy.
peaksofotter.com

BUCHANAN

The Buchanan Rail Car Inn
128 15th St.
(540) 460-1932
buchanarailcarinn.com

CLIFTON FORGE

Red Lantern Inn
314 Jefferson Ave.
(540) 797-5000
theredlanterninn.com

COVINGTON

Cliff View Golf Club and Fly Fish Inn
410 Friels Dr.
(540) 962-2200
cliffviewgolfandflyfishinn
.com

HOT SPRINGS

Winding Ridge Lodge
Gap Road
(757) 723-0644
vrbo.com/404609

MONETA

Bernard's Landing Resort & Conference Center
775 Ashmeade Rd.
(540) 721-8870
bernardslanding.com

ROANOKE

Shirley's Bed and Breakfast
3920 Saul Ln.
(540) 589-5600
shirleysbandb.com

ROCKY MOUNT

Early Inn at the Grove
50 Floyd Ave.
(884) 327-8946
earlyinn.com

WARM SPRINGS

Inn at Gristmill Square
124 Old Mill Rd.
(540) 839-2231
gristmillsquare.com

Places to Eat in the Virginia Mountains

BEDFORD

Olde Liberty Station
515 Bedford Ave.
(540) 587-9377
oldlibertystation.com

BUCHANAN

The Buchanan Fountain and Grill
19752 Main St.
(540) 620-2354

CLIFTON FORGE

The Club Car
525 Main St.
(540) 862-0777
clubcarva.com

COVINGTON

Fudge St. Cafe
109 E. Fudge St.
(540) 962-4700
facebook.com/
fudgestreetcafe

FINCASTLE

Brugh's Mill Country Store
345 Brughs Mill Rd.
(540) 966-4660

FOREST

Carol's Restaurant
15173 Forest Rd.
(434) 525-9181
eatatcarols.com

HOT SPRINGS

Les Cochons d'Or
2829 Main St.
(540) 839-8900
lcdoinc.com

ROCKY MOUNT

The Hub
245 N. Main St.
(540) 483-9303

ROANOKE

Alexander's
105 S. Jefferson St.
(540) 962-6983
alexandersva.com

Carlos Brazilian International
4167 Electric Rd.
(540) 776-1117
carlosbrazilian.com

Coach & Four
5206 Williamson Rd. NW
(540) 362-4220
coachandfour.com

SALEM

Awful Arthur's Seafood
131 S. Main St.
(540) 404-4488
awfularthursseafood.com
also in Roanoke

Mac and Bob's
316 E. Main St.
(540) 389-5999
macandbobs.com

The Pancake House
1840 Apperson Dr.
(540) 389-6549

WARM SPRINGS

Inn at Gristmill Square and Waterwheel Restaurant
118 Old Germantown Rd.
(540) 839-2231
gristmillsquare.com

Blue Ridge Highlands

Bland County

The **Wolf Creek Indian Village and Museum** (6394 N. Scenic Hwy.; 276-688-3438; indianvillage.org) in **Bastian** is a living-history museum, a 24.5-acre re-creation of an American Indian community with a population of about 100 persons that existed nearby approximately 800 years ago. The remains of the original village site came to the attention of state archaeologists in 1969 after highway workers began excavating the area to build I-77. Archaeologist Howard MacCord mapped the area before it was flooded by the rerouting of Wolf Creek, and the catalog of artifacts includes Indian skeletons, signs of 11 wigwams, and several storage pits. The reconstructed village includes wigwams, fire pits, a perimeter fence, and other facilities. Costumed interpreters help you understand the skills that these Indians probably used and how they created their pottery and weavings. A picnic area with 14 tables and grills, a shelter, and hiking trails are available.

Wolf Creek is open Mon through Sat, 10 a.m. to 5 p.m. The admission fee to the museum and the Indian Village is $10 for adults and $6 for children (6–11); a family pass (2 adults and 3–5 children) costs $35. AAA, senior, and military discounts are honored.

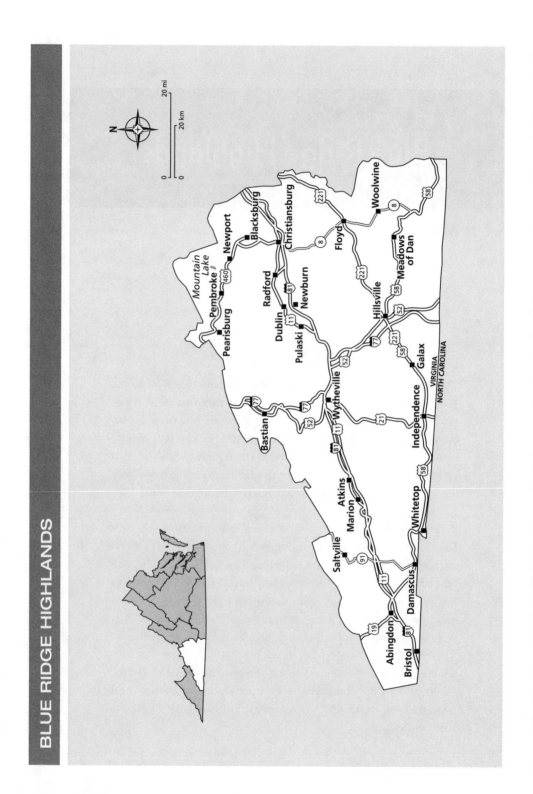

BLUE RIDGE HIGHLANDS

The Bottle House

In 1941 or 1948 (depends on who you ask) pharmacist John "Doc" Hope had a large playhouse (about 15 feet by 25 feet, estimated by the current owner) built for his daughter made out of about 10,000 medicine, wine, and other bottles. I did not realize there are "conventions" about building a bottle house or wall, but apparently there's at least one, and that's the concept of building with both the neck facing outdoors so the inside wall is flat, and building with the necks inward so the exterior is a flat wall. This playhouse is flat inner walls. There's also an "H" (for *Hope*) formed with green bottles on a side wall. The **Bottle House** is on N. Main Street in Hillsville.

Galax

The ***Jeff Matthews Memorial Museum*** (606 W. Stuart Dr.; 276-236-7874; jeff matthewsmuseum.org) in ***Galax*** is housed in two pioneer cabins (one built in 1834). Among the things you'll see are more than 1,000 different knives collected by Matthews; newspapers dating to January 4, 1800, covering George Washington's burial; and 40 mounted heads and animal rugs from other parts of the country collected by Glenn Pless. With today's ever-more-painless dentistry, you might want to notice a collection of old dental equipment from local dentist Dr. Paul Katt, who was still practicing dentistry at the age of 80 when he died in 1988. Among the equipment are his chair, an X-ray machine, and tools of the trade from an earlier generation. A Confederate soldier display in two rooms shows pictures of all the men they could locate from Galax, Grayson, and other nearby towns who fought in the Civil War.

The museum is open Wed through Sat 11 a.m. to 4 p.m. and by appointment. The visit is free, with donations accepted.

funfacts

Word has it that the **Hillsville Diner** (525 N. Main St.; 276-728-7681), established in 1946, was transported from Mount Airy, North Carolina, to Hillsville, and that a young Andy Griffith either worked or visited there (when it was in Mount Airy, of course). It is also said to be the "oldest continuously operating streetcar diner in the state." Open Mon through Sat 5 a.m. through 2 p.m. (except Sat, when it's open only until 11 a.m.)

Floyd County

The **Floyd Country Store** (206 S. Locust St.; 540-745-4563; floydcountrystore .com), "a great little country store in the Blue Ridge Mountains of Virginia,"

All Roads Lead to Floyd . . . or Away from It

If you're looking for a particular place in the town of Floyd, directions will start with "Begin at the stoplight" in the center of town at the intersection of Route 8 and Route 221. You should also note that there's no turn on red. If you go north on Route 8, you're aiming toward I-81 and Christiansburg. Go south and you head toward Stuart. Go west on Route 221 to I-77 toward Galax, or east toward the south side of Roanoke. Because they are all long and winding roads, you need a good map, a GPS system, or a sense of adventure, because using the sun for a compass just won't work.

has a Friday Night Jamboree, where, at 7 p.m., folks bring their banjos, fiddles, guitars, and harmonicas, their old-timer's memories, and the music of Floyd County. The store is open Mon through Thurs 10 a.m. to 5 p.m., Fri until 10:30 p.m., Sat to 8 p.m., and Sun 11 a.m. to 6 p.m.

Giles County

Near Newport, in Giles County, are two of the six (some references say seven) remaining *covered bridges* (Sinking Creek and C. K. Reynolds) that are accessible to the public in Virginia. There used to be more than 100 covered or "kissing" bridges. These are modified William Howe truss bridges (in 1840 he combined iron uprights with wooden supports, creating the forerunner of the steel bridge) and cross Sinking Creek. The first is a 55-foot bridge, which used to be along the Appalachian Trail near Route 700 (Mountain Lake Road) but was bypassed by a realignment of the trail. The bridge was left in place so that the property owner could use it when a new bridge was built in 1949. The second, a 70-foot span, was left in place when a new bridge was constructed in 1963. The bridge indicates it was constructed in 1912; the state says circa 1916. For more information call (540) 921-5000 or visit virginia .org/coveredbridges.

The *George Washington and Jefferson National Forests* (540-265-5100; nationalforests.org/our-forests/find-a-forest/george-washington-and -jefferson-national-forests) blanket 1.8 million acres across Virginia, West Virginia, and Kentucky, and an entire book could be compiled on the various trails and activities within the system. As a sampling I'll use the part of the forest in the area around Giles County that is supervised from the New River Valley ranger district. Among the activities is a 2-mile hike to view the *Cascades,* a spectacular 60-foot waterfall. The approach is via **Little Stony Creek** (stocked with trout), past a steam boiler from an old sawmill (1918–1922) and an awesome look at **Barney's Wall** (a sheer bluff rising from the creek bed to a height of 3,640 feet) from the bottom of the bluff. The hike along this easy-to-moderately-difficult trail should take 3.5 hours (round-trip). You can purchase maps of recreation areas, illustrated trails, Appalachian, Ramseys Draft Wilderness, St. Mary's Wilderness, and Lake Moomaw , in the George Washington and Jefferson National Forests, online and at various retail stores.

Farther up Route 700 in **Pembroke** is the **Mountain Lake Conservancy and Hotel** (115 Hotel Circle; 540-626-7121 or 800-346-3334; mountainlakehotel .com), which has been catering to summer visitors for years. Although former manager Joseph "Mac" McMillin used to say that people would tell him they or their relatives stood on the fire line fighting the blaze that destroyed the old (1850s) wooden structure, in fact it was torn down and rebuilt in 1936 with stone cut from the property. Even if you have never visited **Mountain Lake,** you may feel you know the place, for it was featured in the 1986 movie *Dirty Dancing,* with Patrick Swayze and Jennifer Grey. Word has it that they were fighting Mother Nature toward the end, with crew members spraying the turning autumn leaves with green paint. Apparently, a British reality show, *Dirty Dancing: The Time of Your Life* and a documentary entitled *Seriously Dirty Dancing* were also shot at the resort.

In honor of those films, a Dirty Dancing Weekend is scheduled periodically and includes tours, lessons, and a dance. The dining room offers gracious service, a pleasant house wine, and fairly good food. Of course, after a day of fresh air and exercise, anything is likely to taste good. About 25 non-hotel guests can be seated in the dining room, but reservations are essential.

Mountain Lake is said to be the highest lake in Virginia (4,000 feet) and the highest inhabited mountain in the state. Activities abound, including an adventure center a mile from the lodge

coolwaters

Mountain Lake (near Blacksburg), one of only two natural freshwater lakes in Virginia, was formed when a rock slide dammed the north end of the valley. Debris of organic matter filled around the rocks to form a watertight seal. The lake is fed by underground streams that rarely allow the water temperature to rise above 72 degrees. Lake Drummond in the Great Dismal Swamp is the other natural lake in Virginia.

where you can participate in a sky slide, archery tag, bubble ball, treetop adventure course, and Zorb racing. Photography is marvelous all year, with wild azaleas and rhododendrons in spring, blazing leaves in fall, and crystal snow scenes as winter starts its visit.

Up from Mountain Lake is ***Minie (or Minnie) Ball Hill,*** a great place to find Civil War souvenirs. According to legend, General George Crook, pressed by Confederate troops and bogged down by muddy trails, was forced to abandon an extra weight of ammunition and perhaps even a cannon full of gold (which some say is at the bottom of Mountain Lake). Lead bullets, or "minié balls," left behind on May 12, 1864, are still found by those who search this area. Actually, minié balls do not refer to size, but to French army captain Claude Étienne Minié, who developed the bullet-shaped projectile that could be shot from the muzzle-loading rifle.

Grayson County

West of Galax is ***Independence,*** the Grayson County seat. There, at the ***1908 Courthouse*** (107 E. Main St.; 276-773-3711; historic1908courthouse.org) is the art and cultural center of Grayson County. The former county courthouse also houses the ***Vault Museum,*** formerly the court clerk's vault room, and has a display of an early mountain home, barn, and blacksmith shop, complete with tools and farm implements. There's also the Grayson County Tourist Information Center and an arts and crafts shop featuring Grayson County artists and artisans. The building is open from Mon through Fri 10 a.m. to 4:30 p.m. and until 4 p.m. on Sat.

It's hard to believe that it's been almost two decades (Oct 6, 2001) since the $5.2 million ***Blue Ridge Music Center*** (700 Foothills Rd.; 276-236-5309; blueridgemusiccenter.org), an outdoor stage and amphitheater just off the Blue Ridge Parkway and about 12 miles east of Galax, enjoyed its first concert. Located at milepost 213 on the Blue Ridge Parkway, an interpretive center helps preserve, interpret, and present the unique American music tradition of the Blue Ridge Mountains. The interactive exhibit *Roots of American Music* opened to huge fanfare over Memorial Day weekend in 2011. The complex includes an interpretive center and a 2,000-seat hillside amphitheater, picnic facilities, and a luthier shop (people who make or repair stringed instruments).

Independence

Located 15 miles west of Galax, the town of *Independence* came into being in 1850 over a dispute between residents of two towns about where to locate the county seat. In a Solomonesque decision, adjacent county commissioners chose a site favored by a group of "independents."

The visitor center is open daily from 9 a.m. to 5 p.m. from late May through Oct and Thurs through Mon in late May.

Montgomery County

To learn about the political, geological, and natural history of this area, head to **Blacksburg** and stop at **Virginia Tech,** home of the Hokies. There are a number of interesting places to see, the first of which is **Smithfield Plantation** (1000 Smithfield Plantation Rd.; 540-231-3947; smithfieldplantation.org). When Colonel William Preston constructed it back in 1772, it would have been difficult to predict the influence he would have on the area. Let it suffice to say that the Preston family was a founding family of Blacksburg and Montgomery County. William Preston, born in 1730, arrived here from Ireland in 1738 and served in the militia in the French and Indian and Revolutionary Wars. He then went on to serve in the House of Burgesses, representing several different counties. He built Smithfield in the Tidewater Plantation style and named it in honor of his wife, Susanna Smith.

The plantation is open for tours (beginning on the hour, with the last tour starting at 4 p.m.) with costumed interpreters Apr 1 through the first week of Dec on Mon, Tues, Thurs, Fri, and Sat 10 a.m. to 5 p.m.; Sun 1 to 5 p.m. Admission is $8 for adults, $5 for students (13–23), and $4 for children (5–12).

Driving through this country could stir your interest in the earth sciences, and, fortunately, Virginia Tech has a **Museum of Geosciences** (2062 Derring Hall, Virginia Tech; 540-231-6894; geos.vt.edu/museum-of-geosciences .html) to satisfy your curiosity. Included in its collection is a full-scale model of an allosaurus (a huge carnivorous North American theropod dinosaur of the Later Jurassic period, about 150 million years ago), the OmniGlobe, gemstones, rocks, and fossils. And if that means nothing to you, just check with the

Go with the Flow

The **Eastern Continental Divide** runs through the Christiansburg and Blacksburg areas. All the water to the east of this divide flows through the Roanoke River into the Atlantic Ocean. The water to the west runs into the New River and eventually to the Ohio and Mississippi Rivers and on to the Gulf of Mexico before spilling into the Atlantic. Look for where the New River (which runs south to north, by the way) has etched through limestone, leaving spectacular towering formations hundreds of feet tall.

children; they're sure to know. It also has a seismograph and the largest display of Virginia minerals in the state.

The museum is open Mon through Fri 8 a.m. to 5 p.m. during spring and fall academic semesters, and there is no admission fee.

The **Oaks Historic Bed-and-Breakfast Country Inn** (311 E. Main St.; 540-381-1500; theoaksvictorianinn.com) is the focal point of the E. Main Street Historic District in **Christiansburg**. Construction began in 1889 and was completed in 1893. Modern bathrooms and other amenities have been added, and the original floor plan and elegant interior have been carefully restored and preserved. Look for "inn-dulgences" where you can choose a romance package with champagne and fresh flowers awaiting your arrival or have your bed draped in silk rose petals.

virginiatrivia

In May 1808, Thomas Lewis and John McHenry were involved in the first duel with rifles known to have taken place in Virginia. Both men died. This duel led to the passage of the Babour Bill in January 1810, which outlawed dueling in the state. Dr. John Floyd was the attending physician and later went on to become governor of Virginia and a member of Congress. A marker in Christiansburg at Routes 11 and 460 designates the site of the duel.

The history of a place helps us see how the people of today arrived here and understand what they think, how they act, and where they're going. A good place to visit is the **Montgomery Museum of Art and History** (300 S. Pepper St.; 540-382-5644; montgomerymuseum.org). It focuses generally on southwestern Virginia, particularly Montgomery County, and the works of primitive and 19th-century country folk artist Lewis Miller as well as contemporary art displays. There's also a genealogical research area. The museum is housed in a mid-19th-century Presbyterian church manse of American and Flemish bond brick, made with local materials and hand-hewn oak beams and rafters.

Admission is free to members. Open Tues through Fri 10:30 a.m. to 4:30 p.m.; Sat 1 to 4 p.m.

Bristol

Going south out of Abingdon, you come to **Bristol**, the "twin cities" whose State Street is the dividing line between Tennessee and Virginia. The famed BRISTOL—A GOOD PLACE TO LIVE sign, with arrows pointing to the Virginia and Tennessee sides of State Street, is right outside the train station.

With the thought of observing a solar eclipse on Aug 7, 1869, an astronomical observatory was built on the highest piece of land in the Bristol area where a near total eclipse was predicted. Thought to be an ideal residential neighborhood, the area was named **Solar Hill** (276-669-6457; solarhill.tri pod.com), and the street running along the top of the hill was named Solar Street. The area reached its peak in the early 1900s. Many homes are huge, representing "one of the finest collections of historic residential architecture in the region," and date from the 1800s to early 1900s. You'll see colonial-, Victorian-, Neoclassical-, and Craftsman-style homes. In 2001 it became the first Bristol neighborhood listed on both the Virginia Landmarks Register and the National Register of Historic Places. The Solar Hill Historic District Association was formed in 2003 to provide improvements that include replacing sidewalks, installing decorative post street lights, burying overhead cables, erecting a gateway monument, installing historic markers and landscaping, and offering walking tour maps. Peter Lawrie, grandson of sculptor Lee Lawrie (designer of the *Atlas* statue in Rockefeller Center in New York City), was named the architect for the monument. You can download a walking map tour on the Solar Hill website.

The **Birthplace of Country Music Alliance Museum** (BCMA; 101 County Music Way; 423-573-1927; birthplaceofcountrymusic.org) is based in Bristol, where it focuses on the history of country, bluegrass, and other music that's such a vital part of this area, its influences, and how it has affected the local and national population. The BCMA works to help preserve and promote this musical heritage by showing historically significant artifacts and teaching about the history of country music. Rotating exhibits from guest curators and other institutions (including the Smithsonian) are featured throughout the year. Although there's information from colonial days, it mostly concentrates on the period starting in 1927 through the mid-1970s.

It's "From Bus to Brew" at the Bristol Station Brews & Taproom (41 Piedmont Ave.; 276-608-1220; bristolbrew.com), a 1937 Greyhound bus depot that now serves up brews. Ken Monyak, owner of the transformed brewery, displays a colorful map showing Greyhound bus routes, bus signs, and a waitress uniform on the walls. Look for original woodwork, a skylight, and the area where the phone booths were (the popcorn machine is there now). The original schedule board is still in use to announce new brews. Monvak brings in food trucks so you can eat while you drink. It's a historic landmark.

Patrick County

One of the six (or seven) **covered bridges** remaining in Virginia (there were more than 100 by the early 1900s) are found in Patrick County, named for Patrick Henry. There were two until the **Bob White Bridge**, an 80-foot Theodore Burr–style bridge over the Smith River near Route 8, south of Woolwine, was washed away in a storm on Sept 29, 2015. It was constructed in 1921 and served as the main link between Route 8 and a church on the south side of the river. It was used for more than a half century before it was replaced by a newer bridge. Although it is called *Jack's Creek Bridge,* another covered bridge straddles the Smith River on Route 615, just west of Route 8, about 2 miles south of Woolwine. You can see this 48-foot span from Route 8, where it intersects with Route 615, or travel about 0.2 mile west on Route 615.

As an effort to preserve and promote the bridges, a covered bridge festival was started in 2005. The June event is in *Woolwine,* with live bands, artists and crafters exhibiting and selling, food vendors, and carriage rides between the Jack's Creek Bridge and the site of the former Bob White Bridge. For more information call (276) 692-7949 or visit visitpatrickcounty.org.

Nancy's Candy Company, in business for 30 years, has stores in Salem, Floyd, and *Meadows of Dan,* and in the latter location you can see (through viewing windows) how chocolate is molded into sweet morsels of smooth, velvety candy and watch fudge being made. Skilled craftspeople and candy-makers take special care to ensure quality and superior confections. There are at least 45 different flavors of fudge made daily and 60 varieties of chocolates on display, ready for you to sample. Can you even imagine a half-pound Grand Marnier truffle? Nancy's has it. Call ahead to request a "chocolate talk" and candy-making video presentation. Open Mon through Sat 10 a.m. to 5 p.m., and Sun 1 to 5 p.m. with extended hours in Oct. The factory and outlet store is at 2684 Jeb Stuart Hwy., Meadows of Dan. For more information call (276) 952-2112 or (800) 328-3834, or visit nancyshomemadefudge.com for more information.

Pulaski County

A mile or less off I-81 and away from the rush of today's traffic is *Newbern,* a town from yesterday. The entire 1-mile-long linear town, basically located on the Olde Wilderness Road, was declared a historic district in 1979. The land was granted to early settlers by King George III in 1772, and it was founded as a town in 1810, acting as the Pulaski County seat from 1839 to 1893. At an altitude of 2,135 feet, the town, with its beautiful sunsets and surrounding mountains, reminded the settlers of Bern, Switzerland.

Daisy Williams, born in 1905, was a major force in bringing the past to our present in the form of the *Wilderness Road Regional Museum* (5240 Wilderness Rd.; 540-674-4835; wildernessroadregionalmuseum.com) in *Dublin,* which covers Floyd, Giles, Montgomery, and Pulaski Counties and the city of Radford. It includes rooms furnished in period style and several outbuildings.

A log kitchen has been constructed behind the museum, on its original foundation. The museum committee is always looking for such artifacts as paintings, letters, photographs, and documents from 1810 to 1865 to further document the growth and development of the area. The museum is open from Tues through Sat 10:30 a.m. to 4:30 p.m.

The historic district contains original log and wooden buildings, including a jail, hanging house, store, churches, private residences, and an inn that served as a stagecoach stop. You also can see the waterworks, a slave-built flagstone sidewalk, a pre–Civil War church, the community center, and other points of interest. The original *Newbern Reservoir,* constructed in 1870, also remains. The water system, more than 110 years old, is still intact, and a piece of the original pipe is shown as part of the reservoir display. Various fires destroyed the courthouse in 1893, the Methodist church in 1912, and 11 of the original houses in 1924, but 26 of the original log or wooden buildings constructed between 1810 and 1895 still stand.

A walking-tour brochure about Pulaski County and Newbern (listing accommodations, restaurants, campgrounds, entertainment, a calendar of events, maps, tours, and attractions) is available from the Pulaski County Chamber of Commerce (4440 Cleburne Blvd., Ste. B, Dublin 24084; 540-674-1991; pulaskichamber.info/tourism).

The *Fine Arts Center for the New River Valley* (21 W. Main St.; 540-980-7363; facnrv.org), in *Pulaski,* offers music performances, exhibitions, poetry and literary readings, lectures, private collections, and shows by amateur and professional artists. The Virginia Historic Landmark building, constructed in 1898, is considered an excellent example of Victorian commercial architecture. Free concerts are presented at Pulaski's Jackson Park throughout the summer.

The center is open Mon through Fri 10 a.m. to 4:30 p.m. There is no admission charge. A gift shop is on the premises.

The *Pulaski Railway Station* (20 S. Washington Ave.; 540-994-8600; virginia.org/Listings/HistoricSites/PulaskiRailwayStation) was erected by the Norfolk & Western Railroad in 1886 when passenger service existed here and Pulaski was one of the major stops along its route. The railroad donated this remarkable example of railway stations of the late 1800s to the town in 1989. It was restored in 1994. Unfortunately, a fire in 2008 ravaged the building. The station was restored, once again, with the original stone walls intact.

As you'll learn when you visit the *Shot Tower and New River Trail Historical State Park* (116 Orphanage Dr.; 276-699-6778; dcr.virginia.gov/state -parks/), Colonel John Chiswell discovered lead and zinc deposits in this area in about 1757 while he was hiding from the Cherokees. Shot was made from those deposits for firearms for frontiersmen and settlers at the Jackson Ferry shot tower, constructed by Thomas Jackson about 1807, with walls that are 2½ feet thick on a 20-foot square base. Shot was made by dropping the molten lead from a pouring kettle, through a sieve at the top of the 75-foot tower, down to a kettle of cold water that was 75 feet belowground. The size of the holes in the sieve determined the size of the shot. This is one of only a handful of such towers in the United States. The shot tower was designated a National Historic Mechanical Engineering Landmark in 1961 by the American Society of Mechanical Engineers. There are 77 steps up the winding staircase. The grounds are open from dawn to dusk. The tower is open occasionally on weekends in the summer.

Radford

In 2004, the **New River Heritage Coalition** in **Radford** was formed to improve the coordination and collaboration of the numerous historical sites along New River. These include testaments to explorers, Native Americans, European settlers, and industrial developers. They are working to help you understand how the people and events preceding us have made us and this area what it is today. Many of Virginia's 38 **state parks** and 33 natural areas are located in the Southwest area, with cabins, campsites, trails, waterways, and picnic shelters all available for your outdoor pleasure.

Most of the time, art is inside. That's true for the **Radford University Art Museum** in Radford. However, there's also art outdoors in the **Corinna de la Burdé Outdoor Sculpture Court** (between Porterfield and Powell Halls; 540-831-5754; radford.edu/content/cvpa/home/art-museum/galleries-hours/sculpture-court.html), which features permanent and temporary collections. You'll find contemporary pieces in metal, wood, and cement by artists from the region.

Smyth County

Just as your back (or whatever) is about to give out from hours of driving and riding while you're exploring the back roads and beautiful mountain scenery, along comes **Saltville,** the Salt Capital of the Confederacy. Suddenly, out of what appears to be almost nowhere, is the **Saltville Fitness Trail,** running along the railroad tracks to help you work on your tired muscles and brain cells. The first salt mine in America opened here in 1795. The "mining" operation removed the salt from the ground in liquid form, which was then boiled. Four million bushels of salt were produced in 1864. You can see examples of the big salt kettles around the town.

Time in Saltville goes back a long way. Each summer a dig is conducted by the Virginia Museum of Natural History and the Smithsonian Institution for prehistoric bones, and finds have included a musk ox skeleton and the track of a giant ground sloth. It's possible they've also found evidence of human life in our hemisphere from 14,000 years ago. The floor of the Saltville valley has a flat layer of mud, which is why so many artifacts and fossils have been preserved and not washed away. Stop by the **Museum of the Middle Appalachians** (123 Palmer Ave.; 276-496-3633; saltville.org/museum-of-the-middle-appalachians), your gateway to history. All is not petrified here. They've even had a Night at the Museum fundraiser for children 5 through 12, complete with a flashlight museum tour, a scavenger hunt, games, crafts, a movie and pizza and popcorn. Makes you want to be a child again. Open Mon through Sat 10 a.m. to 5 p.m.; Sun 1 to 4 p.m. Admission is $5 for adults, $30 for seniors (60+) and children (6–16).

The **Madam Russell Methodist Church** (207 W. Main St.; 276-496-5342; virginia.org/listings/HistoricSites/MadamRussellMethodistChurchandCabin/) and cabin are named after Elizabeth Henry Campbell Russell, sister of Patrick Henry. She was a leader of the Methodist Church in the region and is considered by some as the "Mother of Methodism." Construction of the church was begun in 1898, using local sandstone.

Washington County

Probably the best-known historic and tourist area in Washington County is **Abingdon,** the oldest incorporated town west of the Blue Ridge Mountains. One of the better-known attractions in Abingdon is the world-famous **Barter Theatre** (127 W. Main St.; 276-628-3991; bartertheatre.com), with such comic and lightly serious traveling company presentations as the marvelously funny *Greater Tuna* by Jaston Williams and Joe Sears. Other productions might include *Elf: The Musical, The Santaland Diaries, Camelot, Madame Buttermilk, Shrek: The Musical,* and *Exit Laughing.* Bob Porterfield gathered the first production company together during the Depression, when they bartered their presentations in exchange for food and services from area residents. Gregory Peck, Ernest Borgnine, Patricia Neal, Ned Beatty, Hume Cronyn, Gary Collins, and Larry Linville are among more than 100 well-known stars of stage, screen, and television who launched their careers at Barter Theatre. The sculptures surrounding the lighting fixtures were created by Mary Filapek, in the Barter production building. Payton Boyd designed the seat covers, based on the Charles Vess design of the Barter logo. There are about 40,000 stitches on each embroidered pattern, with the embroidery donated by Lebanon Apparel. The lobby drapes were designed by Amanda Alridge, Pat Van Horn, and Amy Fansler of the costume shop, and the stained-glass circular window on the building's facade was crafted by Abingdon artist Allen Boyd. The theatre is open Feb through Dec.

The **Historic District of Abingdon** is about 20 square blocks of restored 100- to 200-year-old homes and buildings, each with its own story. The **Arts Depot** (314 Depot Sq.; 276-628-9091), inside an 1890s railroad freight station, has artists' studios, changing exhibits, and classes. **Heartwood Southeast Virginia's Artists Gallery** (1 Heartwood Circle; 276-492-2400; myswva.org/heartwood) is the latest and largest stab at packaging local artists and their works as a tourist attraction. The facility, housed in a "deconstructed barn" design opened in June 2011. You'll also have a chance to appreciate (and buy, in some cases) traditional handcrafted woodwork, weaving, and pottery.

The Crooked Road: Virginia's Heritage Music Trail, connects legendary bluegrass and traditional mountain music venues together in a 250-mile driving tour through the mountain towns of southwest Virginia. The trail is a driving route along US 58 that features some of Virginia's significant contributions to the music world, promoting Appalachian Virginia's cultural heritage. Starting on the eastern end, it goes through Ferrum (Blue Ridge Institute and Museum), Floyd (Floyd Country Store and Country Records), Galax (Blue Ridge Music Center and the Old Fiddler's convention at the Rex Theater), Bristol (Birthplace of Country Music Alliance Museum), Hiltons (Carter Family Fold), and Norton (Country Cabin), until it reaches Clintwood (Ralph Stanley Museum) on the northwestern end.

Obviously, you can visit as much or as little as you wish, depending on where you're driving or how you like your blend of gospel, bluegrass, and mountain music. Look for annual festivals, weekly concerts, live radio shows, and informal jam sessions throughout the area.

It's said that on the night of the full moon, haunting violin melodies can be heard from the third floor of the **Martha Washington Inn** (150 W. Main St.; 276-628-3161; marthawashingtoninn.com) in Abingdon. Traditional lore says that during the Civil War, Captain John Stoves, a Union officer, was captured near the inn, which was a girls' finishing school at the time. As he lay dying, a "Martha Girl" who was known as Beth played a comforting melody on her violin. Soon after he died, she came down with typhoid fever and died. They're both buried in Abingdon's **Green Springs Cemetery.** More cheerful times at the inn today could include a visit to the year-round indoor swimming pool or the spa.

So much of Virginia is old and wonderful that we sometimes we don't see or appreciate the new and delightful. *Morgan's* restaurant (190 E. Main St.; 276-258-5632; morgansabingdon.com) is in the latter category. Featuring fresh seafood, handmade pastas, local ingredients, and global inspirations, chef Stephen Gilbert says he wants to explore the idea of "Old World, New World, Whole World" with new technologies and styles. Menus are changed season-ally. Gilbert is a native of Abingdon and was graduated from Southeast Culinary Institute in Bristol (the Virginia side). His background includes a stint as sous chef at Bristol Motor Speedway. His wife, Morgan, is a local artist and educator, and her photographic art is on display throughout the dining room. She's an art teacher at Lebanon High School and an art history instructor at Virginia High-lands Community College. She and her students made the artisan-style plates and bowls for the restaurant. The bowls are for sale and help fund the high school arts program. Open for lunch and dinner and Sun brunch (closed Mon).

The *Virginia Creeper Trail* (virginia.org/virginiacreepertrail) is a 35-mile rail trail running from Abingdon to *Whitetop* along an old railroad bed. There is an abundance of beautiful scenery as the trail passes through farmland, a small mountain range, and over creeks and gullies. Thanks to the assistance of the Jacobs Creek Job Corps and the Seabees, there are four trestle bridges, which have been floored for pedestrian use and are provided with handrails. Motorized vehicles, firearms, and alcoholic beverages are not permitted. The trail passes through private property, and you are asked to remain on the trail itself, not trespass, and to please close the gate behind you. Although the trail is fairly level, a shuttle is available from the top of Whitetop (which at 5,525 feet is the second tallest mountain in the state, after Mount Rogers) for those who bike or hike up and want an easier or faster way down.

Wythe County

When you want to see exhibits from the old mining camps, Civil War artifacts, and antique farm machinery, stop by the (Colonel) *Thomas J.* (Jefferson) *Boyd Museum.* Boyd was the Father of Wytheville, and this collection includes his surveyor's instruments, *Wytheville*'s first firefighting equipment, minerals, paintings, tools, musical instruments, antiques and clothing, books, and racks of photographs of early people from and places in the county. Large items, including a buggy, a moonshine still, and business equipment, are in the base-ment. The town's first fire truck is here, and there's a room dedicated to polio in Wytheville. Why polio? Because, it was considered a "polio" town in 1950 and suffered the largest number of polio cases per capita in the country. Of the 1,200 cases reported throughout the state, about 190 cases were reported in Wythe County, with most cases in Wytheville, which had a population of 5,500 at the time. The Museum Resource Center, of interest to genealogists and researchers, is on the first floor. The Discovery Center provides hands-on learning opportunities for children.

The Boyd Museum (295 Tazewell St.; 276-223-3330; wytheville.org/muse ums/museums.php) is open Mon through Fri and the third Sat of the month 10 a.m. to 4 p.m.

Next to the Thomas J. Boyd Musum is the **Haller-Gibboney Rock House Museum** (205 E. Tazewell St.; 276-223-3330; virginia.org/listings/HistoricSites/ HallerGibboneyRockHouseMuseum), an old Pennsylvania gray limestone house that has seen a lot of history. The home was built in 1824 and served as a hospital to both Confederate and Federal troops. Included in its exhibits are furnishings that were transported by oxcart from Pennsylvania, possessions of the Haller, Gibboney, and Campbell families, who lived in the house from 1820 until 1967. Dr. John Haller, the second occupant of the Rock House, was Wytheville's first resident physician. The furnishings are displayed in a parlor, dining room, reception room, and some bedrooms. There are also displays of coins, rocks, and Indian relics of the area, among other regional artifacts. Another Rock House souvenir of the Civil War time is a bullet hole in the wall of the front parlor.

The museum is open Mon through Fri and the third Sat of the month from 10 a.m. to 4 p.m.

Skeeterdogs

Since 1925, *Skeeter's,* E. N. Umberger's store (165 E. Main St., Wytheville; 276-228-2611; skeetershotdogs.com) has been serving its self-proclaimed "world-famous hot dogs" or *"skeeterdogs."* More than 9 million have been sold so far "without a dissatisfied customer." They've been shipped to people in Singapore, Amsterdam, Germany, and Great Britain. By the way, Edith Bolling Wilson, a descendant of Pocahontas and wife of President Woodrow Wilson, was born in the residence above the store. There's a museum next door to Skeeter's that tells the story "from Wytheville to the White House." In Mar 2019, owners Bill and Farron Smith announced they were selling Skeeter's. They've owned it since 1989 and "want to make sure this treasured establishment is in the right hands to continue for generations to come." The Smiths have been the second owners of Skeeter's outside the Umberger family since the business opened.

Virtus in Virginia

So, **George Wythe,** for whom Wytheville is named, never visited the town. He did, however, sign the Declaration of Independence and design the original great seal of Virginia. It's circular, with a figure of Virtus, the goddess of virtue, dressed as a warrior in the center. She holds a spear in her right hand, with its point held downward touching the earth. In her left hand is a sheathed sword pointing upward. Her left foot rests on the chest of the figure of tyranny, who is lying on the ground. Above the figure is the word "Virginia," and under the figures is the state motto, "Sic Semper Tyrannis" or "Thus Always to Tyrants." The seal was adopted in 1776 and modified in 1930.

Wythe also was the first professor of law in an American college, the College of William and Mary in Williamsburg.

Edith Bolling Wilson, the only Appalachian-born First Lady, is sometimes referred to as the United States' "first female president," and this is one of only eight historic sites across the country dedicated to a First Lady. She's honored at the *Edith Bolling Wilson Birthplace Museum* (145 E. Main St.; 276-223-3484; edithbollingwilson.org), opened by Bill and Farron Smith in 2008. She was the first honorary president of the Girl Scouts, so have your Girl Scout daughters check out the patch program. Open Thurs through Sat 10 a.m. to 4 p.m. Admission is $5 a person for the family home tour.

When you head north out of Wytheville, you come to Big Walker Mountain, and the *Big Walker National Scenic Byway and Big Walker Lookout* (8711 Stoney Fork Rd.; 276-663-4016; virginia.org/listings/OutdoorsAndSports/BigWalkerMountainScenicByway) at an elevation of 3,405 feet, in the Big Walker National Forest. Named for Dr. Thomas Walker, who passed through here in 1749, it's frequented because the Appalachian Trail goes through this area, affording many vistas of the farmland below to the north and mountain wilderness to the south. The lookout, with a 100-foot tower, is at the halfway point of the byway.

In spring the view is highlighted by the newborn blossoms; in fall, by the flaming foliage. There's a beginners hiking trail, Monster Rock Trail, that begins behind Big Walker Lookout and follows the ridge of the mountain.

The byway is open year-round; the lookout is open daily 10 a.m. to 6 p.m. Memorial Day to Labor Day, and until 5 p.m. in the spring and fall. The overlook is free. Take exit 52 off I-77 and travel south, or exit 47 of I-77 and travel Route 717 to US 52 and go north.

ANNUAL EVENTS IN THE BLUE RIDGE HIGHLANDS

JANUARY

First Day Hike
Claytor Lake State Park
Dublin
(540) 643-2500
dcr.virginia.gov/state-parks/
claytor-lake#general_information

FEBRUARY

New River Polar Plunge Fest
Bisset Park
Radford
(540) 267-3153
polarplunge.com/new-river

APRIL

The Crooked Road Open Jam at Heartwood
Abingdon
(276) 492-2400
myswva.org/heartwood
through December

MAY

Whitetop Mountain Ramp Festival
Whitetop
(276) 388-3422
graysoncountyva.com/Whitetop_
Mountain_Ramp_Festival.aspx

JUNE

Grayson County Fiddler's Convention
Elk Creek
(276) 655-4866
ecvfd.net

JULY

Smoke on the Mountain Barbecue Championship
Galax
(276) 236-2184
smokeonthemountainva.com

AUGUST

Fairview Ruritan Old Fiddler's Convention
Galax
(276) 236-5725
fairviewruritan.com/
bluegrassmusicvirginia.aspx

Virginia Mountain Crafts Guild Claytor Lake Fair
Dublin
(540) 725-9570
artandcrafts.com/virginia/

SEPTEMBER

Virginia Highlands Festival
Abingdon
(276) 623-5266
vahighlandsfestival.org

OCTOBER

Whitetop Mountain Molasses Festival
Whitetop
(276) 388-3480
graysoncountyva.com

DECEMBER

Parade and Christmas Tree Lighting
Hillsville
(276) 728-2128
townofhillsville.com

OTHER ATTRACTIONS IN THE BLUE RIDGE HIGHLANDS

Calfee Park (seasonal)
Pulaski
(540) 994-8630 or
(877) 474-3567

Damascus Brewery
Damascus
(276) 469-1069
thedamascusbrewery.com

Devault Stadium (seasonal)
Bristol
(276) 206-9946
milb.com/bristol

Glencoe Museum
Radford
(540) 731-5031
glencoemuseum.org

Hungry Mother State Park
Marion
(540) 781-7400
dcr.virginia.gov/state-parks/

Mabry Mill
Meadows of Dan
(276) 952-2947
virginia.org/Listings/HistoricSites/
MabryMill

Mule Hell Trading Co.
Galax
(276) 236-4744
mulehelltradingco.com

SEEDS (Seek Education, Explore, DiScover)
Blacksburg
(540) 552-3914
seedskids.org

Settlers Museum of Southwest Virginia
Atkins
(276) 686-4401
settlersmuseum.com

Starlite Drive-In (seasonal)
Christiansburg
(540) 382-9227
starlitedrivein.info

White's Mill
Abingdon
(276) 628-2960
whitesmill.org

Places to Stay in the Blue Ridge Highlands

ABINGDON

Inn on Town Creek
445 E. Valley St.
(276) 628-4560
innontowncreek.com

Summerfield Inn Bed and Breakfast
101 Valley St. NW
(276) 628-5905 or
(800) 668-5905

BLACKSBURG

Main Street Inn
205 S. Main St.
(540) 579-0533
hotelblacksburg.com

BRISTOL

The Bristol Hotel
510 Birthplace of Country Music Way
(276) 696-3535
bristolhotelva.com

CHRISTIANSBURG

The Oaks Victorian Inn
311 E. Main St.
(540) 381-1500
theoaksvictorianinn.com

DAMASCUS

Riverside View
223 E. Laurel Ave.
(276) 475-5361
ariversedgelodging.com/
rooms/riverside-view-a
-mountain-retreat

GALAX

Chestnut Creek Cabins
1000 Revere Rd.
(276) 236-8455
chestnutcreekcabins.com

MARION

General Francis Marion Hotel
107 E. Main St.
(276) 783-4800
gfmhotel.com

PEARISBURG

Inn at Riverbend Bed & Breakfast
125 River Ridge Dr.
(540) 921-5211
innatriverbend.com

PULASKI

Jackson Park Inn
68 1st St. NW
(540) 509-5164
jacksonparkinn.com/home

WYTHEVILLE

The Bolling Wilson Hotel
170 E. Main St.
(276) 223-2333
bollingwilsonhotel.com/
en-us

Places to Eat in the Blue Ridge Highlands

ABINGDON

128 Pecan
128 Pecan St.
(276) 698-3159
128pecan.com

BLACKSBURG

Cellar Restaurant and 6-Pak Store
302 N. Main St.
(540) 953-0651
the-cellar.com

Joe's Diner
221 N. Main St.
(540) 961-4194
joesdinervt.com

BRISTOL

Bristol Burger Bar
8 Piedmont Ave.
(276) 466-6200
theoriginalburgerbar.com

Lumac
Bristol Hotel
510 Birthplace of Country Music Way
(276) 696-3535
bristolhotelva.com/
drinks-dining/lumac

CHRISTIANSBURG

Dude's Drive-in
1505 Roanoke St.
(540) 382-7901

DAMASCUS

Damascus Brewery
32173 Government Rd.
(276) 469-1069
thedamascusbrewery.com

GALAX

Galax Smokehouse
101 N. Main St.
(276) 236-1000
thegalaxsmokehouse.com

MARION

Wooden Pickle Food & Spirits
120 E. Main St.
(276) 783-2300
facebook.com/
woodenpickle120

PULASKI

Artie's Hometown Diner
4860 N. Jefferson St.
(315) 298-6082

RADFORD

Sal's Italian Restaurant & Pizzeria
709 W. Main St.
(540) 639-9669
salsradford.com

WYTHEVILLE

Graze on Main
Bolling Wilson Hotel
170 E. Main St.
(276) 223-2334
bollingwilsonhotel.com

Heart of Appalachia

Ah, southwest Virginia. This is where mountains—not buildings—form the skyscrapers; where canyons are really canyons (the deepest this side of the Mississippi), not the canyons created by tall structures.

You will note that interstate highways here are more serpentine than ironed-ribbon straight. If you're observant, you'll even notice that one stretch of I-77 and I-81 overlap, and you can go south on one and north on the other and still be on the same side of the road. This is called a wrong-way concurrency, one of maybe a handful of such roadway designs on the continent.

This is where Mother Nature's awe-inspiring works are yours for the looking and hiking and exploring. You will find the frontier spirit and revitalizing natural beauty. You will be able to take time for camping, fishing, and swimming in numerous state and national parks. You will find quaint old mills and summer outdoor dramatic offerings that retell the history and life of mountain days decades and centuries ago. And you will find unusual ways to enjoy yourself, including trekking via llama.

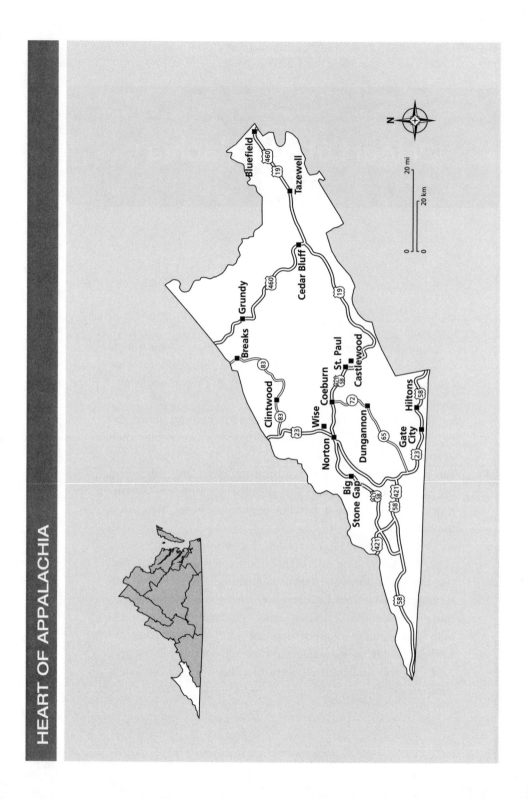

Among the parks, preserves, and management areas are Breaks Interstate Park, Natural Tunnel State Park (see more details in the Scott County listings), Southwest Virginia Museum Historical State Park, and the Wilderness Road State Park.

For more information about these facilities, write or call the Virginia Department of Conservation and Recreation, 203 Governor St., Richmond, 23219 (804 786-1712 or 800-933-PARK [7275]; virginia.org/HABRHstateparks).

Dickenson County

Clintwood is the Dickenson County seat, where Ralph Stanley (1927–2016), noted bluegrass and mountain singing legend, grew up and helped establish the *Ralph Stanley Museum and Traditional Mountain Music Center* (249 Main St.; 276-926-8550; ralphstanleymuseum.com). The $1.4 million complex is at one end of the Crooked Road Music Heritage Trail that starts in Floyd, goes by Galax, and continues through Grayson County, Bristol, Hiltons, and then to Clintwood. Stanley donated old musical instruments and memorabilia collected since he started in the business as a teenager.

The museum is open Tues through Sat 10 a.m. to 4 p.m. and Sun 1 to 4 p.m. (Apr through Dec); Wed through Sat 10 a.m. to 5 p.m. and Sun 1 to 5 p.m. the rest of the year. Admission is $7.50 for adults; $5 for seniors (55+), students, and Dickenson/Wise/Buchanan County residents.

Lee County

Lee County is the southwesternmost of Virginia's counties, where Virginia borders Kentucky and Tennessee at Cumberland Gap, named for the Duke of Cumberland, son of King George II. Getting there along Route 58 is an experience that can almost make you forget there's a highly industrialized civilization just a few miles away. Once you leave Duffield (Scott County), it's a pleasant drive past serene, checkerboarded pastures, little towns, white churches of assorted denominations, tobacco-drying barns, livestock barns, wildflowers, and cemeteries. Norman Rockwell couldn't have painted anything more idyllic.

Historical markers along the road relate the comings and goings of Native Americans, such as the June 1785 massacre of the Archibald Scott family by a notorious Native American known as Benge. Two miles west of Rose Hill is an Indian burial mound, most likely Cherokee.

Once you reach the Gap, you have to go into Kentucky to reach the visitor center, where there are displays on the Civil War and about Daniel Boone and the 30 axemen who cut the Wilderness Trail in 1775. The Cumberland Gap is

In Lee County You Can . . .

- be farther west than Detroit

- be farther west than all of West Virginia

- be closer to eight other state capitals than to Richmond

- see five states at once

- see "black diamonds" (coal)

- walk the "Trail of the Lonesome Pine" (see Big Stone Gap)

- visit the University of Virginia's College at Wise, a place that grew from a home for indigents and the homeless into the only branch of the University of Virginia

both a scenic wonder of the world and a lesson in the significance of geography to history. From 1775 to 1800 some 300,000 settlers traveled this way to get to the other side of the Appalachian Mountains as the Gap evolved into the primary track of an immense trans-Allegheny migration.

Leaves start turning in this neck of the woods as early as 125 days before Christmas, but the peak is late fall. During fall you're likely to find the view fogged much of the time, but at the visitor center you can buy slides of what the view would look like on a clear day.

The trail was an evolving process. Deer and buffalo migrated across the Gap, and Indians followed their path. The Cherokees, leading strategic battles against other tribes, had made the trip on foot from their native North Carolina. An occasional courageous person wandered through, and there was talk of the marvelous bluegrass country and the riches of food, livestock, and logging trees on the western side of the Gap. Eventually coal would be discovered here as well.

choochoo

Supposedly the **Bee Rock Tunnel,** at 47 feet, 7 inches, is the second shortest railroad tunnel in the world (reportedly, the Westmoreland Tunnel in Gallatin, Tennessee, is the shortest, at 46 feet). At one time the town of Appalachia was the center of eight coal camps constructed by the Louisville & Nashville Railroad and the Southern Railroad: (276) 565-3900.

Then, Richard Henderson, a lawyer and land speculator, formed the Transylvania Co. to establish trade with the Indians. Daniel Boone was hired to cut and mark the trail known as Boone's Trace, or the Wilderness Road, between areas now known as Kingsport, Tennessee, and Fort Boonesborough, Kentucky. It wasn't very wide in places: In some areas it was barely a horse path;

others were just large enough for a wagon to get through. Some say it was littered with the bleached skeletal bones of history.

Then the Revolutionary War began, and the Gap just wasn't on anyone's front burner for a while. In fact, because the British stirred up the Indians against the settlers during the American Revolution, Kentucky was a downright dangerous place at the time.

The Wilderness Road eventually became a two-way thoroughfare. As some settlers trekked westward, others brought cattle, sheep, pigs, and turkeys eastward to the markets along the Atlantic Ocean. At the turn of the century, other means of transportation were developed, including the Erie and Chesapeake and Ohio Canals, the Pennsylvania Main Line, and even steamboats up the Mississippi. The Gap was of extreme strategic value during the Civil War and changed hands a few times, but mostly it languished.

On June 11, 1940, the area was declared a National Historical Park, and no matter how many people are visiting the park when you're there, you're bound to think you're one of the first to discover its rugged beauty. It's one of two historical parks in the state and of 45 in the country, which are different than historic sites because the park includes multiple components. The National Park Service says the 24,000-plus acres of the Cumberland Gap area is one of the "lesser-used" areas in the system and therefore offers an above-average park experience.

There are more than 85 miles of hiking trails (from 1 mile to the scenic 21-mile Ridge Trail), a developed campground and primitive camp areas with summertime campfire programs and daytime activities, Hensley Settlement, caves, and the *Pinnacle Overlook.*

The Pinnacle is reached via a 4-mile drive from the visitor center. The drive is off-limits to trailers and vehicles more than 20 feet long because the road can give a new meaning to the term *hairpin turn.* Additionally, due to inclement weather (ice, snow, lightning), the road to the overlook may be closed. Depending on available staff, a shuttle runs to the overlook; the charge is $5 per person. As staffing and crowds fluctuate throughout the year, you might want to let the staff know you'll want a shuttle ride so they can try to schedule you on your desired day.

On a clear day at the Pinnacle you can easily see the three states of Kentucky, Tennessee, and Virginia, and, of course, the Gap, approximately 1,000 feet below you. On exceptionally clear days you can see the Great Smoky Mountains of North Carolina, and possibly even South Carolina and Georgia. More likely, you will see a lot of mist and will have to rely on purchasing slides and pictures of the spectacularly sweeping vistas.

The plants and wildlife here are seldom seen elsewhere, and they abound in much the same setting as when the Gap was first described. There are hardwoods (majestic virgin hemlock, oak, and magnolia) and pines. There are clumps of mountain laurel and rhododendron, so spring and early summer fill the landscape with fragrant wildflowers and brilliant redbud and dogwood. Although you'll periodically come across some rocky outcroppings, the area is fully clothed in greenery because the glaciers never came this far south, so the hilltops weren't denuded of valuable plant-supporting dirt. Because of the various elevations, each season's exotic blooms last a long time, and you need only climb up or descend a few feet for a different botanical view.

From 1903 to 1951 the Hensley and Gibbons families (who intermarried) occupied the **Hensley Settlement,** a plateau that is almost 1,000 feet higher than the Pinnacle Overlook. It was unreachable by our current standards of accessibility. Everything had to be made or grown there or carted in on mule-drawn sleds or by hiking. They lived without roads, electricity, or other conveniences. Sherman Hensley was the last to depart. The Park Service is re-creating this last settlement, and several buildings and farms have been restored.

Tours, including a shuttle bus and a 1-mile walk through the settlement, are offered daily at 9 a.m. and 1:30 p.m. from late May through Oct 31. Tickets are $10 for adults, $5 for seniors with a Senior Passport and for children under 12. Bring a light snack and drink. Reservations are strongly suggested because the tour has a limited capacity.

The biggest change to come to Cumberland Gap National Historical Park is the completion of two 2-lane, nearly 1-mile-long tunnels that cut off 3.2 miles of curving, dangerous winding roads. This is allowing the old Wilderness Road (now US 25E) to be restored and revert roughly to the way it was in Daniel Boone's days. First, the trail will be narrowed down to a 10-foot wagon path. Native seeds of grasses, shrubs, and trees have been collected and propagated to be used to restore the gap. This method is less expensive than buying nursery stock and is a lot more natural. It probably will be well into the 21st century before the area looks the way it did 200 years ago, but the work is providing a major head start.

You can join park rangers on a moderately strenuous 1.5-mile, 2-hour hike through the Gap Cave, looking at stalagmites and flowstone cascades, maybe seeing a bat. Should your passion include spelunking, note that the white-nose syndrome is killing hundreds of thousands of bats, incredibly handy animals that eat thousands and thousands of nasty insects and bugs. Therefore, some caves may be closed or you may be requested to wear appropriate clothing and footwear that either has not been in another cave or has been decontaminated.

Check with the rangers to see whether that cave is open to the public or if they have specific requirements in place.

Hike tickets are $8 for adults, $4 for seniors with a Senior Passport and for children (5–12). Be sure to wear appropriate hiking boots. The tours are offered at various times of the day (sometimes once a day; sometimes twice) depending on the season and day of the week. Call or check the website to confirm a hike reservation.

The visitor center has films, exhibits, overnight camping passes, and general information. It is open daily 8 a.m. to 5 p.m., except Dec 25. For more information call (606) 248-2817 or visit nps.gov/cuga.

Russell County

The old ***Russell County Courthouse and the Dickenson/Bundy Log House*** (Route 58; 276-889-8000; virginiaheritage.org/russell_co.htm) on Copper Creek in ***Castlewood*** was the first landmark in Russell County to be nominated to the National Register of Historic Places. It was built by Henry Dickenson to replace a log courthouse that was burned during the Revolutionary War. The courthouse was used from late 1799 to 1818, when a new county seat was designated. It was a residence until restoration began in 1976. Many antiques are included in the display (they're always looking for donations if you have a piece that is appropriate). Self-guided tours are encouraged. There's also a covered picnic area and a log house on the property that's used for craft sales. Open Tues through Sat 10 a.m. to 4 p.m.; Sun 12:30 to 4 p.m.

Scott County

The ***Natural Tunnel*** (1420 Natural Tunnel Pkwy.; 276-940-2674 or 800-933-PARK; dcr.virginia.gov/state_parks/nat.shtml) is part of Natural Tunnel State Park. The tunnel is 850 feet long and as high as a 10-story building (100 feet) that began more than a million years ago in the early glacial period as the persistent waters of Stock Creek eroded the limestone rock of Powell's Mountain. It's large enough for trains to go through. William Jennings Bryan called it the "Eighth Wonder of the World." Other scenic features include a wide chasm between steep stone walls surrounded by several pinnacles, or chimneys. Facilities include picnic areas and an amphitheater. The park also offers cave tours and canoe trips on the Clinch River, and the Cove Ridge Center, which offers environmental education, conference facilities, and overnight dorm accommodations. The only chairlift in Virginia state parks is at Natural Tunnel. It runs daily from Memorial Day through Labor Day and on weekends in May, Sept, and Oct. Cabins and a campground were added in 2007. Each campsite has a campfire ring grill, with firewood and ice sold at the park. RV sites are up to 38 feet and have electric and water hookups. Summer swimming (with a 100-foot slide) in a 5,400-square-foot pool is free to campers. A visitor center sits atop the mountain and is open weekdays daily from 8 a.m. to dusk.

Nashville, Tennessee, may claim to be the home of country music, but the Carter Family Fold in **Hiltons** claims that A. P. Carter, his wife, Sara, and her cousin Maybelle (mother of June, Helen, and Anita Carter) were the pioneers of this music form. The Carter family recorded 300 songs between 1927 and 1942, 100 of them written by A. P. Now the **Carter Family Museum, Memorial Music Center, and Music in the Fold** (3449 A. P. Carter Hwy.; 276-386-6054 or 276-594-0676; carterfamilyfold.org) on Sat nights at 7:30 p.m. show what country music, clogging, and buck dancing are about in a rustic country setting. A 1,000-seat music "shed" is the site for traditional country music every Sat night. You can see displays about the role the Carter family played in developing and promoting traditional bluegrass and country music, shown through instruments, original records, photographs, and personal family items. The museum is their old home, and A. P. Carter's general store is "the fold" where the shows are held. An annual festival, with only acoustic music, celebrating the first recordings by the Carter family, is held the first weekend in Aug.

The museum, cabin, and the Family Fold are open Mon through Wed from 10 a.m. to 2 p.m. during the season. Admission is free although donations are gladly accepted. Concert tickets are $10 (unless otherwise noted) for adults and $2 for children (6–11).

Tazewell County

The **Historic Crab Orchard Museum and Pioneer Park** (3663 Crab Orchard Rd.; 276-988-6755; craborchardmuseum.com) displays photographs, multimedia presentations, and artifacts dating from millions of years ago to the present in a 110-acre area near **Tazewell** (it's a short "a") designated as a prehistoric and historical archaeological area. Among the regular exhibits are a leg bone and teeth of a huge mastodon that roamed the area millions of years ago, the double palisades (protective fortification wall of tree trunks) of the Native Americans, and relics from the Revolutionary and Civil Wars. Many of these "souvenirs" of the past were uncovered during the construction of US 19 and US 460. A **"lepidodendron tree,"** which is really sandstone rock, might be the first thing you see as you enter the museum. The lepidodendron was a popular growth item about 300 million years ago and grew in the water that then covered the area. Eventually the trunk would break off, and water would rot the interior, which would then fill with sand and form a cast of the inside of the tree trunk. Some of the wood would adhere to the stone, carbonize, and form bituminous coal. I'll admit it, the Historic Crab Orchard Museum and Pioneer Park in Tazewell is one of my favorites, no qualifiers attached.

Crab Orchard, however, is more than what's past and gone. There's a new exhibit every quarter: perhaps photographs, a history of railroading, German Expressionistic art, or the paintings of local artist Tracy Ratliff. The activities calendar is filled with such items as a May Civil War reenactment and, on July 4, a community festival that's attended by several thousand people with crafts and home-baked goods. In Sept there's a storytelling festival.

Crab Orchard is open Tues through Sat 9 a.m. to 5 p.m. (Labor Day to Memorial Day); Sun 1 to 5 p.m. (Memorial Day to Labor Day). Admission is $5 for adults; $3 for seniors and AAA members; and $2 for children (7–12) for full site privileges. Event day demonstrations may have an extra charge.

Not too far from Tazewell is **Burke's Garden** (276-322-1345 or 800-588-9401; visittazewellcounty.org/burkes-garden-2), which was surveyed in 1748 and is now designated a Virginia Scenic Byway. This beautiful valley is unique because it is surrounded by only one mountain. The collapsed dome is also the highest, coldest, greenest, and maybe the prettiest in Virginia. James Burke discovered the area in the 1740s when he followed a wounded elk there. Legend says he planted the potato peelings that provided food for the Irish surveying party that came through in 1749, who jokingly named the place "Burkes Garden." The Burke's Garden Fall Festival is scheduled for the last Sun in Sept. To get there, take Route 623 east and south out of Tazewell for about 15 miles.

Wise County

The **Big Stone Gap** welcome center, **Interstate 101 Car and Visitor Center** (619 Gilley Ave.; 276-523-2303; bigstonegap.com), is located in an 1870 Pullman Company passenger train car. It had two staterooms, a dining area, kitchen, and an observation room. The president of the Interstate Railroad Company used it when it was purchased in the 1920s. The car was retired in 1959 and used as a hunting cabin on Dorchester Lake on Black Creek in Wise County. Eventually, it was donated to the Gap Corporation in 1988, when it was restored. Stop by the center to learn about sights and activities in this area and about the car's history.

The **Harry W. Meador Coal Museum** (570 Shawnee Ave. E.; 276-523-9209; bigstonegap.org/attract/coal.htm) is operated by Big Stone Gap Department of Parks and Recreation and exhibits artifacts collected by the late Harry Meador Jr., who went from being a union laborer to the vice president of funfacts

This area may look familiar to those of you who've seen the movie *Coal Miner's Daughter*. Some filming for the movie was done in Bee, Haysi, and Wise (fairground scene).

coal development for a local coal company. Other items have been painstakingly assembled from private homes and public buildings, which illustrate the coal-mining heritage of the area and coal mining's profound effect on the local lifestyle. Among the more interesting exhibits are photographs, mining equipment and tools, and coal company items. There's also a 1900s dentist office tucked in there. The museum is open Wed through Sat 10 a.m. to 5 p.m., Sun 1 to 5 p.m. and by appointment. There is no admission fee.

For the longest continuing outdoor drama in the United States, see **The Trail of the Lonesome Pine** (518 Clinton Ave. E.; 276-523-1235; trailofthelonesomepine.com), the official outdoor drama of Virginia, telling the story of the romance of a mountain girl during the development of the coal industry. The drama is adapted from the book by John Fox Jr., which was the nation's first million-selling novel (and was later made into a movie), and it has been presented every year since 1963. The doors open at 7 p.m., pre-show entertainment starts at 7:15, and the show starts at 8 p.m. Ticket prices are $18 for adults, $15 for seniors, and $10 for students.

June Tolliver was the heroine of Fox's book, and her home is open as the *June Tolliver House and Folk Art Center* (522 Clinton Ave. E.; 800-362-0149 or 276-523-4707; junetolliverhouse.com) for tours Apr through mid-Dec, Tues through Sat from 10 a.m. to 5 p.m. Fantastic local craft offerings from the gift shop and special events are scheduled regularly.

funfacts

John Fox Jr., a Rough Rider with Teddy Roosevelt, and author of *The Little Shepherd of Kingdom Come* and *Trail of the Lonesome Pine,* used the building that is currently the coal mine museum as his study and library.

To see authentic Fox family furnishings, visit the *John Fox Jr. Museum* (118 Shawnee Ave. E.; 276-523-2747; bigstonegap.org). The house was built in 1888 and was opened in 1970. It's filled with beautiful furnishings and mementos of the Fox family. Visit Thurs through Sat 2 to 6 p.m. from the Thurs following Memorial Day until the Sat before Labor Day. Admission is $3 for adults, $2 for seniors (65+), and $1 for students.

The *Southwest Virginia Museum* (10 W. 1st St.; 276-523-1322; swvamuseum.org) is in a 4-story mansion bequeathed in 1946 by Congressman C.

Bascom Slemp. Opened in 1947, it strives to preserve a picture of the early southwestern Virginia pioneer lifestyle and the boom and bust times of the late 19th century. You should note the use of local materials, including locally quarried and hand-chiseled sandstone and limestone and the extensive use of red oak in the interior and as decorative flourishes on the doors and windows. You can also see custom-made china commissioned by Queen Victoria of England and Oriental antiques. The museum is open Mar through Memorial Day and Labor Day through Dec 31, from Tues through Thurs 10 a.m. to 4 p.m.; Fri 9 a.m. to 4 p.m.; Sat 10 a.m. to 5 p.m.; Sun 1 to 5 p.m. Mon hours are added

ANNUAL EVENTS IN THE HEART OF APPALACHIA

JANUARY

First Day Hike
Southwest Virginia Museum
Big Stone Gap
(276) 523-1322
dcr.virginia.gov/state-parks/
southwest-virginia-museum

APRIL

SWCC Festival of the Arts
Cedar Bluff
(276) 964-7348
sw.edu/swccfestivalofthearts

MAY

Mountain Man Rendezvous
Historic Crab Orchard Museum
Tazewell
(276) 988-6755
craborchardmuseum.com/
mountain-man-rendezvous

Clinch River Days
St. Paul
clinchriverfest.com

JUNE

Best Friend Festival
Norton
(276) 679-1160
nortonva.org/490/Best-Friend-Festival

JULY

Drums of the Painted Mountain Pow Wow
Cedar Bluff
(276) 596-9281
visittazewellcounty.org/events

SEPTEMBER

Benge's Revenge Challenge
Norton
(276) 679-0961
bengesrevenge.com

OCTOBER

High Knob Hellbender 10K
Norton
(770) 654-3942
highknobhellbender.wordpress.com

DECEMBER

Frontier Christmas
Historic Crab Orchard Museum &
Pioneer Park
Tazewell
(276) 988-6755
craborchardmuseum.com/
frontier-christmas

OTHER ATTRACTIONS IN THE HEART OF APPALACHIA

Lincolnshire Park (seasonal)
Tazewell
(276) 988-5404
townoftazewell.org/lincolnshire-park

Scott County Lavender Farm
Dungannon
(423) 753-2351
facebook.com/ScottCountyLavender

Wilderness Road Blockhouse
(summer)
Gate City
(276) 386-6521
explorescottcountyva.org/history/
wilderness-road-blockhouse

during the summer. Closed Jan and Feb. Admission is $5 for adults and $3 for children (6–12).

The *University of Virginia's College at Wise* (1 College Ave.; 276-328-0100; wise.virginia.edu) is the only branch of the University of Virginia. It was founded in Wise in 1954 after local citizens petitioned UVA to build a college here. Until then, access to public higher education in far southwestern Virginia was minimal, limited to a few extension courses. Wise County donated the land and two old stone buildings (still standing and in use) that had served as the Wise County Poor Farm, a home for the indigent. The state offered up a total of $5,000 in appropriations for the first year. Local citizens contributed twice that to furnish and equip the school. One hundred students entered the first class in 1954. Until 1968 the school was a two-year "feeder college" for UVA (and other universities). It's grown up since then, and the 369-acre campus is one of the most picturesque campuses you will ever see. This is the only four-year state college in Virginia west of Radford (the college became a four-year liberal arts school in 1968; it was never a community college). Ties with UVA have strengthened considerably in past years. As with any college, there are numerous cultural activities, including recitals, exhibits, and an international movie series.

Places to Stay in the Heart of Appalachia

BREAKS

Breaks Park Rhododendron Lodge
KY-VA 80
627 Commission Cir.
(276) 865-4413
breakspark.com

Breaks Interstate Park Luxury Cabins
627 Commission Circle
(800) 933-PARK
breakspark.com

GRUNDY

Comfort Inn–Grundy
22006 Riverside Dr.
(276) 935-5050
choicehotels.com/virginia/
grundy/comfort-inn-hotels/
va079

ST. PAUL

Mountain View Lodge
16602 Wise St.
(276) 395-0546
mountainviewlodgestpaul
.com

TAZEWELL

Foxtail Orchards Cabins & Campground
148 Macky Ln.
(276) 200-4176
foxtailorchards.com

WISE

The Inn at Wise
110 E. Main St.
(276) 321-7600
innatwise.com

Places to Eat in the Heart of Appalachia

BIG STONE GAP

Four Seasons Farm Produce
231 E. 5th St. S
(276) 523-4317

BLUEFIELD

The RailYard
530 Raleigh St.
(304) 800-4141
railyardwv.com

CLINTWOOD

Valentino's
Dickenson Highway
(276) 926-4222

COEBURN

Wakame Japanese Steakhouse
509 Front St.
(276) 807-7118

GRUNDY

Southern Smoke BBQ
19547 Riverside Dr.
(276) 935-0600

NORTON

The Wood Booger Grill
921 Park Ave.
(276) 325-0551

WISE

Moon Dog Brick Oven
302 W. Main St.
(276) 321-7452
facebook.com/
moondogwise

Index